MARINER'S VOYAGE

Mariner's Voyage

Dr. Ray Solly

Whittles Publishing

Published by
Whittles Publishing,
Dunbeath,
Caithness KW6 6EY,
Scotland, UK
www.whittlespublishing.com

© 2008 Ray Solly
ISBN 978-1904445-50-0

Typeset by Ellipsis Books Limited, Glasgow

Printed by

CONTENTS

FOREWORD

I very much enjoyed reading *Mariner's Launch*, and so it was a great pleasure to be asked to write the foreword for *Mariner's Voyage.*

With these volumes, Dr Solly has very cleverly woven together a social history of seafaring in the post-war years with a semi-autobiographical account of the experiences of a young man making his way in the world.

There is, of course, no requirement for a seafaring background to read *Mariner's Voyage* – these are essentially tales of adventure, after all.

But if you have served at sea, and especially if you did so during the 1960s and 1970s, before the twin forces of globalisation and containerisation ushered in the modern era, this is also your story. If so, your first reaction on picking up the book will probably be to flick through the pages to spot familiar references, such as the names of ships you have sailed on and the places that figured in the social life of your youth. But it is only when you sit down to read it properly that you discover just how well the author, through the character of Jonathan Caridia, has captured *the experience* of being at sea. Although some of that experience is located very firmly in the period, in the ships and trades of the time, much of it is timeless – officers of every generation know what it feels like to hold that precious first certificate of competency, and the feeling of nakedness on being left alone on watch for the first time.

It would be remiss not to mention the skilful way in which photographs and drawings are used to complement the text. There is one cartoon which reminds me instantly of the day in 1975 when I joined my first ship, the MV *Clan Robertson*, in Southampton. It shows an anxious-looking young man at the foot of the accommodation ladder, suitcase in hand, with a stern-looking senior officer in uniform looking down at him from the deck. As a polite young man, I foolishly asked the harassed Chief Officer for permission to bring my gear onboard. "Well, it's not much bloody use down there, is it?" came the reply …

Mariner's Voyage is a wonderfully evocative read, and an important contribution to the history of the period.

John F Millican
Director
Warsash Maritime Academy

PREFACE

Jonathan Caridia the narrator of this book made his debut in *Mariner's Voyage* as he set off to sea in the mid-1950s as a sixteen-year-old navigating officer cadet in the Merchant Navy. His innocent naïvety at that time provided valuable insight into those uncertain inner feelings experienced by most of us when young and faced with new and apparently overpowering life situations that challenge resources and abilities – even if our 'sea' is very different from that of Jonathan. In these conditions, we survive, become submerged, or give up, probably to seek an alternative career. Chatting with today's modern generation of mariners I remain convinced they fare little differently from our narrator. Jonathan survived his (literal) 'rite of passage' and *Mariner's Launch* recounts how he did this. That the pathway to his success was comparatively easy was not dependent purely on his own strength of character, temperament and perseverance, although these elements played a decisive role. It resulted from a series of circumstances involving people – the support of caring parents coupled with chance encounters involving others wielding influence. Jonathan was fortunate in meeting a sympathetic marine departmental manager before he went to sea, a sensitive nautical college superintendent, a sensible older cadet, and the 'fate' that determined he would sail with a responsible shipping company. The sound quality of officers responsible for his training and development at sea was equally an essential matter of chance, rather than design as many cadets and apprentices in the 1950–70s, and today (from all reports) have discovered to their cost.

In *Mariner's Voyage*, Jonathan is a newly qualified twenty-year old navigating officer and we share his development as he continues to face unforeseen challenges in his chosen career emanating from unexpected obstacles. Once more, we share his private thoughts as he calls upon his previously sound training and experience gained gradually as both ship's officer and man, to support new areas of responsibility. We find ourselves living the situations with him, and almost willing him to discover the correct way forward to succeed – and then heaving sighs of relief as he gains the further requisite steps in self-confidence. When we leave him at the end of this book, he has survived service as third and junior second mate across a range of trades and crew experiences, and is offered further promotion.

Mariner's Voyage once again is a semi-autobiographical account. The continued persona of a narrator permits the relating of incidents experienced by the author during his service in the Merchant Navy. Such adoption permits the relating of pursuits at sea which border still dangerously close to libel, but allows also the narration of numerous events gleaned from other reliable service sources. The book, like its predecessor (and the final part of the trilogy, *Mariner's Rest*) stands as a socio-historical account relating how effectively Merchant Navy personnel confronted some very significant economic and social changes affecting directly UK shipping and port cargo handling developments during the 1960s and 1970s. In these respects, it possesses genuine educational value in its depiction to a new generation of an insight into a way of life now overtaken by events.

Ships and trades are completely different from fifty years ago, with computerised navigational, engineering and cargo practices – especially containerisation – replacing much of the drudgery and lengthy periods spent in port. Certainly, today's generation of seafarers would not tolerate absences from home and family of a year or more so easily as Caridia and his generation. Yet, in some respects, the ethos of 'going away to sea' retains a taste of why Jonathan was attracted to the lifestyle, for quotes from present young seafarers reflect very closely desires of their predecessors as they too 'sign Articles'. It is still true to say that 'scratch the surface of any Briton and underneath you will find a seaman' and it would seem that little has changed concerning the need to satisfy that almost indefinable aspect of seafaring that Jonathan confronts and attempts to solve as a young officer. A need continues to exist for 'seeing something of the world' and hopefully capturing a sense of adventure.

'The Ellerton Shipping Group' is a title chosen purely for convenience. It does not represent any single shipping company, but is an amalgam of the best of two regular cargo lines plus a dry-cargo tramp and a coastal company with whom I served as a navigating officer.

Ray Solly

ACKNOWLEDGEMENTS

I am indebted to a number of people and organisations who have provided photographs included in this book. Every effort has been made to attribute correctly the copyright of each photograph, but some images are around fifty years old and it has not been possible in all instances to ascertain original ownership. The author would be pleased to receive appropriately verifiable proof of ownership and assign copyright correctly in future editions. As with *Mariner's Launch*, the photographs serve only as representations illustrating situations described in the text. They do not portray people, places or ships actually served with or on: so there is no direct connection between text and attributed copyright owners.

I owe a considerable debt to BP Shipping Limited for again allowing me unlimited access to their photographic archive at the University of Warwick. Specifically, to Peter Housego, BP's Global Archives Manager of Communications and External Affairs, and Bethan Thomas, an Archivist, for giving so freely of their time and assistance. Shell International Trading and Shipping Company Limited also granted use of historical photographs and I am grateful to the Estates of Gerard Manley Hopkins and Rudyard Kipling for allowing publication of extracts from works of these poets.

Chapter 1

CASTING OFF

———

PRIORITY — URGENT YOU CONTACT CAPTAIN FORD LONDON OFFICE STOP
ELLERTON SHIPPING STOP ENDS.

I waved the Company's recall telegram around the room encompassing parents and fiancée Sue with, it must be confessed, some affected agitation. Frankly, it was difficult to suppress a sigh of relief. The gathering looked in my direction expectantly, emotions briefly freezing their enquiring faces. The arrival of this small brownish-orange envelope, with its strikingly wide blue side panel, caused more than a cursory lull in the animated conversation of relaxed people who feel safe in each other's company. We knew the import of an oblong sheet of white paper, but no one wished to express the common thought. Instead, my 'nearest and dearest' looked at me intently, clearly awaiting my confirmation.

Reading aloud the fateful words, with a feeling of almost guilty detachment, I saw looks of resigned acceptance sweeping over their faces. Each confronted the inevitable in characteristically different ways. Dad remained stoic as ever, but the torn feelings of Mum and Sue were painfully evident. On my part, shore life had undoubtedly acquired certain attractions. Initially, being at home had been thoroughly enjoyable: days of comparative idleness being pampered by Mum, experiencing a new more relaxed relationship with Dad and discussing generally tentative arrangements for a (much) later marriage. Recently however surreptitious strains of an additional ingredient had been unresistingly infiltrating. Shore life was ceasing to satisfy and I felt there was definitely something lacking.

Standing quietly looking at each other, collecting our thoughts, my mind reflected over the last few months. Of course, the period at nautical college had been extremely pressured, although not particularly stressful. Accompanying the confirmation that I had passed as Second Mate, the next four weeks had proved genuinely idyllic. A letter of congratulation had been received enclosing a generous cheque from Ellerton Shipping with whom my deck cadetship had been completed. It took little imagination to realise the acceptance (and spending) of such extravagant bounty, tacitly and morally (if not legally), assumed my signature on a two-year contract of employment as third officer.

From a coat-hanger on the door of my bedroom wardrobe hung a new Number One doeskin uniform – very casually displayed and showing, to maximum advantage, the traditional Ellerton rank style of a thick gold stripe surmounted by a diamond on each sleeve. It had taken quite a bit of discreet rearranging before both sleeves became so nonchalantly visible. On the tabletop, my Discharge Book and new-style Seafarers' Identity Card were partially hidden (equally casually, of course) by a brand-new Second Mates' certificate. Contrasting colours of gold lettering and coats of arms on light blue, red and black covers appealed to that aesthetic sense in my personality. Under these documents however (but very definitely hidden) lay my latest bank statement. It did not require an accountancy qualification to prove there was a certain impracticality to living very much longer on love alone.

'The situation is simple really,' I explained to the family, stuffing the telegram into my pocket and happy to accept an irrefutable excuse to hide the deeper truth of my feelings: 'Until I sign Ellerton's contract – or find another shipping company, which is not my intention – there is no income. Although,' I added, 'the urgency of a priority delivery telegram seems to show undue haste in Ellerton's desire to recruit my services.'

The silence was broken in time honoured way by mother stating that a pot of tea might be in order. Her suggestion eased the tension, letting me off the hook a little. Only two days earlier, over Sunday lunch, my father had mooted it could not be too long before Ellertons contacted me. With customary perception, he had added I was 'no doubt eagerly anticipating this', although his unexpected remark left me floundering a bit. Sue and Mum, with glass and fork respectively raised halfway, had also looked in my direction almost willing me to offer even a thinly disguised denial. Much as I had smiled weakly – trying to oblige them – it was really of little use, hiding my true feelings had always proved difficult. I would have made a quite appalling poker player – a thought which reminded me of an aphorism from my mother – something about 'being behind the door when the gift of subtlety was distributed'.

Captain Ford was in charge of seagoing appointments at second and third mate level, but there was a subtle difference since I had joined the Ellerton Steam Ship Company as a cadet over four years previously. It seemed employment and loyalties were no longer with 'Ellerton Lines', as they were more colloquially known, but had been transferred recently to Ellerton Shipping Group. A warm smile accompanied his invitation to sit, whilst a welcome cup of coffee and a large plate of biscuits were passed casually across his desk. As I sat happily sipping and munching, the good captain explained some implications in these changes as they directly affected my service: 'You will understand, Mr Caridia, although we most certainly continue to take officers' preferences into consideration as seagoing appointments are discussed, these are now subject to what is termed a "manning rule". In practical terms, any junior mate may argue against an offered posting, but now 'the most pressing urgency' determines in which of the Group's companies and ships he will serve. You will need to be aware of these changes before considering whether you should sign an employment contract with us.'

Whilst I deliberated 'Hobson's nautical choice', the title 'Mr' in recognition of my promotion was silently savoured. By using this honorific, and throwing off the surname-only merchant naval reference traditional to all cadet officers, the superintendent acknowledged my 'arrival'. With a brief glance of appraisal, he turned to an impressive array of documents on the desk blotter before him. The inevitable contract was then passed for my signature and, after signing both copies, we discussed a few salient points. I noticed also a set of joining instructions and a travel warrant previously hidden behind other papers. The original contract was grabbed from my hand – with almost undue haste in case I changed my mind – and placed inside a folder (presumably my record of progress). Although I was left in no doubt who was conducting this interview, the efficacy of the 'manning rule' seemed a suitable target for testing: 'Is there any opportunity of a posting to one of the group's six *Empress* tankers, discussed a few months ago with the chief super? He did suggest I wait until qualified before enquiring about a transfer.'

A disarmingly warm smile accompanied his reply: 'Regretfully, it is not possible on this occasion as no vacancies are immediately available because all our tankers are properly manned and on passage. We are aware that the Group will almost certainly be interested in seeking officers such as your good self for this class of ship, but unfortunately that is not the situation now.'

I was offered instead, in a tone boding little room for manoeuvre, an Ellerton vessel – the MV *Earl of Gourock*. Following a nineteen-month voyage, the ship was returning early next morning from deep-sea to commence cargo discharge at Southampton, after which she was bound for unspecified UK coastal and then continental ports. A relieving third mate was required immediately enabling the deep-sea officer to go for a well-deserved leave. This at least explained the priority cable. The ship was an 8945 gross registered tonnage (grt) dry cargo vessel of 489 feet overall and 67 feet beam; a six-hatch job, six years old, with a cruising speed of 15 knots. She was one of the Group's twelve-class passenger ships, although none was currently carried and berths would not be filled around the coast. I was instructed to return home, pack my gear and catch a

Southampton train early next morning. This proffered trip was (as far as requirements allowed) a typically short run for all newly-qualified officers with Ellerton's, offering a chance to 'dry the ink on their certificates' as the superintendent commented wryly. I was sufficiently shrewd to realise a short voyage afforded also a golden opportunity to examine Company new recruits to see if they would prove useful, prior to foisting them onto some unsuspecting master for a more prolonged foreign-going voyage.

In the comfort of my bed that night, with suitcases packed and taxi ordered ready for an early morning start, it was difficult to settle immediately to sleep. My insomnia was caused not so much by the hectic yet comparatively uncomplicated events of the day, but came from a need to unravel and fathom out reasons why 'going away to sea' was so eminently important. Such thoughts seemed especially relevant in the light of my recent engagement to Sue. I tried to control struggling thoughts into a rationality that might find some possibly productively useful answers. Yes, 'the sea' was missed, but it was not merely the physical contribution of moody excitement from uncontrollable weather and restless waves. There was far more to seafaring than that – there simply had to be. Absentmindedly studying the pattern on my bedroom wallpaper helped thoughts and feelings to become focussed whilst I attempted defining the indefinable.

Then the penny dropped, well, at least for a certain way as (even at my age) I recognised such things were really far too complex for easy unravelling. What was being missed – and so yearned for – was the ethos of seafaring life. Ninety per cent of me yearned to savour again that peculiar atmosphere unique to working a ship in port or at sea. There was more to being at sea than actually being aboard a ship in the knowledge that she would shortly be moving on – to sail elsewhere – with constantly challenging seas and ever changing glimpses of intriguingly new vistas of ports, jetties, docks and river banks. There was an involvement and, being part of, numerous minor impressions alien to life ashore. Such trivialities as the invariably nerve-racking 'venturing into unknown waters' by clambering up a bouncing gangway on joining, and the smiled greeting from an Asian duty *secunny*. This contrasted vividly with the relaxed anticipatory excitement generated by signing-off to go on leave. There were unique sounds. The clanking rumble of McGregor's hatches closed or opened by jocular *khalassis* working amicably with their British officers. The sense of achievement and finality emanating from an unmistakable roar as anchor cable rushed through hawse-pipe signifying termination of another successful passage. I felt a need to experience again sounds of cargo gear, creaking and protesting under heavy load and abuse from indifferent shore handlers, as topped married derricks moved boxes or bales from deep within the hold to dumb barges below. Other contributions came from smells such as funnel exhaust mixing with assorted aromas from a *bhandary's* galley; well-oiled derricks (and satisfaction at no longer having to apply the stuff myself), of assorted paints and greases in the fo'c'sle head stores, and variegated whiffs from sacks of Far Eastern cargoes. Intermingling amongst all other sensations rode that unmistakably permeating aroma – and taste almost – from the heady salt tang of the sea itself. Additionally, on this forthcoming voyage a brand new personal challenge was present: I would be a member of the bridge team aboard a ship again (*in charge* this time for two four-hour periods) as an integral part of that quietly determined air of responsibility attendant with navigational watch-keeping. Seafaring was proving a delightfully nomadic restless existence, always 'going to somewhere from somewhere – to do something else'. Even in port there was movement: wandering off to experience different countries, peoples and situations many of which, for some, were not the kind they would wish to be reminded about when reunited with their families.

Such thoughts racing through my mind helped clarify what seafaring meant to me and reinforced my need to be part of once more. This was how I had to spend my immediate future. Yet simultaneously there was awareness that going away for a typically prolonged voyage would cause pain to my family – especially Sue – and create paradoxically a sense of inordinate loneliness within me. This was the essence of my personal maritime dichotomy. It would not take the most 'dippy' of psychiatrists long to deduce that I had been bitten deeply by 'the sea bug' – perhaps even more than I suspected.

It seemed almost the next moment that my cab deposited me at Waterloo railway station. Even before we came to a complete halt and my luggage had been removed, another potential passenger inserted himself into the opposite door shouting urgent instructions to the driver. I wondered sardonically if he might wish to pay my fare so they could set off together that much quicker, but sanity prevailed and I dropped a handful of notes into an outstretched hand, thanking my cabby for a safe, if chatty, start to my trip.

Waterloo certainly lived up to its customary hustle of bustling concourse life recalled from cadet days travelling to Portsmouth for Royal Naval Reserve training. Handicapped by my two suitcases I was soon entangled with hundreds of people forming the tail end of early morning rush-hour – a newly-coined word imported (along with Coca-Cola and increasingly heady rock music) from the United States. After changing my travel warrant – simultaneously keeping an eye on my gear – I fought a path to the Southampton–Weymouth platform barrier, leaving a host of cursing office-workers in my wake. Regular travellers were obviously used to warfare in which no quarter was given so, for self-preservation, both suitcases simply had to be used as a battering ram. Overhead, frequent yet unhurried train announcements competed with soothing music, fragmented conversations, noises from steam engines, and a characteristic burp from an occasional new-fangled diesel unit – 'travel propulsion of the future' we were informed. Smoke and fumes settled everywhere contributing to the atmosphere. Eventually, I nestled in a lavishly-cushioned empty compartment corner and watched, through a rapidly closed window, countless swarms of people rushing from an adjoining platform to an equally diverse array of offices. It reminded me of my own brief spell in a shipping company headquarters prior to attending navigation school. I felt no superiority over these 'office *wallahs*', but most definitely (especially following the previous evening's ruminations) did not envy their lifestyle in preference to my own. A packed incoming train suddenly clanked alongside that platform. The movement broke both view and reverie. It eased my sense of relaxation, and gave a chance to glance again through joining instructions and seaman's documents, whilst awaiting departure on what proved an uneventful journey in a virtually empty carriage.

Upon leaving Southampton Central railway station, while waiting to enter yet another taxi, my attention was diverted by the disembodied range of superstructures and funnels belonging to liners in the New Docks. Union-Castle colours, P&O, together with United States and Royal Rotterdam Lloyd lines were immediately recognisable, towering over wharfs, sheds, dwellings and intervening buildings – although none fired me with sufficient enthusiasm to consider joining this class of vessel. Approaching the entrance, by the dock offices in Canute Road, I smiled inwardly at seeing two men with red flags waving down our cab and accompanying convoy of lorries and cars on each side of the railway track. The reason for such an archaic (to my mind) method of traffic control was explained away by the driver as 'traffic lights broken down yet again'. Soon an Ocean-Liner Express trundled past blowing a thick whiff of cinders and smoke through the open window. Cursing quietly while closing this rapidly, he explained over his shoulder that passengers aboard the train were joining Union-Castle Line's *Carnarvon Castle* lying at Itchen Quays, just outside Empress Dock where the *Earl of Gourock* was moored. Apparently, this large passenger company occasionally used these berths in preference to those normally taken by their regular-run '*4 o'clock PROMPT SAILING Thursday*' mail ships – one of whose funnels had been recognised in the New Docks. I accepted this information happily but without total concentration for, as reality loomed closer, that very slight apprehension of last night was again experienced concerning joining my own ship in a brand new capacity. Although undoubtedly proud of achieving full officer status, slight doubts infiltrated my sense of well-being. One major gremlin in particular dwarfed a few minor fellows, namely bridge watch-keeping and being there mostly alone. Certainly, this was definitely what I wanted, but previously there had always lurked a reassuring senior officer at the back of the wheelhouse ready to offer a quick word and divert potential emergency. Still, I assured myself, the master would presumably never be much further away than the nearest telephone – although this thought also lacked a certain conviction.

Before any morbid introspection could intervene, we drew alongside my ship. On leaving the cab a glance forward along the black hull showed clear evidence in spattered and besmirched paintwork of some heavy weather sustained crossing the Atlantic. Subconsciously I recognised the correctly adjusted moorings, rigged safety net and height of gangway above the quay – each offering reassuring evidence of a typically Ellerton conscientious crew. The driver gave a hand up the gangway with my gear and we were guided by a smiling *secunny* to the third officer's cabin. A quick glimpse along the port side main deck showed that all too familiar view of starboard swung derricks, and dock cranes nodding as they slickly discharged slings and pallets of boxed cargo and dropped these close to a convoy of forklift trucks waiting on the jetty. It was comforting and reassuring to hear the constant bustle of familiar shipboard crashes; assorted train, tug and ship whistles from adjoining docks, and an even drumming of different machines, all mixed with a variety of voices and accents. I caught sight of the distant fo'c'sle head through a jungle of masts massed by supporting wires, cluttered by contactor houses, winches, deck cleats, rails with paint slightly eroded from sea air and awaiting attention, and mooring bollards encircled with heavy wires or ropes restraining ship to jetty. Suddenly I realised my musing was holding up a chain-gang of Goanese stewards as the pursers' laughing and joking crew darted in between cargo slings with cases of saloon stores. Standing aside, and grinning infectiously, I caught a waft of that singular curry smell from Asian galleys aft, and distinctive cabin smells of varnish and polish − and a quick aroma of that day's lunch from the European kitchen. Merging with impressions from the jetty, the scenario seemed almost welcoming. It was as if I had arrived home and confirmed my decision that returning to Ellerton's had been the correct one to make.

I had no sooner dropped my bags than Derek McFay, the deep-sea third mate, came in. It was encouraging to see the Company grapevine working so effectively, for I had certainly been unaware of any officers noting my arrival alongside. Still, his joy at seeing me was perfectly understandable. So would mine have been if I have been at sea for such a lengthy period whilst *Earl of Gourock* wallowed her way around the Far East, then onto Australia (with endless dock strikes) for the wool sales, thence discharging and loading at Japanese ports en route to India for Africa and the United States Gulf. He could not wait to get away and I suspected he had after all been looking out for my arrival. I accepted his effusion with contentment, for my policy was always one of spreading a little happiness and then, as past experience invariably dictated, sitting back to see whatever might develop. The only discernible follow-up on this occasion was for him to change into civvies and pop his uniform and some final gear into an awaiting suitcase. In between these agitated functions he advised me regarding the status quo of fellow mates and cargo. He had already signed-off with most other officers before the captain and shipping master in the saloon earlier in the day when deep-sea Articles closed and coastal ones opened. The voyage chief officer was still on board, but the coastal master and second mate had already relieved their opposite numbers. Neither of the two cadets remained and there were no rumours of any to join. The ship had taken diverse general cargo for discharge in London, Hull, Newcastle, Copenhagen, Hamburg and Antwerp, afterwards being scheduled to load in Rotterdam and the UK for deep-sea. Well, at least that was the existing plan … He left that comment open. Currently, she was discharging all hatches: tinned fruits from Tampa and Mobile, along with synthetic rubber from Beaumont, and cartons of wax from Galveston.

Before we could develop our conversation further the chief officer and another taxi driver arrived simultaneously at the cabin entrance. The former shook me warmly by the hand whilst the latter took Derek's two cases and holdall into the alleyway. The mates' parting offered an opportunity to take stock of Ian Windsor. It was with some diffidence that I began using Christian names with all officers above third mate, junior engineers and Sparks, but this soon came naturally. The captain of course, to all ranks, remained firmly within the 'Sir' bracket – whilst 'the chief' engineer remained precisely that.

Ian also was impatient to leave the ship, but had been informed by Head Office – or, the 'Kremlin' as we respectfully referred to the place – that there was immediately no relief available and he would have to take the ship round to London, at least. This worrying news was consistent with a chronic shortage of officers over all deck and engineering ranks, not only within the Group, but across the Merchant Navy generally. Ellerton's had recently followed wider company shipping policy of offering a magnificent bounty to all recently qualified cadets. They had recently introduced berths to officers' wives around coastal voyages, and this was rumoured soon to be extended deep-sea. Both incentives were purely an effort to retain men. There was even talk of recruiting female deck cadets. This rumour filled the mess rooms of most ships with unbelievable horror – almost akin to a forecast attack of beriberi or blackwater fever. Universal disapproval abounded leading to cries of 'it's no life for a girl – they'll not be able to cope physically with the deck work – there are accommodation difficulties on most ships – it will upset the social life of the voyage' – and similar negatives. The only whimsical acceptance perhaps came from certain male cadets whose minds abounded enthusiastically in delightfully erotic dreams of tropical nights alongside some eager and nubile female in a closely adjoining cabin. The industry clearly needed time to adjust even remotely to this novel idea – let alone accepting it as fact. My own views were consistent with the general outcry for, to be honest (like railway diesel engines), I also could not see this 'new fangled idea' working in practice – possibly because I was now no longer a 'forward-looking' cadet. Whilst turning over this information, the steward sounded a timely gong so, as Ian went to discuss 'something nautical' with a runner from the Inward Freight department, we parted on the way into the saloon for lunch where I joined the junior deck officers' table, after dropping off my joining expenses chit with Danny the purser/chief steward.

Following my quick meal, I reported to Captain Davies' cabin with Discharge Book and brand new Certificate to make my number and sign Articles. This indicated little more significance for me than having an *Earl of Gourock* entry inserted to start the second page. This was satisfying in an odd sort of way. It was a sobering reflection that it had taken four years to 'turn a new leaf', as it were, and led me to wonder just how long it might be before completing all sixty entries necessary to finish the entire book.

The Master's friendly, firm manner immediately put me at ease. He recognised this to be my first trip as a newly-qualified officer and unequivocally reinforced his ready availability at all times: 'The yardstick is really quite simple, Mr Caridia. When you are on watch as my third officer, if you even *think* perhaps you might need to call me to the wheelhouse – then *that* is the time to do so. I shall never be angry if it turns out to be a false alarm.' He looked at me intently, and then smiled gently, 'Much rather you did that, you know, than left things too late'.

In relaxed mood I moved from his to my own accommodation, exchanged civvies for working gear of battle-dress uniform with cap, and went to relieve the second mate covering discharge now from numbers one, three and five hatches for cargo watch. I was to be on deck until work stopped around 1700 hours and then be on duty until 0800 next day. James Parsons had been with the company for ten years, since his cadet days, and exuded that confidence associated with the two-and-a-half stripes on his epaulettes of an Ellerton senior and very experienced second officer: one not far off promotion to mate. His greeting was cordial enough as he passed across the cargo tally book and filled me in regarding the discharging situation. His wife was doing the coastal trip, along with those of the master and second engineering officer, but all three were currently ashore together on a 'spend, spend, spend spree', as it was caustically described – the twinkle in his eye belying too serious a concern in his statement.

I was kept extremely busy tallying broken cases of tinned fruit – ones that had been broached probably by dockers 'somewhere' and their contents removed – so, by the end of the day, skeletal remains of sixteen were stowed in the Mate's office. It was amazing really, because not even a hint of anything going on was detected and no one was actually seen leaving the holds with bulging pockets. It could not possibly have happened in Southampton for, I mused quietly to myself whilst gazing in frustration down number one hatch, 'were not 2½-sized tins of assorted fruits quite large cans and therefore impossible to smuggle safely ashore? Unless they had 'vanished into thin air', as my mother used to say when things went mysteriously missing at home, they could only have been stolen. The few remaining cans I did find lying loosely in the 'tween-decks were taken to a locker for handing over to the freight department. As these were rarely collected we usually gave them to the chief steward as supplements to his catering rate (unless of course they were of a more delectably desirable nature, when – hypocrisy notwithstanding – they found their way discreetly to the arresting officer's cabin for personal consumption). Following my deck watch there was time only for a quick refreshing wash before joining the single sitting at supper. A wave of hilarious laughter met my ears long before I entered the saloon as officers and wives exchanged stories across the tables of amusing events occurring ashore. James was sitting with his wife at our table and soon included me in the general repartee – which extended to coffee in the smoke-room afterwards. The friendliness of my colleagues and the introduction of wives on the coastal trip were certainly conducive to further relaxation. It seemed there would be much hilarity over the coastal trip, but I retained my doubts concerning the efficacy of 'this alien wives arrangement' during a prolonged deep-sea voyage.

Within an hour of supper all other officers, apart from the duty engineer, had gone ashore leaving me nestled in the comfort of a deep armchair glancing idly through the local newspaper. Regardless of wherever in the world I found myself there was always considerable interest gained from browsing through any 'local' – doing so seemed to add colour to the port in which we were staying, however casually might be our visit. Roland the third engineer had to pop below 'to check his rubber bands' as I teased him, so I toddled along to my cabin to unpack gear, place photographs and trinkets and stamp the place with something of my own personality. Once this was done, Roland knocked on the jalousie inviting me to a few lagers and a couple of crib games, 'assuming of course I could draw myself away my window watching'. Smiling acceptance of his 'oily-water revenge' we then spent a couple of hours in serious and intense competition with me, as the marginal loser, signing the bar steward's chit for

Officers and their wives enjoying a social evening in the ship's lounge and bar –
very much the focal point of social life aboard most ships (courtesy BP plc)

the ale consumed. My leisurely yawn indicated that it was time to turn in. As I stepped onto the gangway for a quick check on deck, a sudden blast from a cold wind caused me to make an immediate about-turn for a windproof, causing my Asian watchman to express a smile. We exchanged a few pleasantries, but I did not spend too long checking moorings, gangway and the like, before returning and advising the *secunny* where I would be until 0800 next day. It was then a grateful return to my cabin where I passed James and his wife returning from a visit to friends who lived in a nearby suburb of Southampton.

The one thing really appreciated accompanying my promotion was the privacy of a single-berth cabin which, in effect, was home for the duration of the trip. This provided a safe haven where I could be myself and recharge social batteries so, despite my tiredness, I played some music quite loudly through headphones (to prevent disturbance and for deeper appreciation) whilst simultaneously reading a favourite book.

Later, snuggling into a comfortable bunk, I allowed my mind to run again over events so far encountered on board before dropping into a deeply-restful slumber. In a strange sort of way, memories were evoked of joining my first ship the *Earl of Bath* in Amsterdam, as an extremely green and unbelievably naïve seafarer. Certainly this second stage of newness was far more under control, for the years of my cadetship nullified

A newly-appointed third officer in the comfort of his cabin catches up
with ship's paper work (courtesy BP plc).

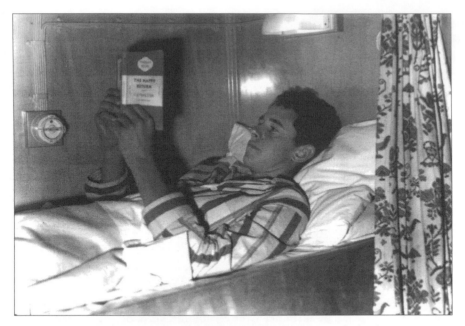

*The best part of any day after Watches was to relax in the bunk
with a favoured book (courtesy BP plc).*

*A gentle sifting through the ship's library – another essential part of the procedure
for settling into a new ship (courtesy BP plc).*

considerably the sense of apprehension which had then been experienced. My meetings with the captain and chief officer who, so far as my professional and indeed social welfare were concerned represented the two most important people aboard, had offered particular reassurance. Further comfort came with the confidence that my work could be handled competently, and the idea of taking my bridge watches was now positively anticipated. The informality of meeting fellow officers led me to fear few difficulties in meeting social obligations of an officer on board. I had started also cementing crew relations whilst joking with the *serang's* deck ratings as I kept an eye on them whilst they stored ship.

Heavy rain next morning prevented further cargo work and afforded time to study an assortment of ship's plans, including the distribution of fire-fighting appliances and general arrangement and capacity drawings. I also updated our lifeboat and emergency stations muster list. This was quite a simple task involving removing the names of officers who had been relieved and entering those newly joined. Although this introduction to responsibility (under the first or third mates) for all life-saving appliances aboard had been done in latter stages of my time, this was my first solo act and confirmed again my sense of arrival. It was therefore with some satisfaction that I entered my own surname at the head of number four boat, the after one on the port side. Taking charge of a ship's lifeboat, and indeed fire fighting and rescue parties during drills, had also been encouraged whilst a senior cadet, so few worries existed now I was to do these duties for real. Our Indian ratings were all on one-year contracts, so the crew invariably remained unchanged, apart from occasional alterations due to hospitalisation – and an ever rarer desertion. This was the reason why, unless returning from a prolonged foreign-going trip, officers on Asian-crewed ships signed Articles locally before the Old Man and not at the shipping office. All ranks were now paid salaries through their bank account, obviating the need for cash exchanges during pay-off times, and generally there were so few men joining and leaving ships that changes occurred in the Old Man's cabin – with the Board of Trade notified through the second copy of Articles lodged with them prior to sailing from any port.

There was little time available whilst sailing around the coast to offer anything other than a cursory look over the boats and their equipment. The completion of after-lunch coffee in the lounge coincided happily with the cessation of heavy rain, appearance of a welcomingly hot sun, and the Mate. All three encouraged me on deck to supervise opening of numbers two and four hatches and recommence cargo discharge. We worked continuously until early evening after which, following a quick supper and change into civvies, I suggested to Sparks that we go ashore. Our foraging in Southampton proved little more dangerous than visiting a local cinema to watch an intriguing film about bomb disposal in the Second World War – entitled, as I recall, *The Small Back Room*. This was followed by a fish and chip supper and 'phone call home before returning safely back on board to our respective 'snuggies'.

A couple of evenings prior to sailing were occupied with ship visits. Not wanting to go ashore every evening, I sometimes spent time after supper wandering alone

RMS Queen Elizabeth *always made an impressive sight lying quietly at her berth in Southampton's Ocean Dock (Author's collection).*

around nearby dock complexes freely savouring the contrast between the quietness of our ship with that atmosphere of hustle and bustle as cargo loading continued aboard other vessels well into the early hours to hasten turn-rounds. The Royal Mail Lines' *Andes* frantically loaded endless sacks of mail and I exchanged passing rueful comments with the second mate as he checked these onto the ship into 'tween-deck lock-ups. My main objective on one occasion was the liner *Queen Elizabeth* in the adjacent Ocean Dock whose impressive superstructure and funnels had been visible from our boat deck. Dwarfing sheds, cranes and even the roof of the passenger terminal they could hardly have been missed, but had aroused an uncharacteristic desire to enquire about seafaring life aboard one of these marine monsters. Making myself known to the quartermaster, he telephoned the duty mate who instructed a nearby steward to take me along seemingly endless brightly lit alleyways that gradually ascended to officer territory abaft the bridge. Considering I had very much dropped in out of the blue, my reception was very cordial indeed and a junior deck officer was soon hosting me around a wheelhouse that extended about 130 feet – or almost a quarter the length of my own ship. It appeared enormous – and took a seemingly inordinate time to cross from port to starboard bridge wings. The other impressive factor was the distance from wing to jetty, which looked 'an awful long way down'. Chatting over a beer later, it seemed that once at sea the vast expanses of water cut her down to size a little and, although large, she handled similarly to any other vessel. I kept my own counsel on that having nothing within my experience to compare. The officers were of similar background found with many traditional first-class UK shipping companies including Ellertons – until, that is, the precedent of my arrival amongst ranks of the latter.

The second ship visit was more surprising. I had just settled to an evening as duty officer relaxing in the lounge with the second mate and his wife when the captain's steward (or 'tiger' as he was known universally) came with a written note summoning me to the Old Man. James was equally bemused and could offer little in the way of explanation whilst I hastily adjusted my shirt collar and tie and, buttoning my reefer jacket in the process, made my way aloft. A quick smile from 'father' was the initial reassurance that there was nothing amiss. He explained part of my duty that evening would be to escort a visiting party from a local ship society and show them around our vessel. It seemed the Company had issued a dock pass to eleven of these gents authorising them to develop their inherent interest in 'matters maritime' and it would be my lot to host this enthusiastic gathering. They were due in about half an hour's time and the Old Man had forgotten entirely they were coming until, with some prescient instinct, he had fortunately glanced at his desk diary to which was attached a letter from Ellerton's Southampton office. I went immediately to the duty *secunny* at the gangway instructing him to show them upon arrival to the lounge where I promptly repaired, explaining the nature of this unusual calling to James. He recalled doing something similar years previously with a group of elderly Women's Institute ladies, whilst a cadet aboard the old *Earl of Madras* in East India docks, and roughed an outline itinerary which excluded the engine-room, but included virtually everywhere else.

So far as it was possible to deduce the group seemed to enjoy their visit. They were a cheerful crowd, none of whom had served at sea in any capacity, but proved extremely (and even embarrassingly) knowledgeable about the Group's fleet such that, in many respects, I learned much from them. We ventured around the main deck where I pointed out features of interest concerning gear and cargo for about forty minutes. After this, it was a case of 'into the wheelhouse' where explanations about navigation, the equipment and its uses, and my own career to date, were followed by questions and answers of a vicarious nature that extended over the next hour and a half. There were too many of them to invite into the smoke-room for drinks so we animatedly chatted our way to the gangway and the termination of their visit. In such manner passed an unusual yet interesting duty. James and his wife had retired to his cabin when I returned to the lounge so, making a thick sweet cup of cocoa and grabbing a couple of biscuits, the rest of the evening before rounds was spent relaxing quietly in my cabin.

My first stand-by as third officer was a hectic affair. Shortly after the pilot boarded whilst awaiting tugs, I tested all gear, synchronised clocks with the duty engineer, hoisted the appropriate flags and ruled up a much-used Movement Book. Performing these familiar routines was found comforting and quietly reassuring so I felt totally

The first stand-by in the wheelhouse as third officer was exciting in anticipation of an unknown voyage in a new rank (courtesy BP plc).

at ease as both Captain and pilot entered the wheelhouse chatting casually. The latter gave me his name and that of the tugs and, confirming with the chief officer that all was in order and we would be using their towing wires, Ian disappeared forward whilst the pilot set about taking *Earl of Gourock* off her berth and into the narrow shipping channel of Southampton Water. I must confess a touch of envy as we passed Fawley Refinery with a full quota of tankers. The 36,000 sdwt *Esso Portsmouth* – 'a recently rebuilt chap' as the pilot laconically referred to her – had smoke bursting impatiently from her funnel and, with tugs in attendance, was merely waiting our departure before going deep-sea to the Persian Gulf for a further load of crude oil. Picturing my opposite number in her wheelhouse rekindled my interest in serving on tankers . . . some day.

Turning to my more immediate station, I savoured the peaceful quietness in our wheelhouse and watched as pilot and Master concentrated on moving our ship between opposing yachts whom our pilot referred to as 'the Twickenham navy'. This name was applied to them as a sardonic reference to their supposedly middle-class and quite well off owners. As one crossed our bows, inordinately closely, he also referred to them as '*WAFIs*' - which was interpreted caustically to my enquiring glance as 'Wind assisted ****** idiots'. His remark clearly arose from professional concerns for safety

Passing the MT Esso Portsmouth *evoked images of the third officer on her bridge performing similar duties preparing and taking his ship to sea (courtesy World Ship Society).*

at sea and resulted not only from this occasion, but also a host of near misses whilst piloting deep-draught ships in dredged channels as some 'yachties' attempted to sort out their obligations under the collision regulations. In fairness, he did admit that 'some of these people holding BOT/Royal Yachting Association (RYA) Yacht-Master certificates, were very competent' but, the problem was, he never knew if any of these 'professional amateurs' (I loved this expression) were aboard – until it was too late.

We competed also with coasters, fishing boats, and Royal Navy vessels in the Solent, after which I kept an eye on larger traffic entering the main channel bound for the two major regional ports. My task was simply to plot our position by regularly putting 'a dot on the chart' as we were in close waters; transmitting helm orders from pilot to the *secunny*, working Movement Book to engine-room telegraph orders and, by request, feeding radar information on closing craft. Just south of Portsmouth we dropped the pilot. This was a few miles north-east to the area of my Royal Naval Reserve manoeuvres in picket boats. I shuddered on recalling memories encompassing my ten-day period of what was known in the trade as 'a time of mixed fortunes'. In agreement with Captain Ford my decision whether or not to proceed with an application for commissioning was to be deferred until after my first voyage. It was then I decided that, unless Ellertons really wanted me to, papers for a RNR List One Commission – with Service in the Merchant Navy – would not be submitted. I experienced an accompanying inward peace over my decision.

Having returned to the bridge from seeing the pilot away the Master had already commenced the wide turn necessary to come out of the lee we had created enabling the pilot safely to board his cutter. By the time I had struck the pilot flag, and stowed this neatly in the flag locker fixed to the after-part of the wheelhouse, the ship was settled on her course line to head a couple of miles south of the Owers light vessel. The Old Man had already rung FULL AHEAD and, pausing, looked at me very directly as I glanced up from leaning over the chart fixing our position. He advised the *secunny* should be left on the helm for a while, before adding, 'You know where to find me if you want me – and she's all yours'.

Before I had even entered the time against my 'fix', the wheelhouse door clanged-to with seemingly certain finality – and the realisation dawned that I was in the chart area alone. Feeling momentary panic, I over-carefully replaced our 2B pencil between parallel rules, went into the wheelhouse and altered the pegboard against which 'my' quartermaster steered. Everything seemed very quiet – and surprisingly normal. The gyrocompass ticked away contentedly as the quartermaster casually kept the course: passing ships actually passed without incident – wide and clear – whilst Coast Line's battered old tub *Atlantic Coast*, being overtaken on our port side, continued behaving herself with commendable placidity, even to the extent of issuing enormous clouds of thick dark grey smoke from her tall angular funnel.

Conning our ship back onto her course-line when the coaster was well clear aft coincided with Sparks popping along with the latest weather report. In matter-of-fact tones he commented on the age of the thing wallowing in our wake. We could just make out the duty mate aboard her talking to his able-seaman (AB) on the helm. Having looked her up in a shipping register we found she was built in 1934. He expressed no surprise finding me on watch alone and, following a few other casual comments, returned to his shack. Such automatic acceptance gave me an enormous boost, and it was with considerable confidence that I fed the *secunny* instructions so we could gradually alter course to round the Owers and head two miles south of the *Royal Sovereign* lightship. It was interesting watching variations in the gradually passing coastline and following these down on radar and chart. There was a fair density of shipping (yachts and cabin cruisers) but nothing to cause immediate problems, although the 24-mile range showed an increasing build-up in the vicinity of Dungeness pilot station – which anyway would be the second mate's problem by then.

My next set of fixes put the *Gourock* setting slightly north of her course-line as she caught the strong easterly current prevalent in this area five hours before high water at Dover. By the time two degrees on the gyro had been allowed to compensate for this set and drift, it was approaching noon and James came up to relieve the watch. His wife Sheila accompanied him and stood by quietly as we passed information regarding shipping, courses with set and drift, radar and the like after which, following some inevitable jokes, I entered events of my first solo watch in the Mate's rough logbook. Feeling a tremendous sense of self-achievement I went below to the saloon for luncheon.

The Old Man glanced up upon my entry and smilingly quietly enquired if 'all was well'. I detected a delightful ambiguity in his remark which could have referred equally to me upon completion of my first bridge watch, or the situation concerning the shipping. I nodded an affirmative and, joining in the repartee between Sparks and two junior engineers, enjoyed a satisfying meal.

With the South Channel pilot on board from Dungeness, we were entering Princes Channel in the Thames estuary when I was next called on watch. It was quite a long haul for I remained in the wheelhouse until we were safely moored alongside the familiar Elllerton berth in King George V Dock, but an interesting time for all that. Passing shore marks familiar from my own teenaged pre-cadet days aboard harbour service launches with my uncle was now, as an officer, extremely satisfying. Our stay in London covered a partial cargo discharge which included streamlined Chevrolet saloon cars, along with cellulose products originally loaded in Charleston and Fernandia Beach respectively.

I was fortunate in having a long weekend local leave before rejoining the ship early the following Monday morning. This proved a welcome and unexpected break made all the more agreeable by receipt of a letter from Captain Mobbs, the superintendent of my pre-sea nautical training college. Apparently, he had noticed my name amongst other successful candidates for Second Mates' and higher grades which were reported weekly from examination ports in *Lloyd's List and Shipping Gazette*. I obtained a copy of this publication and admitted a modest thrill sharing this within the family. I had no idea my progress had been noticed by him in this way and, feeling guilty at having not written before, penned a short account of experiences encountered during my cadetship and outlined plans for my future seafaring.

Returning aboard, I immediately (and not surprisingly) commenced an all-day cargo watch. Apart from noting a couple of broken headlights, and one dented chrome rear bumper, the day passed uneventfully. On the way to my cabin, I unexpectedly encountered a newly-joined uniformed cadet complete with gear who looked both lost and yet vaguely familiar. We had obviously never encountered each other before because he showed no sign of recognition as we introduced ourselves and I shunted him towards the Mate's cabin so he could report aboard. Helping move his gear into the cadets' cabin, the penny suddenly dropped that he could only be Frank Dow, the nineteen-year-old brother of Graham whom I had met as a cadet when he was third mate on the *Earl of Melbourne*. The resemblance was uncanny. Well into his cadetship, he was assigned to the second officer for supervision of his final stages of training prior to taking Second Mates' early the following year. It seemed he was staying with the ship after Tilbury.

Frank and I were given the job of lugging the ship's box down the gangway and into a taxi. This was a large black tin trunk containing sundry documents pertaining to the deep-sea voyage which, considering the time she had been away, turned out to be quite considerable. We had to deliver this to Ellerton's head office near that bastion of shipping business in the City of London colloquially called 'Leadenhall Street'. Whilst in Southampton, I had been instructed by the Master to work in his office, attempting to bash some sense out of his battered typewriter, commencing his own coastal voyage report. The first stages of this he had completed whilst on passage off the Kent coast.

An unexpected trip by road proved quite interesting as we exchanged witticisms with the driver, but lugging this awkward box into the Kremlin was not quite so amusing. Frank inevitably dropped the edge of the thing so close to my left foot that I almost felt the wind of its passing. My instinctive verbal admonition to him, in terms perhaps more appropriate to the main deck of a ship, was most certainly not appreciated by the sombre clerical staff in the office, and a host of extremely black looks pointedly came our way. There was at least some compensation in that his unrestrained semi-apologetic laughter at this situation received also a fair share of the disapproval shot in my direction. Although our objective had certainly been achieved in completing delivery of the thing I was left with a distinct feeling that our trip could hardly have been described as propitious. This visit was in marked contrast to my very first call there some five years previously whilst arranging my cadetship: a considerable amount of water had passed under the bridge since those halcyon days. Probably resulting from our *contretemps* we were not invited to lunch in the company's refectory, but were issued with a surprisingly generous wad of luncheon vouchers and directed to a hostelry just across the road in Camomile Street.

After luncheon, as we were virtually *in situ*, the opportunity was taken to visit another bastion of maritime knowledge known to generations of seafarers' as Potters of the Minories. This was a bookshop 'crammed to the gunwhales' with nautical gems essential to mariners studying for all grades of the Board of Trade Marine Division's Regulations governing the issue of their Certificates of Competency for masters and mates – and indeed engineers. I had recommended to Frank that he should acquire a textbook which complemented admirably, and offered an alternative view, to that nautical bible for Second Mates, *Nicholls's Concise Guide – Volume One*. This was *The Cadet's Manual of Navigation and Nautical Astronomy* used by students at Southampton University's School of Navigation at Warsash. I had met this modestly presented tome in my study as a first trip cadet. Some pre-examination candidate who had outlived its use had clearly deposited it there (no doubt thankfully – a spirit in which I gratefully accepted this little gem). The diagrams, explanations and examples offered were found immensely valuable to my own studies – to such an extent that I had purchased my own copy from Potters during my first leave period. Frank, like me, had attended only a three-month pre-sea training college – where nautical astro-theory was of necessity non-existent – and, with exams looming, had expressed interest in my enthusiasm for this volume. A book or two was required also for my own First Mates study

– such as *Nicholls's Volume Two* – and Captain Denne's *Magnetic Compass Deviation and Correction*, a lively tome describing the vagrancies of the deviascope (an interesting maritime machination with which I would eventually have to come to terms). It was a good opportunity whilst among the dimly lit, crowded and cramped shelves, to see what other more general 'goodies' might be available. Eventually, our browsing produced some useful books sufficient to keep us out of mischief on long ocean voyages and, more immediately, during the short train haul back to the ship.

Over supper, Sparks suggested a trip ashore might be in order for a glass or two of English ale so, having nothing else better to do and with insufficient time for a quick visit home, I was easily persuaded. We invited the cadet to join us and, for the want of anywhere better, decided on a visit to the much-maligned Kent [Bent] Arms public house. This was an appropriate perversion of the true name very much consistent with many of the clientele – especially when any of the European-crewed liners were in dock. As Shaw Savill's *Dominion Monarch* and Union-Castle's *Bloemfontein Castle* were berthed in the Royal group, and their 'queens' were out in full force, a delightfully 'entertaining' evening ensued. Although a new experience for Frank (surprisingly, mindful of his time already at sea) Sparks and I had been there before so knew what to expect. Most of the stewards were in drag and, whilst some looked undoubtedly more female than male,

A deck cadet writing letters home or to 'the girl friend' in the comfort of his cabin (courtesy P&O Lines).

I felt their combined effect was one of utter revulsion. The expression on Frank's face was the picture we anticipated as neither of us had thought of warning him beforehand. The public, private and saloon bars were packed, but eventually we found seats sharing a table with a trio of engineer officers from Royal Mail's *Loch Gowan*, bound shortly for Ilheus, Recife and a variety of South American ports. The noise was deafening. The floorshow lived up to hilarious expectations – even if these were slightly risqué. One of the queens was standing near the bar stroking a kitten perched precariously on 'her' shoulder. Our minds boggled at the thought of where she had found it and the implications of bringing it on board ship. Our speculations concerning the captain's possible response, when discovering it during his inspection, left us creased with laughter. With the other hand, she was caressing equally as tenderly her 'friend' until, that is, the barman hollered out for her to stop. She drew herself up to full height and, in haughtily piercing tones, waved a limp wrist whilst declaiming he should 'be like that then'.

Such parts of the conversation we could hear were notable for slick-fire spontaneity and *double entendre*. The comments were extremely funny if largely unprintable. The Royal Mail officers soon left and, as it was my round, Sparks accompanied me to the bar to help carry our glasses. Waiting to be served was a marathon in itself, but we were finally chosen and made a delicate way back to our table. As we approached, I turned to Sparky pointing out that Frank was in the process of being 'chatted up' by one of the stewards. Joining him at the table, his sense of relief was almost palpable, but his unrequited companion made no effort to leave, but included us by asking the usual questions concerning which ship and what jobs we did. The effect was dramatic. She exclaimed: 'Oooooh – officers, and so lovely. How I wish our officers were *mates* like you. They are a rather stuck-up lot – in a manner of speaking, but naturally if unfortunately, not towards us.'

We felt there was little answer against this delightful if challenging sally and that clearly we were going to be dragged in against our wills – if we were not too careful. Fortunately, she was lured away by one of her fellows and we were left in comparative peace to finish our drinks. It was not long after this that we also departed mainly because we could sense trouble brewing between factions of the stewards from both ships, and considered it advisable to make ourselves scarce before encountering a possible introduction to the local law. Of course, we agreed whilst returning to our ship, perhaps we should not have gone there, but still regarded the experience as quite entertaining – if rather harmless.

For me, in an odd sort of way, it was an important visit. Coming ashore to take Second Mates had meant living at home for a few months and this, combined with my leave and concerns over the new third officer posting, had contributed towards a more sober approach to my chosen life at sea than was warranted. Our visit to the Kent Arms helped me regain a more relaxed perspective. Of course, my attitude towards duties remained responsible, but neither my colleagues nor I were taken quite so seriously. I began to see again that more humorous side to seafaring, which had been so much a facet of my later cadetship days.

It was on the 'lunch time tide' (as I cynically referred to it) a few days later that we sailed and by early evening were heading off Harwich. It was a clear night when I relieved Ian on watch with the ship heading sedately for Hull. He was in the middle of quite a bold alteration of course for a combined fishing fleet and coastal ménage so, following the practice of watchkeepers in letting the officer on watch sort out his own situations before handing-over, I waited until he had settled *Earl of Gourock* back onto her course-line before going through the necessary procedures. After completing his logbook entries, he remained for a while chatting generally and enjoying sharing that customary pot of coffee normally made to greet the relieving mate. He had not been let off the hook (as I put it) in London, but this had been promised for Hull. Unable to resist introducing puns in to our conversation (a sure sign of my relaxed composure) I commented that, if he had been 'Itchen' to get away in Southampton, then he was doubtless 'hauling' to go in Hull – a comment which earned from him a spontaneous smile – despite his rather jaundiced glance in my direction. He did express the view, on his way to the bar for an evening 'sup' that I was plainly beginning to settle well into my new role even if I should be punished for making jokes of such dubious nature. Managing to throw a quick 'with impunity, no doubt', as he disappeared out of the wheelhouse door, left us both chuckling mildly. I reflected that such humour cemented comradeship – indicating a ship upon which it was good to serve.

The tow wire parted as we were heading into Hull's King George locks. It was invariably up to the pilot whether or not we passed a ship's towing wire to the tug or took one from them but, on this occasion, the wire passed was plainly past its sell-by date. As we took the tug off our port bow, making the incident visible to me at the centre-line, I immediately reported to the pilot on the starboard bridge wing. He quickly stopped the ship and instructed me to go astern on the engines, which brought her up before she could do any harm to vessel, quay or even the tug. The Mate had a towing hawser available so the practical aspects of this situation were soon remedied. As it transpired, the only damage sustained by our ship was a slight scraping of the paintwork on our shell plating, to the relief of everyone – except perhaps the chief officer who would have to report on and make good the damage or, alternatively, bequeath the latter to his relief. The incident evoked memories of my cadetship involving the debacle of sinking a tug whilst that ship was manoeuvring in Nagoya harbour.

In the lounge over drinks, the incident led to another – perhaps inevitable - exchange of triple punning built around the word hull. Even if Ian had been present, he would have been far from caring, as his relief had been waiting on the quayside along with the local marine superintendent. I had never before encountered such a rapid 'baling out'. He was due back on board at Tilbury for the next deep-sea voyage so a considerable curtailment had been made of his leave period. By the time our super had settled immediate ship's business with the Old Man, Ian was packed, signed-off and ready to join him hotfoot for Hull railway station. His sights were set hopefully on a mid-afternoon train to London, and hometown Brighton, before the day's end.

The new chief officer who joined shortly after we berthed was Jim Gaskell, with whom I had sailed previously as a first trip cadet on the *Earl of Bath*. It was not too long before the smoke-room echoed with hoots of laughter surrounding incidents that had occurred in my past. As these were of some embarrassment to me at the time, let alone after a lapse of five years, no holds were barred or anecdotes withheld, as I squirmed whilst sins from my naïve youth were 'blatantly uncovered', as he put it. Luckily, the three wives took my part and my pride became cushioned from too many extremes, even if this was more by their presence than their kindness. It seemed, following Mr Gaskell's revelations, that my reputation was made (or ruined – depending on point of view) as far as the *Gourock* was concerned. Luckily, the relating of my fivefold-downfalls on that ship led us to share memories that soon spread across ships and colleagues worldwide. The result was for an evening of unrestrained laughter as tongues became further loosened by lager. It was in a sense of such bubbling fun and more than slightly inebriated that I finally turned in – well into the early hours of the following morn.

Cargo watch next day was not a great success. Turning-to was a nightmare – breakfast a nonentity – and for the whole period, my head swam with every banging crash from swinging cargo gear and cranes, as crates were crunched onto the quayside, and buffers on wagons clashed with lorry engines and the customary cursing of dock workers and railway engine whistles, to compose a cacophony of noise. I ruefully relegated my originally pensive thoughts at home, on such 'contributions towards ethos', to the muck pile. Luckily, we were discharging bagged soya beans from New Orleans and wood pulp board from Jacksonville, so the cargo was 'very third mate friendly' as far as supervision was concerned. I could not face more than couple of slices of dry toast for lunch in the duty mess and, by 1700, even after the thankful stopping of cargo, my head was splitting sufficiently to burst. I felt like death warmed up so, missing supper, dragged a suffering body along to my cabin, drew the port curtains, and crashed into a welcoming bunk. With pillow wrapped tightly around my head, I fell into a deep sleep until woken by the officers' steward with a welcome cup of tea next morning – feeling, it was a relief to say, considerably better and able to face breakfast in the saloon. My absence for supper the previous day had, as I feared, been noticed and led to some pretty heavy flak from my little friends in the engineering department across the saloon. Luckily, the Old Man and entourage of senior officers entered which put a welcome end to that particular barrage.

Newcastle was significant only for an increasing number of incidents involving broached cargo as we discharged more tinned fruits from US Gulf ports. James came close to catching a carton being opened, but was thwarted by some secret sign code amongst fellow hatch workers that prevented a red-handed haul. The men concerned undoubtedly looked very guilty as James glared down at them from the coaming. But as Captain Houghton, the local company dock superintendent explained, even if the duty mate had directly caught a broaching there was in reality very little that could be done without creating the possibility of a prolonged labour dispute. It was better to let things go as he despondently put the situation. It was a sign of the times – apparently devoid of solution.

The night was pitch-black and pouring with wind-swept rain when I relieved the chief officer for my bridge watch. The ship was on course for Copenhagen taking Force 8 (gusting 10) north-westerly winds down our port side. We were shipping green seas as the bows plunged into surging water, with heavy spraying elsewhere for'ard, causing the ship to adopt a severe corkscrew motion. Progress through the water was handicapped by our partially loaded condition, which made the ship what is termed 'tender', causing her to roll very slowly port to starboard and taking additional time to recover. From previous experience, similar wind over tide conditions combined with such heavy swell had usually proved a rather uncomfortable combination for my stomach but, as it happened, there was far too much happening to allow myself to feel ill.

A considerable density of shipping was in our vicinity. Twinkling side and masthead lights from some coastal traders and deep-sea ships combined with a myriad of signals from numerous fishing boats. It seemed as if the nation's entire in-shore fishing fleet was congregating near our track with trawlers, drifters and other assorted craft making the North Sea look as if it were setting up in opposition to Blackpool illuminations. I felt it prudent to make a number of bold alterations to our course-line, although the situation was not sufficiently tight for me to summon the Master. It was not too long before I put the stand-by *Laskari 1* to act as lookout and moved the *secunny* to alternating duties with him on the helm – an action which allowed more effective ship control.

The Old Man popped up earlier than his usual 2200 spot to share a cup of cocoa and, sipping from his mug, commented that 'things seem a bit lively up here this evening, but you're coping extremely well'. Smiling agreement with another of his bland ambiguities in the former part of his comment (referring both to the motion of our vessel and the number of other ships around) and accepting his encouragement, I gave a large starboard course alteration, swinging the ship well clear off the stern of yet another recalcitrant trawler. We all had to hang on grimly whilst our ship 'rolled herself silly' under the influence of such temporarily heavy beam seas. He grunted approval of my turning-to the spare hand and, in fluent Bazaar Bat Hindi [nautical colloquialism for low-caste Hindustani dialect used by ship's officers], exchanged a few pleasantries with the sailor at the wheel. After a while, giving his customary noncommittal nod, he informed us 'You know where I am if you want me' and left the bridge, presumably to turn in. The casualness of this act again inspired wonders for my self-confidence.

It was just before seven bells, whilst noticing vaguely how gusting rain falling onto heavy swell was being reflected in our sidelights, that I caught momentary glimpse of what seemed to be an extremely faint red light, quite low down, about two points – or roughly twenty-two degrees – off the starboard bow. By this time the local fishing fleet had returned (presumably towards Britain) and, apart from a few ships on either side well over and clear, traffic had quietened considerably. I strained again my eyes in the Stygian blackness ahead of us. The radar on this occasion was next to useless, for all that could be seen on the PPI (Plan Position Indicator – the 'picture' painted electronically onto the physical screen) for the immediate three miles ahead of the ship was 'sea clutter'. This was created by a reflecting of both rain squalls and wave crests detected by the scanner that threw variegating patches of diffused light immediately ahead of the ship – the area where the set would have proved most useful. Even reducing range and adjusting clutter and gain controls did little to improve the situation. The reflected squalls were not too much of a problem – in fact, it was interesting watching them slide apparently across the screen. Automatically picking up binoculars and moving onto the starboard bridge wing I again strained into this utter darkness. My *lascar* glanced at me, but indicated he had seen nothing as otherwise he would have reported the sighting. My agreement and confirmation of his efficiency reassured him, but did little to convince me I was imagining things. The only sound was from a swishing of waves below the bridge over the muffled throb of our engines.

Then we both simultaneously caught sight of a red light – much stronger on this occasion – as it crested a wave very low down about ten degrees on the starboard bow, and probably less than a mile distant. In the absence of a masthead light, my first reaction was to think perhaps that it belonged to a yacht under sail which had been caught out in this appalling weather for no one, other than a complete nautical idiot, would have ventured forth willingly into these severe sea conditions in such a small boat. Then reason asserted itself. Few yachts could survive under sail in such heavy wind-blown seas: canvas would have been ripped to shreds and they would simply have headed into the wind to prevent being overwhelmed. I could only assume it was a small craft, perhaps a cabin cruiser under way which had lost its masthead light. Whatever it might be, my first duty was to avoid clouting it by giving way. As the light had again become lost amongst the waves, I had little time to ponder further any mysteries, but broke both silence and tension by poking my head inside the wheelhouse and ordering a firm 'hard a starboard', which would enable us (hopefully) to cross astern of this intrepid little craft. The *secunny* duly repeated the order and, a few moments later, confirmed it had been carried out – not that I needed his repetition on this occasion as the ship swung heavily again under impetus of both engines and helm. The familiar sequence brought normality back into the situation and my sigh of relief must have been almost tangible. Apart from catching occasional glimpses of his white stern light abaft our port beam there was no further sighting. Later, I sent my *lascar* to call his and the *secunny's* relief, whilst 'phoning James his 'quarter-to' call and, by the time he came

Lifting the wheelhouse binoculars to focus on a ship detected initially by radar was virtually a reflex action to all navigating officers (courtesy BP plc).

up to relieve me (wifeless at this time of night) I had brought *Gourock* back onto her course-line. I was the first to admit to James when relating the incident that, had my experience been greater, the ship could have been put back to automatic steering (or the Mad Mike as it was colloquially known) much earlier. He was cautiously judicial, stating merely it was only by working through these situations, in the knowledge of the Collision Regulations, that 'experience becomes experience', as he adroitly put things. It was reassuring to note that he also retained both sailors in their existing capacities for at least the initial stages of his watch. Concerning my 'solitary red light on our starboard-bow', he agreed it might well have belonged to a small power-driven craft whose masthead light had become extinguished. His only further comment was to the effect that 'at least you managed to miss the thing'.

*   *   *

We discharged crated machinery and engines from Pensacola, more cars from Charleston and cotton goods from Corpus Christi alongside a berth in the outer harbour at Copenhagen. This modern city offered very agreeable opportunities for shore leave as well as the chance of a rip-roaring party in the officers' smoke-room on the first Saturday evening, which lasted well into the early hours of Sunday. Girls seemed to appear everywhere from nowhere, as it were. It is true to say that a good time was had by hosts and guests alike. There were more than a few thick heads when cargo recommenced on Monday for the celebrations had continued among the junior engineers well beyond the weekend. I never ceased to wonder at the stamina of some fellow officers, but did ponder what the wives made of some of these observed excesses – questioning quietly if thoughts crossed their minds concerning what their own husbands 'got up to' in port when their opposite numbers were safely ashore. To me, the situation was largely academic as I was adopted, for want of a better word, by a local pilot with whom a friendship was established as he brought our ship alongside. The pilot's wife had lived in south London very near to my home and, guessing she might wish to discuss old times, he invited me to spend a couple of days with her and their young family. Ian willingly granted me local leave enabling that otherwise fateful weekend of some debauchery to be spent in the pilot's home and visiting places of interest. For me at least it was an innocent time of genuine pleasure. I was able to reciprocate to my colleagues by doing a two-day stint on cargo work allowing James and Ian their chance of a prolonged run ashore. We co-opted Frank to keep the best part of a few watches alone for, as Ian put it 'there was little damage he could do supervising discharge of crates and bags'.

We were greeted by dense fog on approaching the Belgian coast with visibility so reduced we could not see the fo'c'sle head from the wheelhouse. Port Control told us unequivocally to anchor off Flushing until the visibility improved sufficiently for a pilot to board at 1022 hours the day following our arrival. The 57 miles along the River Scheldt was completed in not far short of three hours as visibility continued to wax and wane erratically. It was always interesting in a deep-sea ship to negotiate the very sharp bend in the river at a place called Bat. The acute turn required large ships to run fine to the bank ahead and, as we approached this jockeying with other ships for position, our pilot proceeded into the bold alteration of course at a speed just above steerage way. Owing to the restricted visibility, our Scheldt passage was about twice longer than normal, and the time was well past 2200 before we were brought up fast alongside in Leopold Dock. Following such a prolonged trip, which necessitated most officers working continuous relieving duties, there was little enthusiasm for shore leave that night so, uncharacteristically, apart from duty officers we took enthusiastically to our bunks.

James, his wife, Frank and I managed to go ashore the following evening to visit a bar remembered from my cadet days as providing a good evening's entertainment. We eventually managed to track down the place amidst quaintly cobbled streets seemingly very similar. The bar certainly lived up to forecast expectations (to my great relief) for

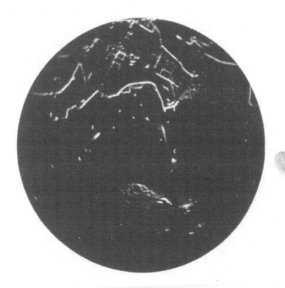

The difficulty of the sharp turn at Bat on the River Scheldt can be seen clearly from this Radar Plan Position Indicator. This is a true motion photograph and 'own' ship is steering about 340° in the buoyed channel. A large ship on the port beam is moving up river and a smaller vessel on the port bow can be seen passing outside the channel buoys (courtesy Racal-Decca).

the music was of the 'marching song' type encouraging everyone to form a sort of conga around the tables singing enthusiastically. Frank had been assigned to James's watch and they seemed to relate extremely well so the unusual evening was thoroughly enjoyable – once we had overcome initial British reserve and let ourselves go as wholeheartedly as the locals. That we did not know the words was unimportant – we still managed to participate fully in the fun. It was well past midnight before we made our way back on board ship.

Upon completion of deep-sea cargo, we shifted berth to commence loading a mixture of machinery, bagged cement and sundry manufactured products for Far Eastern ports. The company cabled the Master confirming Frank's deep-sea appointment; whilst I was informed they required me to remain for the forthcoming deep-sea trip. These were both very acceptable pieces of news. Mr Gaskell was told that, upon opening new Articles in Tilbury, he would be promoted Master and take command of the ship. I knew he was a senior chief officer by now, but had no idea quite how close he was to achieving 'that ultimate step'. Needless to say a level of modest celebrations greeted this appointment but, following an evening when 'sir' was tagged to each and every sentence, we almost imperceptibly found ourselves practising those reservations for one in whose professionalism ship, cargo and our lives would soon become entrusted. Yes, we rejoiced with him in his well-deserved promotion, but were well aware he had now attained new responsibilities for which all deck officers strived (even if to some – as the rot set in – for only early stages in their careers). It remained still very much my desire to attain both my Masters' certificate and eventual command. I did ponder however now that he had joined a very exclusive club by 'putting up his fourth stripe' – whether or not, or how long it might be, before he also would succumb to tradition and become 'bloody-minded'.

We completed a partial loading in Rotterdam of additional manufactured goods together with a deck cargo comprising some sixty 40-gallon drums of chemicals. These were roped very securely to the after rails equally on both port and starboard quarters. We also enjoyed a roaring unplanned evening of typical self-entertainment produced spontaneously by having a Ships' Officers Dramatic Society (SODS) opera. All this really entailed was a casually commenced meeting in any officer's cabin during which

To a newly-appointed third officer, the friendly and experienced eye of the master was invariably very reassuring (courtesy BP plc).

tales of the sea and large quantities of lager, beer or spirits were consumed. Inevitably, this led to an equally spontaneous sing-along of increasingly popular airs from Elvis and other artists. Alas, they all too soon degenerated into sea shanties during the course of which 'On Ilkley Moor…' (to which tune I had coined some delightfully filthy rhymes) and other old favourites, became interspersed with originally home-spun words composed to a variety of popular airs – most of which were unprintable, libellous but often extremely funny. Enquiries were never initiated concerning what the wives might have made of our little efforts, but around 2200 hours I suddenly noticed they and husbands were no longer present. The captain's wife, with long experience, had excused herself to join the Old Man, well before the more risqué contributions began to emerge. Cargo watches the next day were a nightmare, evoking echoes alas of all too many similar occasions extending over my previous years in the Merchant Navy. Equally of course, loading was carried out with some degree of reasonable efficiency. There seemed to be some sort of guardian angel who took good care of well hungover duty officers.

Rotterdam certainly lived up to its reputation of being a free port in more ways than one – depending of course on the nature of entertainment that passed for being liberated. Our junior engineers managed to find considerable variety amongst the fleshpots constituting the red-light district, returning on board dreary-eyed and shattered at various hours the following day. The electrical engineer (Lecky) managed to get himself arrested by the police – much to his shock – and the surprise of every other officer. He was the least likely person for anything in the nature of a mishap to befall as he was a middle-aged pleasant, easy-going and happily married man with five children. He had certainly not joined in with his colleagues' 'Danish pastry' – as I had nicknamed their party. It seemed that whilst happily humming away quietly to himself whilst shopping for family presents and souvenirs in stores near the red-light district, much loved by certain of our officers, he suddenly found himself accosted by two police officers. They came from behind, catching him totally unawares. One minute he was contentedly browsing, the next he was grabbed by each arm and then, with considerable embarrassment and shame, frogmarched into a van and taken to a nearby constabulary headquarters. There, much to his horror, he was confronted by a middle-aged women, obviously a victim, and accused of being a persistent flasher for whom the Dutch police had been looking over some weeks. Jim thought perhaps that it might have been wishful thinking on her part… That he was plainly English, and a visitor at that, soon led to his release with many apologies and rueful smiles all round.

Lecky was released into the custody of the agent who returned with him to the ship – and that was where his problems really started. The agent related what had happened to the Old Man as a much shaken and abused officer was sent about his business. The matter would probably have gone unremarked if the captain had not been discussing 'matters maritime' with Mr Gaskell. In keeping with the comradeship of the sea (and of course the fact that he was an engineering officer), the Mate lost no time in relating Lecky's downfall at the earliest opportunity to the smoke-room at large – where his friends had no hesitation in adopting such a god-given opportunity to offer their support. Whilst the wives were full of compassionate sympathy for his predicament, the officers most definitely were not and poor old Gerald could hardly show his face in saloon or lounge for a few days without receiving considerable stick from his fellow officers. That he was such an unlikely person to have committed such an unseemly crime only added zest to the teasing. A certain third mate even managed to rhyme his surname 'Walker' with the words 'flasher and hawker' which were integrated as a limerick into the next available SODS Opera – thus perpetuating Lecky's downfall for all time – as the verses tended to be lugged around the fleet as officers moved from one ship to another.

It was with considerable relief (especially to a certain electrical officer) that we sailed for Tilbury, completion of loading and eager anticipation of the delights to be found in Far Eastern waters – for those remaining with the ship. The voyage from Rotterdam was very busy. I was on the bridge with the Old Man from berth stand-by to dropping the pilot, and then as we neared the English coast. Initially he left me to handle the numerous alterations of course necessary for collision avoidance caused by close-quarter traffic in the Felixstowe approaches. Although there was much discussion in maritime circles concerning possible introduction of Traffic Separation Schemes around British and Continental coasts, this remained currently something of a pipedream. As it was, the proximity and quantity of shipping crossing – at all angles – in the southern part of the North Sea and navigation channels off Harwich were formidable. As we approached a six-ship collision situation off Trinity Buoy to pick up a pilot, the Captain took over and used both helm and engines to weave *Earl of Gourock* judiciously between coasters, anchored tankers, cargo and fishing boats – and numerous shallow areas. It was traditional when deep-sea for navigating officers to use only the helm to avoid collision. This was perfectly acceptable as radar (and the 'Mark One eyeball') between them picked up targets in clear weather in excess of 10 miles distance. This allowed ample time for course alterations to be made imperceptibly. The engine-room was frequently unmanned under these circumstances, although there was some talk that newly-built ships were soon to be fitted with direct bridge-control over the engines. That however would also be well into the future – even if it happened at all. We could see the yellow of low tide sandbanks passing seemingly just a few feet from the ship as we kept well over the starboard side of Black Deep Channel. I was perfectly happy to stand by the radar, advising master and pilot regarding courses, nearest approaches and distances off, as well as putting a dot on the chart at frequent intervals. It was an ideal opportunity for simply observing experts at work and learning from their experience. It was also during this watch that the lesson was learned never to be afraid of using the engine in our manned engine-room during passages in coastal waters to get out of trouble. I was the first to admit that, as a newly-qualified officer, there was still much for me to gain from the hard school of practical experience.

We exchanged pilots off Gravesend and, taking tugs fore and aft, entered the familiar Tilbury lock leading to Ellerton's berths in the Eastern Arm. There was considerable movement of shipping within the dock with a host of barges alongside ships, a few tugs and bustling coasters. Our passage across the main branch was almost stately in its ponderousness. We commenced loading as soon as *Gourock* was in position and made fast, both from barges alongside which had come from up-river, and a regular convoy of lorries that had deposited outward-bound goods in the adjoining shed. There was not a great deal of cargo to be taken and this was mainly 'tween-deck general. As I was duty officer first night in I 'phoned Thames Navigation Service headquarters, just across the river in Gravesend, where my Uncle Wag was employed as a senior river inspector aboard Harbour Master service launches, to see if he was available to come on board for the evening. He was at home in Northfleet, so a quick telephone call

Putting the cadet on the helm for entering or leaving harbour was an essential part of his training (courtesy BP plc).

induced him and my aunt eagerly to accept an invite to pop over for a drink. Wag arranged for a colleague to take them across the river and return for them later that evening, and so he and aunt appeared for an enjoyable and completely unexpected mini-family reunion.

The coastal crew had signed-off the ship (along with a greatly relieved Lecky), deep-sea articles were opened and, as the weekend came upon us, the ship was conspicuous for its absence of officers. No cargo was being worked anywhere in the docks and an ethereal silence covered this normally hectically busy area. I was duty officer for much of this period, but managed to shoot off to Gravesend with the newly-appointed radio officer for a final afternoon's shopping and meal ashore. In the absence of any other deck officers Frank, to his unmitigated delight and joy, was left in charge of the ship for a few hours. We did not foresee that much could happen and the chief engineer remained aboard anyway – otherwise I also would not have been entrusted with this unique responsibility. Captain Gaskell was returning late Sunday.

Gravesend was hectically busy with weekend shoppers, itinerant seafarers, (such as ourselves) together with a number of cadets from the training ship *Worcester* up river at Greenhithe, conspicuous by their uniforms and clear enjoyment at being released for a while from a fairly disciplined regime. I took Sparks past the promenade, active with boys from the ratings' sea-school canoodling with girl friends on the lawns, into the old Basin in which were berthed yachts and other sundry local craft. The dock had in ancient days of sail served as the terminus of numerous colliers but, with the advent of motor vessels and their non-reliance on wind power, the need for this haven had decreased considerably. Sparks had an interest in ex-RN ships so it seemed an ideal chance to show him round an old motor gunboat that I knew to be moored, apparently deserted, alongside the western wall. On this occasion to my surprise, the owner was there and proudly showed us around his still seaworthy craft for an hour or two. It was fascinating learning something of the boat's history and his plans for the future. He had served in command aboard a sister ship in the last war as part of a flotilla based in Harwich and, as the opportunity to purchase this boat arose had taken full advantage of being able to do so – even though it had cost much of his savings. He was renovating the thing throughout – changing three engines to one, introducing direct engine control from the bridge (I was particularly interested to observe), renewing deck planking, and the like –doing much of the work in his spare time. Ultimately, he hoped to use the craft in the Mediterranean, but seemed a little vague about specifics. In the light of recent news reports concerning smuggling syndicates in these waters we were left wondering.

On the way back to the ship we passed the very famous Royal Clarendon public house on the waterfront and were immediately attracted by the happy sound of an obvious wedding reception about to commence. Sparky suggested, as we were going into that particular pub anyway for a steak meal with all the trimmings, we sort of join in with the reception and partake of some of the generous buffet so enticingly laid out.

This we casually did and, being smartly attired in ties and sports jackets (in keeping with our status as officers and gentlemen) sidled in with the guests to merge between two generous lounges laid open for their use – and, of course, a veritable bounty of free grub and wine. We worked on an assumption that the bride's family would regard us as guests of the groom and vice versa. This seemed to work out reasonably well – at least for the initial stages of our venture – but I gradually became aware of suspicious looks being shunted in our direction. Frantically grabbing Sparks by an unwilling arm, we stepped out of the nearest exit and ran hell for leather to the safety of nearby Royal Terrace pier, from whence sailed the harbour service launches, tugs and assorted official craft associated with the river services. Fortunately, the wedding guests were not permitted entry to this jetty and they were stopped by the pier-master from following us. Thanking our lucky stars that this attendant knew me from travels on the launches with Wag, we managed to scrounge a lift from a departing tug that dropped us off at Tilbury Landing Stage whilst en route down river to service a departing tanker. It was a very close run thing though and we balked at the thought of what might have happened had we been caught by representatives of this irate party.

The boredom of being duty officer was relieved next morning by a sergeant and constable of the PLA police coming on board enquiring if we knew anything about a couple of youngsters barge-hopping across the dock around midnight the previous day. It seemed that two cadets (it just had to be) from the Asian-crewed *Clan McIntyre,* at Number 17 Berth in the East Branch diagonally across from where we were moored, were faced with a long walk up our part of the East dock and down the other arm – something to the order of ten ship lengths. They had subsequently succumbed enthusiastically to the temptation of crossing the dock by jumping across the strings of barges set out alongside our ship, the one astern of us, and their own. The night police patrol had observed them doing this 'particularly dangerous act', but wished to establish more witnesses before taking further action. Even if we had seen this, it was unlikely we would have volunteered such information – especially as it was the kind of act we ourselves might have perpetrated had we also been berthed there.

A new chief officer, James Dexter, joined the vessel on Monday for the deep-sea trip. It seemed that some senior superintendent had clearly relented allowing Ian Windsor additional time on leave with his family. This was only right (not, I was learning, this always followed) considering the 21 months of his previous trip. I took the opportunity of popping over to Gravesend again to purchase my own sextant – that inevitably handy gun constituting the professional tool immediately identifying (to those in the know) any navigating officer. From amongst the selection of instruments available locally, I chose a Cooke's of Hull Mates' Three Circle Micrometer – very much the traditional model in frequent use as a ship's sextant aboard many merchant vessels, and a popular one owned by most officers. It was with some modest pride that I returned on board with my purchase and shared comparison of this latest model with colleagues.

Moving around peacefully on watch, supervising loading into Number Three 'tween-deck, Frank came up and told me the Old Man wanted to see me. Needless to say, my immediate thoughts centred around my past weekend absence and whether or not repercussions were to follow for leaving a cadet in charge of the ship. It transpired however that nothing could have been further from his mind. He glanced up at my knock and told me to be seated. Wondering what was going on, and with slightly dry mouth, I did as commanded, reflecting how strange it seemed seeing Jim Gaskell with 'four rings up' accepting so naturally his promotion. Pausing from talking across to his wife (who was there until the ship sailed) he explained there had been a change in my sailing orders and they would no longer be blessed with my presence on the forthcoming trip. Sadly, the third officer currently serving aboard Ellerton's *Countess Elizabeth* had been informed of the sudden death of his father and was being sent home on compassionate leave. I began to sense the drift of what was being said. Inevitably therefore, with that ship due to sail for African ports within a couple of days, I was being transferred forthwith and should collect my gear and sign-off without delay, and return home to organise my deep-sea stuff and then report aboard the good *Countess* at her berth in the Royal Albert Dock. I was sorry to hear of my colleague's unfortunate news, and even more so about leaving *Earl of Gourock,* but breathed a few sighs of relief that my indiscretions over the weekend had apparently passed without notice, and at least the RAD was only just up river, so sparing me a prolonged journey to join her elsewhere.

After Captain Gaskell had lifted the Articles from within a cavernous drawer in his desk, I signed both the Master's copy and that which was deposited before sailing with the Shipping Master. He then smiled and offered my very first Certificate of Watchkeeping and Service. This was an essential requirement when eventually I presented myself for First Mates', and confirmed my performance of eight hours in sole charge of a navigating watch over the duration of the voyage. On the reverse, he had commented very favourably on my conduct, ability and sobriety during Captain Davies and his own time in command.

Glancing through my Discharge Book on the train homeward bound it was interesting to see that, with the resigning for deep-sea – and signing-off again so rapidly, in just under four months, this had been blessed with a further four entries. Relaxing in the compartment, watching the Thames off Greenhithe flashing by, I felt an overwhelming sense of peaceful achievement. Clearly there was much still to learn both on bridge and deck, and the single ring on my sleeve retained much of its crisp brightness. Yet there existed also the realisation that a navigating officer's work was within my ability. I looked forward to joining the passenger liner and practising my skills deep-sea.

Chapter 2

LEARNING ON A LINER

—

Following a quick overnight visit home collecting deep-sea gear, I joined the Group's *Countess Elizabeth* at her berth in London's Royal Albert Dock, a couple of days prior to sailing. The largest of their four 13,000-ton-plus passenger-cargo liners, she was engaged on regular return runs to southern and eastern African ports from Cape Town to as far north as Beira. The deep-sea trip of just less than three months was well established, 'almost a bus route' Captain Gaskell had called it, so officers and crew knew for how long they would be away. This was a rarity indeed with Ellertons and very different from the nineteen-month trip of the *Earl of Gourock*.

The *Countess* had capacity for 106 first-class passengers. She had almost loaded her general cargo and, when I joined, was taking on board Royal Mail bags for transit in secure 'tween-deck lock-ups specifically designed for this purpose. Cynics amongst the officers declared that this dual-purpose vessel indicated shrewd foresight from Ellertons' founding directors, over one hundred years previously. Passenger liners carrying over the magic century of passengers conformed to African port regulations permitting direct entry. This resulted in the privilege of reserved berths, enabling them to sail regally past other dry-cargo vessels forced to 'lay off the hook' (as anchoring was romantically termed by her crew), often for many days. Ships carrying mails had similar port privileges, guaranteeing lucrative trade and fast reliable trips. It proved also the adage that 'Ellertons never looked backwards when hedging their bets'. We were carrying only 96 passengers this voyage and they were due to arrive by train alongside our berth next day after which, once tucked-up safely on board, we could sail.

I reported to the chief officer in his cabin on the starboard side of the sports deck situated below the navigating bridge. Richard Smart had served Ellertons since gaining Second Mates twelve years previously after serving a cadetship as a midshipman with 'Blue Flue' (the nickname colloquially attributed to Alfred Holt's Blue Funnel Line). Now, with a Master's certificate behind him, he was awaiting promotion to his first command, almost certainly one of the group's cargo ships, so calling him Mr Smart as deference to his seniority came naturally. I would have done this automatically for there was a definite glint in his eye as we introduced ourselves that took me back a little. Instinctively, my approach was cautious. Offering me a seat in the armchair of his luxurious cabin he gave instructions regarding my immediate duties.

'It's really good to welcome you on board. I am glad you've joined to help us out over your predecessor's personal difficulties, especially at such short notice. His family circumstances are very sad, and quite unexpected. We knew Donald's father was ill but no one, not even the family, realised how widespread was the cancer which resulted in his sudden death. It is good also that you have arrived early today for there is much to be done. On leaving my office, you should change into working uniform and report to the Master. Then you had better go with the junior second officer to the Shipping Office, taking your Certificate and Discharge Book, and sign Articles. You will find him on deck somewhere supervising the last of our cargo. Tell him the senior second should relieve him whilst he is away. Once you have done this, I want you to obtain a crew and passenger list from the purser's bureau and, collecting our junior cadet Gary Faulkner, up-date the lifeboat and emergency stations lists. When this has been finished, you can turn him to with the bosun. Then, it would help if you grabbed a selection of ship's arrangement and capacity plans from the bottom drawer of the ship's office and thoroughly acquainted yourself with the vessel. The senior cadet Geoffrey Whitehead can show you around afterwards. This will give him wider experience seeing as he will be doing a third mate's job himself some day. Now, have you any questions to ask me regarding any of this?'

I sat quietly for a moment digesting these clearly unequivocal instructions. On one hand my path and mind were eased considerably, for it had occurred to me some guidance would be useful concerning the nature of my immediate duties. On the other, it saved me asking him, but his stern manner left me feeling a little bewildered, wondering with what kind of chief officer I was due to sail. He glanced at me as I confirmed 'all had been taken on board' and smiled, clearly aware of my discomfort. This transformed his face and he continued in less serious vein.

'In their wisdom, the superintendents have cordially invited (in other words instructed) all officers', including our two cadets, to attend a pre-sailing meal tonight in the ship's saloon to assist hosting a special evening dinner for shippers. These are managers, accompanied tonight by their wives, who give cargo inducements to the company upon which all ship-owners and us mariners rely for our income. You missed the Old Man's briefing yesterday, so I'll impress upon you the importance of treating these people with considerable respect. Each junior officer will host a table of less important guests whilst us seniors, and various superintendents from the London office, will look after those more esteemed. Normally junior officers dine in the saloon before passengers come in for their meals. There is the duty mess for those below senior rank whose meal times might clash with the 'bloods', as passengers are traditionally called.'

He sensed my quizzical look and continued by explaining how this term originated from large Cunard, P&O and Orient liners: 'Passengers on these august ships were traditionally bled white by being parted from their money by enterprising (some might say mercenary) stewards in the catering department. Each one of whom,' he continued in cynical vein, 'enthusiastically helped their passengers experience the voyage of a lifetime.'

I found myself laughing outright at these remarks. As to the rights or wrongs of his assertion, I could only guess, but this more relaxed style, following the laying down of boundaries by his previously formally-delivered orders, appealed to my sense of humour. It helped me see another side to his personality. He continued, before dismissing me, by talking about both the second officers carried, the cadets, and my various duties. It seemed I would be sharing his four-to-eight bridge watch, as the third officer was always doubled on watches until he possessed a Mates' certificate, by which time 'he would be due promotion to second officer, anyway'. Once we were deep-sea, clear of land, and *if* I had 'proved myself', the Old Man and he would probably leave me to it on the bridge, depending upon the density of shipping.

Captain Douglas Browne, DSO, RNR, was the fleet commodore. He wore the two-inch gold band of his rank on each sleeve surmounted by the Elllerton diamond. His cabin was abaft the separate wheelhouse and chart-room on the navigating bridge. Having served the company since his apprenticeship, he stood as ample proof that 'each lowly cadet carries a commodore's telescope within his gear'. His Distinguished Service Order had been won whilst serving as Commander, Royal Naval Reserve, in command of an escort flotilla on Atlantic convoys in the Second World War, during which time they had bagged a couple of German U-boats. His greeting was courteous and friendly as he glanced through my Discharge Book and casually discussed mutually recognised ships and the names of relevant Masters covering my seafaring experiences to date. He laughed when he saw my *Earl of Bath* entry, leading me to wonder if my indiscretions as a first-trip cadet had become known to him, or whether he merely knew the captain, although neither of us passed any comments in that area. He explained that *Countess Elizabeth*, whilst engaging traditional Asian petty officers and ratings from India, Pakistan and Goa, carried additionally a few British senior petty officers, some leading hands across all departments, plus three European quartermasters. This was the reason why a visit had to be made to the Mercantile Marine Office Establishment in East India Dock Road with whom were lodged our ship's Articles of Agreement. Normally, as I knew, we signed-on in the captain's quarters, and signed-off after arrival deep-sea in the dining saloon before a shipping master. Up until then my experiences with the Board of Trade (or Ministry of Transport as they now wished to be known) had been whilst collecting my Seaman's Identity Card and Discharge 'A' Book from Dock Street upon joining the Merchant Navy, and then for gaining Second Mates, so this would be a first visit to sign Articles. He also acquainted me further with information regarding the important shippers' dinner that evening.

Before anything further happened, a visit had to be made to the Shipping (Officers) Federation to obtain clearance from them which the shipping master at the MOT would need to see prior to signing-on. Pete Davison, the junior second mate, came along after arranging his own relief. We returned to our cabins and quickly grabbed duffel coats to cover our uniforms, and exchanged the usual 'where and what have you done' information in the taxi as we went to the various shipping offices. Pete was an Ellerton man, but we had neither met before nor sailed with mutual acquaintances. This was not as surprising as it sounds, for this company alone (not including associates) ran 90 ships, employing over 500 officers across all ranks, a personnel figure that excluded cadets. Our experiences in the Officers' Federation proved both salutary and a culture shock. As company contract officers we rarely visited them. In fact, the last time our paths had crossed was upon my initial entry into the Merchant Navy as a deck cadet following pre-sea training at Keddleston. Their clerks on this second occasion were, for some reason, abrupt to the point of rudeness and treated officers and ratings (in the same room, but a different counter) alike, as just so many inferior beings. Pete, in the process of recovering from shock, suggested they might have had bad experiences with a previous tramp-ship mate or engineer and had adopted this attitude as a form of self-defence. Whatever, we were glad to shake the dust of the place from our feet, muttering imprecations upon their heads, which probably did little harm to either party. Affairs at the Mercantile Marine Office were much more civilised and Articles were duly acknowledged, following which we rejoined our vessel.

Whilst Pete went back on cargo watch, I collected the crew and passenger lists and popped into the cadets' cabin, between the second officer's and my own looking forward across the main deck, to see where they might be hanging out. Their quarters were neat and tidy, but encouragingly empty. Eventually, I ran them to ground in the Mate's office. Both lads were there listening intently as Andrew Causley, our senior second officer, completed instruction on rigging the ship's 50-ton jumbo derrick serving number two hatch – the largest hold on this and indeed most dry-cargo merchant vessels. The ship had a few days earlier loaded some heavy generators for Capetown and Durban, which required this monster to be rigged, so as they had helped use the gear practically, he was using the manufacturer's manual to point out some finer theoretical points. They all looked up as I entered and we introduced ourselves, following which the senior second officer and I exchanged details of our previous service. Andrew and

I had never met before, but it transpired he had sailed deep-sea with Peter Dathan (a fellow trainee from Keddleston) when the latter was a second-year cadet on the *Earl of Ottawa* and he was first-trip second mate. He had also served on the *Earl of Bath*, when still commanded by Captain Henderson-Jones, but had signed-off well before I joined her in Amsterdam – seemingly light years away now. Causley had transferred to Ellerton's after serving a cadetship with the Harrison Line – more widely known as 'two of fat and one of lean', from the red band interspersed between broader ones of white on the funnels of their ships. He spoke extremely highly of both present master and the Mate, stressing quietly the latter was 'a stickler for detail, but really very human'. This helped confirm my own brief impressions. I found it very reassuring – and relaxed.

The two boys listened politely whilst 'their seniors' (it still seemed strange to be so regarded) exchanged news and views, especially as our research uncovered other officers with whom we had mutually sailed or encountered in some distant port – although at different times. The cadets were very senior, with Whitehead due up for Second Mates' after this forthcoming voyage. As they told me about themselves, it transpired both were ex-Plymouth School of Navigation cadets prior to which they had attended grammar schools. They had just a one year difference at pre-sea training, but had not met again until Gary joined in the RA Dock three weeks' previously. Andrew suggested that Geoff, who had already completed two trips on the *Elizabeth* amuse himself for an hour by offering me a Cook's tour. I immediately told him of the Mate's instructions regarding the LSA (lifesaving appliances) duties so, after pointing out where everything necessary was to be found, he released Gary to learn and help. He suggested that after I had looked through the plans the senior cadet could 'do the Cook's tour, if I felt this could prove useful, whilst the junior cadet turned-to with the bosun. I was delighted to accept and, once the other job was completed, Geoff and I started at the stem and finally ended up at the stern. We took in passenger accommodation, engine-room and various nooks and crannies, including a trip to the top of our streamlined funnel, and a journey up an internal ladder extending from officers' quarters to engine-room.

On the way along the main alleyway outside the purser's bureau, we watched with interest as the Goanese staff struggled to remove the protective covering placed upon the lino in port. It seemed from the frantic efforts and appalling language from the assistant purser supervising this operation, that somehow (or due to the bad intentions of someone) a large portion of this had become stuck to the deck and was proving extremely difficult to remove. Smiling ruefully, Gary told me after we had passed and were on our way back to the officers' deck, he and his sidekick had done this in the early hours of one morning. This apparent enemy action resulted from efforts of Graham Parslow, the assistant purser, who in his cups had attempted to ingratiate his way into the cadets' bunks. 'Oh dear, yet another one' I found myself thinking.

We arrived back in our respective cabins with just sufficient time for me to remove boiler suit, shower, change into something respectable and go along to the passenger lounges for pre-dinner drinks as the shippers joined. I mused whilst knotting my tie

Two cadets were invariably carried deep-sea, gaining continued training in their cabin (hopefully) to assist each other with theoretical learning (courtesy BP plc).

Completing practical chart-work exercises set by the second officer (courtesy BP plc).

*Cadets were frequently employed during the watch
on lookout duties (courtesy BP plc).*

*Part of cadets' training – receiving instruction
in sight reduction (courtesy BP plc).*

Practical chart-work fixing the ship's position (courtesy BP plc).

that, even as a cadet, a momentary sense of satisfaction was always experienced whilst wearing number one doeskin reefer set. My reefer jacket felt smart and helped provide a sense of self-confidence which calmed uncertainties just below the surface of my outwardly placid demeanour.

I welcomed the buzz of animated conversation which hit my ears long before entering the smoke-room. Graham met me, showing his professional smile (which fooled no one – amongst the officers at least), offering cocktails from a tray carried by an immaculately-dressed Goanese steward. We separated to mingle amongst the guests, pausing only to refill our rapidly emptying glasses from the seemingly endless trays of drinks, and enjoy numerous assorted canapés. Captain Ford smiled a welcome as we casually encountered each other in the writing-room and arrested my progress by motioning me towards him with his glass. He made encouraging small talk for a while until the question of my RNR commissioning was raised so, treading very carefully, I voiced the decision made on the *Earl of Gourock*, leaving open an opportunity to reverse this if the heat in that particular kitchen suddenly became too hot. He was pleasantness personified, stating: 'Mr. Carridia it is really up to you whether or not papers are submitted for List One. After all, it will be your good self who will have to negotiate with the Navy and re-attend the Admiralty selection interview board as well as completing their annual two-weekly training commitments. Ellertons are quite happy to support any officers who wish to join the RNR – as indeed we have in the past and continue to do so – but if you do not wish to become commissioned, this decision will not stand in your way regarding future promotion within the Group. On the contrary, in a practical way of course, we can always use your services ourselves during these periods with the fleet.'

As I breathed a sigh of relief, he continued by telling me about the very satisfactory reports received from the captains of my two coastal voyages, and expressed particular appreciation that I had agreed so readily to leave *Gourock* and help out the company by joining this larger ship. Reflections afterwards enabled me to put this fortuitous meeting with my direct boss firmly under the heading 'company progress'.

Strongly reassured (once again) I entered enthusiastically into circulating and chatting casually with small groups of shippers. This certainly proved a novel experience. One party in the veranda café ignored me completely as I hesitatingly smiled a welcome on approaching them. They simply nodded vaguely in my direction, offered a watery grin in return, turned their backs, and continued talking. Somewhat abashed but not defeated (being made of sterner stuff) I continued circulating back in the smoke-room until a particular trio of shippers and their wives stopped me. They introduced themselves and questioned me in friendly terms about my job on board and other seagoing experiences. It turned out they were the chairmen and executive directors of an internationally-known machinery manufacturing company in the Midlands and possessed that very poised confidence emanating from an educated and, what my father would have termed, privileged background. They made me feel at ease and important in a strange sort of way – almost as if they were the hosts and I a guest, and one far more senior than a mere very junior third officer. As our conversation developed the dinner gong sounded so I accompanied them to the second-deck restaurant.

A table plan was displayed at the entrance and, as we gave names to the English leading saloon steward, Goanese waiters directed us to appropriate tables. I found my seating card at the lower end – as expected – and prepared to meet my fellow diners. Whilst standing behind my chair, awaiting grace to be said by the Commodore heralding a start to the meal, I noticed my recent sextet being seated with him at top table. I was with five other shipper guests and smiled across at the cadets who were each hosting adjacent tables seating six persons. My lot were a very different bag indeed from those met previously. After we sat, mutual introductions were made and it soon became apparent why they and I had been landed with each other. Commencing that necessary conventional small talk appropriate to these occasions, I told them about my work on board, thus breaking the ice and permitting them to reciprocate. They were certainly not backwards in coming forwards, as my mother used to say – in fact, they were totally uninhibited. It seemed they were all company directors, but in a much different league to my previous party. From the remarks airily exchanged, it appeared the two couples were in rival scrap metal businesses. The two ladies (using the term guardedly, I am afraid) exchanged thinly-veiled sarcastic comments regarding the dress of the other, whilst their husbands and the other male, talked about recent ventures – apparently trying to out-do each other in a mixture of tricky deals and near-the-knuckle skulduggery. This led me to bless the pursers' staff who had arranged such delicate groupings.

Apart from occasional smiles I was blatantly ignored – apart that is from the attentions of the odd male whom, it transpired, was chairman of a greengrocery concern based in Southwark Market, who supplied provisions to many Group ships. It soon became apparent why he was not married. In between visits from both the Goanese steward and the wine steward, he expressed interest concerning how we conducted ourselves at sea in the absence of women. It was quite noticeable that he could not keep his eyes off young Gary sitting at the next table and, as he imbibed more glasses of wine it became quite obvious he would appreciate being introduced to our still comparatively innocent-looking junior cadet. With the flow of yet more wine, the chatter around our table became as heated as the temperature in the room. Luckily, the noise was such that what was passing for repartee at our table was easily lost amongst the more general mêlée. The latter stages of the meal were notable for two significant events: an indecent proposal from the 'fruit man', as I was graciously regarding him; and one of the husbands who, as the steward placed a finger-bowl in front of him, promptly picked this up and drank it. The expression on the steward's face was a picture – oh for a camera! Keeping a deadpan face over the latter incident, whilst simultaneously under the table, gently removing the hand of 'fruity' from my right thigh, I picked up the bowl and asked the steward to refill it and return it to us. This proved a subtly legitimate way to at least get some of my own back – without being reported for insolence. Thus, on such a cordial note, the meal (thankfully) drew to a close. My reflections on leaving the restaurant were that in the space of one evening my horizons had been widened yet again in the fields of human nature.

The cadets' cabin afterwards resounded to hilarious laughter as Geoff, Gary and I exchanged experiences. They also had a number of tales to relate which collectively helped us place the range of personalities amongst those for whom we relied for our salary and jobs. Hearing the commotion, Peter came in and treated us all to a sup of beer as we exchanged experiences – although his were pretty mild compared to ours. The senior officers may well have enjoyed more salubrious company, with guests clearly from higher up the social scale, but they certainly lacked the informal cabaret to which I in particular had been subjected.

After smoke-oh the next day our passengers joined. They were channelled from the boat train through the adjacent shed by a temporary ropewalk rigged by our crew to the gangway. Looking casually over the rail from the boat-deck led me to wonder if this seemingly inelegant method of boarding was to protect or separate them (or both) from our erstwhile collection of uncouth dockers. Andrew and the Mate joined us and we watched as they were greeted at the top of the gangway by Geoff and the English duty quartermaster, before being grabbed by Graham collecting their passage tickets. They were then led by stewards to their respective cabins. Mr Smart explained this method of boarding was an alternative to collecting them from Tilbury Landing Stage whilst outward bound, 'a far more civilised option' as he put it. He did not know the factors which determined either way of taking them on board. Seemingly, our passengers preferred to travel upon a smaller, but in many respects equally comfortable one-class ship, rather than the larger Union-Castle liners with their thousand or so 'bloods'. The Mate (it just had to be, with his caustically dry humour) again elucidated: 'Our lot clearly prefer a much quieter life to the champagne and sin routines of our larger cousins. We in Ellertons offer our passengers a more subtle approach to enjoyment than blatant bonking on the boat deck, amorous adultery in the alleyways, or crusty crackling in the cabin – or all three simultaneously, for that matter.'

His spontaneous pronouncement was delivered in tones more appropriate to a perverse and lurid advertising poster than the reasoned comment emanating from a very senior chief officer. He was fast helping me regard passengers and liner life (also indeed senior officers) with a different perspective than previously imagined.

It transpired our passengers were mainly expatriates returning to businesses or plantations in southern and eastern Africa. Independence had been granted to the old colony almost two years ago and many English civil servants, entrepreneurs and the like, were slowly allowing (or being encouraged to prepare) white South Africans to take over their duties as they departed from what was clearly regarded in some areas as a hostile regime. Discussing politics in the smoke-room one evening – very unusual aboard a merchant ship – Pete related how he had been in Durban, serving aboard the *Earl of Oswestry,* on the night South Africa became a republic. He and a number of officers had ventured ashore that evening, contrary to advice from the ship's agent, but reported there were absolutely no celebrations in this predominantly pro-English city, and the streets were completely deserted. Such a cool reception to the glories of republicanism were seemingly common throughout Natal, in marked contrast to other parts of the country where apparently wild parties had continued well into next morning.

Just a couple of hours after the last family joined, the Ministry of Transport surveyor, who was an ex-master mariner with command experience, appeared and the ship was put through her paces for very thorough emergency boat and fire station drills. I had discussed and cleared my efforts at distributing passengers amongst the boats with Mr. Smart and, on this vessel, was placed in charge of number three boat starboard side. My fire-station for the inspection was to lead a mixed Asian deck and catering group on an exercise in the passenger accommodation.

*The third officer joined the second and mate in taking turns
running his own lifeboat (courtesy BP plc).*

*Supervising crew during a fire drill. These were times when experiences
proved practically useful (courtesy BP plc)*

Shortly after we passed muster, as it were, the pilot appeared on board, 'Stations' was piped by the Mate, and I repaired to the bridge for my first stand-by. By the time all gear had been tested and Gary had been sent to look after flags, our tugs had come alongside and were made fast. Out of deference to the passengers, we commenced our voyage in typically lively mood, with records playing a selection of Royal Marines music – especially (and inevitably) *A Life on the Ocean Wave*. And so, with strains of martial airs ringing out the *Countess Elizabeth* cast her last lines and was towed slowly towards the locks and Gallions Reach in the Thames.

I remained on the bridge until we cleared the river pilot at Gravesend. Much interest was created amongst our deck officers as we passed the *Worcester* off Greenhithe, for three of them (including Commodore and Mate) had commenced their careers at varying intervals from this training ship. Once stood-down after supper in the duty mess, the success of my first stand-by was celebrated with a pint of English ale in the officers' smoke-room. It was in a mood of excitement, relaxation and peacefulness that I went on deck to savour the atmosphere of embarking on another voyage. Below, I could hear muffled sounds from the passengers enjoying the luxury of evening supper. The rail vibrated softly below my elbows and I caught occasional whiffs of funnel exhaust intermingled with that smell of muddy river and sea salinity as 'my ship' followed the familiar Thames-side banks sliding away quietly to port and starboard. I remained for a while watching the passing of familiar landmarks until we cleared Southend and the passage through the Thames estuary channels, after which I turned in for the briefest of snoozes on my day bed.

My first watch initially with a European quartermaster on the helm was without incident. The chief officer remained with me as we steamed off the Sussex coast, leaving the commodore free to entertain his passengers. Once the local shipping density had decreased and our quartermaster was stood down, the vessel was placed onto automatic pilot or as it was universally called, Mad Mike. A *secunny* was turned-to on the starboard bridge wing for lookout duties and Mr Smart, from the comfort of the wheelhouse (and for the want of anything better to do) explained something of the perils of being Master of a passenger ship. Chugging smoothly clear of Beachy Head light, with strains of his by now customary humour, he related experiences concerning another of the 'big four' captains. It seemed he had taken to the demon drink over a series of voyages and, one Sunday morning during the church service, had appeared under the influence to conduct this religious rite. He was quite a small man in stature so the purser's staff had, with goodly (if not godly) intent built up the lectern, which formed the base of his altar. This hid the Captain so effectively that only the top of his head and eyes were visible. As he entered the lounge, before the assembled gathering of passengers and all off-duty officers, it was quite apparent the fly of his white number ten uniform was undone. He missed out chunks of the printed order of service and

Certainly for the first deep-sea voyage aboard passenger-cargo liners the chief officer offered close supervision during navigating watches (courtesy BP plc).

rearranged the liturgical Lord's Prayer. His misdemeanours were compounded with the introduction of a 'home made' contribution. This was a rambling sermon that lacked continuity and focus (rather like his good self) and eventually petered out. He led the singing of the final hymn 'Eternal Father Strong to Save', (a distinct lack of originality in choice, conditioned largely by the senior purser's opinion of 'what the passengers expected'), by singing alternative words long known to generations of seafarers. I had participated enthusiastically in this, admittedly *sotto voce,* with my fellow midshipmen during the end of term service concluding my RNR training. The delightful perversion had proved one of the few positive elements to emerge from this engaging venture and had remained indelibly engraved on my memory – if not my conscience:

> *It almost broke Lord Wentworth's heart*
> *When Lady Anne became a tart.*
> *But blood is blood and race is race,*
> *And so to save his daughter's face,*
> *Her dad bought her a cosy retreat*
> *On the shady side of Curzon Street.*

Apparently, he followed this with a couple of further verses including ones describing her exploits with an inhabitant of Buckingham Palace, and a viscount of the realm. By that time, I had long forsaken any pretence of concern regarding what my mother and choirmaster might have made of things. Chuckling loudly, the master had then staggered from the service without offering any conclusion. The chief officer, once he had recovered from shock, completed proceedings by exercising that versatility associated with senior rank. He promptly stepped forward and invited participation (appropriately enough) in the grace. Mr Smart, who was serving aboard as second mate, stated the atmosphere in the lounge could be 'cut with the proverbial knife'. He and his fellow officers were almost paralytic with subdued laughter whilst simultaneously forcing themselves to remain solemn-faced. They adjourned immediately, bursting at the sides, to the smoke-room where followed a period of uproariously hilarious – near-hysterical – laughter. The Master's social error was sufficient in itself to have attracted considerable attention from the Kremlin, but it was compounded on this particular voyage by the presence as passengers of a distant member of the royal family and his countess wife, plus a journalist attached to an international British social glossy magazine.

Following the furore raised (even before) the ship reached UK, the Company had no option other than to dismiss the Master, with publicity appropriate to the incident. Once the dust had settled however, and his period of extended leave had been extended even further, they quietly arranged for him to serve in command of a Lamport and Holt (or 'Lean and Hungry' as it was colloquially known in the Merchant Navy) cargo ship, by mutual arrangement between directors of both concerns.

It was then that I was informed of a hidden agenda that apparently existed in higher echelons of the shipping industry. As far as it proved possible, they very much looked after their own in some circumstances – a practice which extended to almost a mutual club encompassing various company directors and superintendents. I learned also the origins of some nicknames given to many shipping companies. These apparently stemmed from the bad old days of the 1920s and 30s and the depression when berths on ships were hard to come by. Master mariners and certificated officers across all ranks were often reduced to signing-on as able seamen – and left considering themselves fortunate in finding any seagoing employment. Never ones to lose any opportunity, it appeared that even some major and reputable shipping companies took advantage of a difficult situation to offer their officers and crews basic Board of Trade scale rations. Hence the delightful attribution of appropriate epithets, such as Hungry Hogarths, were more in the line of barbed humour than the innocent fun I had originally thought [Hogarth was a shipping company notorious for its appalling food during the Depression.] A rhyming sobriquet applied to Union-Castle however originated not from pre-war days, but was attributable more to the energetically enthusiastic antics found amongst certain gay stewards serving this company's catering department, representatives of whom I had already met ashore in various insalubrious bars worldwide.

As my contribution, I related how as a cadet on the *Earl of Melbourne* it had been my privilege to sail with an ex-captain from one of these sister ships that had experienced similar disgrace. In this instance, the master had been relegated back to command of a cargo vessel within the Group. Mr Smart knew of the incident and eagerly, even joyfully one might say, contributed to my existing knowledge some additional pertinent details. Thus was enjoyed quite an engagingly revealing watch before he left me on my own for the remaining couple of hours, as we cleared a few miles off the Casquets light. After he had gone, I spent a few moments reflecting how the mighty may indeed fall from great heights: that even captains were not immune from similar (albeit more intensive) foibles that I knew from bitter experience to affect so frequently the lesser ranks.

Leaving the bridge at 2015, after savouring the quiet solitude of a not particularly busy watch, Graham banged on my door offering (inevitably) a nightcap in the form of cocktails before turning in. Geoff had stated he was really quite harmless and very good company, once the true basis of relationships had been firmly established, so a pleasant couple of hours were spent in his cabin outside the bureau on B deck. He was extremely poised and well educated, having attended a major public school prior to taking A levels and commencing his seagoing career. As the evening progressed, it seemed he had an intellectual and academic potential totally unfulfilled by serving at sea. Discussing this later very casually with other officers we reached mutual agreement and, in the way of seafarers generally, considered this business was not really ours to dissect – not that this stopped us doing so with, it might be suggested, a marked level of enthusiasm.

Crossing a surprisingly calm Bay of Biscay coincided with Christmas – a celebration at sea aboard this hooker that proved a hoot. All watchkeeping officers were sober – the seniors very wisely saw to that – whilst our 'bloods' clearly enjoyed themselves, something determined by the amount of noise in the early hours of the morning, and the cavorting antics witnessed in the public rooms and saloon after leaving the bridge. I was invited to a party hosted in Graham's cabin, which every off-duty officer attended (apart from the seniors in all three departments who were entertaining passengers). Inevitably we ended up with the traditional SODS Opera, but this had to be transferred to the third engineer's cabin, further aft along the same deck, once it had attained more riotous heights (or plumbed even lower depths) with a corresponding increase in near-riotous noise. It was well past three in the morning before I trundled up the inner staircase and tumbled gratefully into my bunk. It required considerable effort of will to respond to the duty *secunny's* call – less than forty minutes later - and, on reflection, I decided it had probably not been very wise of me to have turned in at all. It would have been far more effective for me to have remained awake.

I just managed to throw down a quick black coffee, report to the bridge with one minute to spare and, trying to look intelligent, join Mr Smart in relieving Andrew. The Mate gave me a very direct look and smilingly enquired if I had enjoyed myself at the

'Third's do', as it was already known. Graham had passed out somewhere along the line and had been left in his cabin to recover. The senior purser could not have been a particularly happy chap next day as he gazed in the direction of his erstwhile assistant – propping up his head and gazing bleary-eyed, with haggard features, whilst attempting answers to passenger enquiries, sorting out foreign currencies and simultaneously preparing port entrance forms. Luckily, most of the bloods were themselves a little worse for wear so no apparent harm was done. It seemed that yet another hazard of the sea had been successfully surmounted.

Mr Smart invited the Bosun to join all off-duty officers' – including our cadets – for a pre-luncheon Boxing Day drink in the officers' smoke-room, prior to my grabbing a few hours snooze before going on watch at 1600. 'Bose' was an elderly seafarer who had spent his entire life in the Merchant Navy – going away as a deck boy at the turn of the century and serving on every class of ship before joining Ellerton's as a quartermaster some twenty-five years previously. He was held in considerable esteem by officers and crew. Now approaching retirement age, he held an easy informality (without familiarity) with all officers that made possible this invite. We all rose as he came in, jostling around to make room for him on the settee. With his large whisky encircled in a massive calloused hand, Bose leaned back with a huge sigh, contentedly joining in with the general buzz of conversation, but also clearly listening to the background music of Tchaikovsky's Piano Concerto No. 1 in B Flat played quietly on the stereo system. During a lull in our hilarious chat, he asked the cabin at large who might be the composer. Upon being told, he sighed again – readjusted himself further into the soft back of the settee and uttered this immortal comment – more or less along the lines: 'You've got ter 'and it that **** Tchaikovsky – he certainly knocked out some ***** good toones!' Our outburst of spontaneously unrestrained laughter at the incongruity of this remark left him totally unmoved, but left us with an intense realisation that we were in the presence of a maestro of musical appreciation. After all, not one of us could have equalled such intensity of expression. We felt sure that a certain long-dead composer would have heartily approved at least the fervour if not perhaps the exact expression.

We called at Las Palmas for bunkers and the chance for passengers to experience their first port of call. I was reassured that traditions were well maintained on these larger ships, notwithstanding their status, by receiving a share of perks proceeding from a deal which had been arranged between the Mate and agent. This appeared in the form of six bottles of Williams and Humbert's delicious sherry, which brought back memories of previous visits to both here and Madeira. Visitors to the ship included a party of flamenco dancers to entertain those passengers not going ashore, and traders, who laid out their wares on the boat deck offering a variety of local goods including very fine craft- and lace-work. It seemed a good opportunity to stock up on some goodies for Sue and the family.

It was a novelty to sail with European quartermasters and felt strange to be greeted at the gangway by one of these smartly-dressed leading hands instead of a duty *secunny*. They were carefully chosen from the shipping pool and offered company contracts to reward their loyalty and, as they invariably remained with Ellerton's for long periods, ensured a permanent supply of first-class men available to serve these magnificent ships. Their sense of humour and fun was without question an experience in itself. 'Geordie' Hall assigned to my watch, for instance, never failed to have an appropriate quip for every occasion and was the proud owner of an inexhaustible fund of risqué stories that were nearly all hilarious but unrepeatable. He also possessed the ability, at least initially, of producing an endless stock of excuses for never being where I wanted him during the morning watch, although he was excellent on lookout/steering duties in the evening. His reasons were always apparently plausible yet so convoluted that any investigation would have taken hours. I gave him the job, one morning shortly after leaving London, of cleaning both port and starboard ladders leading from the after part of our bridge to the sports deck abaft our smoke-room, and radio office on the port side. Many of these routines were carried out early before the passengers commenced their morning meanderings. All that was required was a general sweep-up, afterwards polishing brass on handrails and step edges. I used to do this job as a cadet in about thirty minutes but, after two hours when it was still not completed, my patience snapped. Cutting short his long rambling explanations of 'how this was missing and how that had to be fetched from for'ard…the Brasso tin was empty and had to be replaced…', I told him directly that if the task were not completed to *my* satisfaction within ten minutes he would be reported to the chief officer. The Mate (unbeknown to either of us) was in the chartroom talking to the Commodore and, upon entering the wheelhouse and seeing Geordie working as if his life depended on the results, smiled his approval over my actions, stating to the effect he would not try it on with this particular junior mate again. Honour was clearly satisfied but, more importantly, a certain stability in relationships became established. I 'felt my arrival' with both Mr Smart and the Commodore. The realisation also came of why it had been so essential for me to have done these menial tasks during my cadetship – even if they had not been enjoyed particularly at the time.

It was whilst on watch off the Liberian coast that Mr Smart discussed with me the option of being commissioned in the RNR. It seemed as if this particular gremlin was determined not to lie down, notwithstanding my decision a few months earlier, aboard the *Gourock,* and having this confirmed by Captain Ford at the shippers party. He was very persuasive – which was not surprising seeing, from the passenger list with its inclusion of our senior officers, he was a full commander holding an RD, or reserve decoration. Certainly, he made the advantages sound very attractive. I related my experiences as a cadet serving aboard HMS *Beautiful,* receiving in return an hilarious response – not quite the one anticipated – and his comment to the effect that my attitude might 'need a little refining', but generally it was one very much in a mode that would

*One of the duties of the watchman was to hose down the bridge wings before
the passengers rose to commence their daily activities (courtesy BP plc).*

lead to a successful career in the Reserves. He stated that not taking the RNR (or the
Royal Navy for that matter) too seriously was probably 'a damned good thing for all
concerned'. I listened carefully to all he offered but, frankly, apart from the generous
uniform allowance – of which I was already aware, and some of which continued to
enjoy – shared little of his enthusiasm that my nose could be kept sufficiently clean to
prevent a continuous rain of trouble from falling upon me. Fortunately, the plumber
(himself an ex-regular Royal Navy chief petty officer) appeared at that moment to
discuss a minor bedevilment with his tanks and soundings, thus letting me off that
particular hook – at least for a while.

In the officers' smoke-room later that evening, it appeared a row of momentous
proportions was brewing in the engineering department. It must have been something
quite phenomenal to allow even a whiff (which was about all we of the deck department
could discern) to become public knowledge. All disputes were invariably kept within

the particular department. Playing chess in my cabin with the third engineer later on, prior to turning in, his mind was clearly not on the game. This led him to make some appallingly trivial mistakes with the result that I thoroughly thrashed him. Putting away the pieces (both literally and metaphorically), we agreed mutually, and for me charitably, to declare that particular game void. He then opened up a little hinting at the row between the engineers and their senior officers – the chief and second. I listened, but offered little encouragement by asking questions (filing those away carefully for later dissemination amongst the mates). Of such nefarious substance is the nature of shipboard loyalty. As next senior officer, he found himself a buffer between opposing factions, even though his own sympathies were with the juniors. The dispute apparently revolved around dirty job money paid as a bonus for specifically unsocial jobs falling by definition to the lot of engineer officers. He shut up then, realising that he had already mentioned too much, being aware that rivalry on the chessboard was invariably reflected in social areas. Anyway, it seemed the matter was being reported to the Merchant Navy and Airline Officers' Association (MNAOA) and cables had already been exchanged confirming that their local representative would come aboard at Cape Town to attempt arbitration. I had joined this Association as a cadet and valued my membership. This was not so much for the fringe benefits of discounted purchases at selected stores, but more for the insurance cover provided should any officer's certificate of competency be attacked in circumstances which needed defending by a barrister in a court case anywhere in the world. I had heard discussed periodically at sea how supportive and valuable were the services provided, and indeed had met their representatives when they visited ships. I had not focussed particularly (not having had need to do so) on their intervention when requested in internal disputes. Mentioning the matter to Mr Smart whilst on watch the following morning, he confirmed much of what the third had told me. His sympathy appeared also to be with the juniors on this occasion.

We crossed the Equator about eleven days after leaving London. There were no real high jinks amongst the passengers. In fact the ceremony, in which each who had not crossed before was hauled before Neptune's court and dunked in the ship's small swimming pool, was mundane relative to the antics which occurred aboard larger liners. Geoffrey was set up as King Neptune, but a less likely monarch could hardly be conceived. He had filled himself with quantities of gin and consequently had problems retaining not only his crown but also his equilibrium. He was aided by the cadets and the European deck steward but, as the event anyway was one of relaxed hilarity, managed to get away with his indiscretions. He told me later that this part of his duties to entertain passengers was the only one that he dreaded. For me it was more of a financial consideration than a social one. Once it leaked out that I had crossed the line only as a cadet, being thus spared any expense, all officers benefited from a round of lunch-time drinks before the passengers' debacle in the afternoon. I accepted my 'crossing the line' certificate which, on balance probably cost more than my Second

At times during the voyage the Old Man would tear himself away from his duties to passengers and join his officers in the lounge 'for a breath of sanity'(courtesy BP plc).

Mates' but, at the end of the trip, it had been 'caught up in something somewhere' and was nowhere to be found. I was not particularly heartbroken.

Cape Town lived up to the reputation previously experienced (although on this ship this was no chance of a jeep finding its way on board for onward passage up and down the coast as an officers' pleasure boat – as had occurred on a cargo ship during my cadetship). Del Monico's and Darryl's Bar remained flourishing, but the visits I made to these establishments turned out to be pretty mild compared to those during previous voyages. We deck officers had all visited these ports before and the regularly serving officers seemed to have made firmer friendships in Durban and Beira than anywhere else around this coast, so we looked forward to renewing – or making – acquaintances in these ports. I shared in a general discussion one quiet evening on board and related my experiences in wild Africa during preceding trips. This hilarity continued until it was time to turn in prior to commencing a cargo watch at 0600 the following day.

True to his promise, the MNAOA representative arrived on board and immediately went into conclave first with the junior engineers and then the chief and second. The senior officers then adjourned to the Old Man's lounge and discussions appeared to be of such import that the local chief engineering superintendent found himself invited to subsequent sessions. The rest of us were agog to learn the outcome – although motives of deck and engine-room were diametrically opposed. The worried faces of the juniors were greeted with enthusiastic (if hardly-secret) glee from staunch supporters of their friends amongst the mates. It was all in the name of good fun of course and emanated from traditional rivalry which had existed ever since steam replaced sail as a means of propulsion. Inevitably, a compromise was reached which apparently appeased the juniors more than the Company – at least, the latter were paid dirty money by the former. The general consensus was that Ellertons should never have introduced such a ridiculous ruling and, if subsequently they ended up with egg on their collective faces then it was their own fault. And so, peace was again restored to our engineering department; the Second was restored to favour in the eyes of his juniors, and the third engineer ended up with some convincing wins on the chess board – although my own efforts were not complete disasters, and I won some significant battles.

A favourite navigation watch was between East London and Durban, following the coastline with its rivers and scenery looking very similar, both visually and on the radar, for a considerable range of range of miles. The river names simply 'rolled off the tongue': Mewasa – Umtata – Unlakatyi – Umgazi – Unzamba, conjuring in the mind's eye a kaleidoscopic variety of images. On one occasion, I saw ahead of me eight assorted merchant ships coming on virtually a reciprocal course, so altered wide to starboard passing them wide and clear down our port side. The Commodore chose the moment of the widest swing to pop up on the bridge, offered his customary sweep of the horizon, following this with a glance into the radar, saw how far off course we were, looked again, grunted and went as silently as he had appeared. I took his adenoidal noise as agreeable confirmation of my actions – and relaxed.

Durban was again the 'port of all ports' for all concerned – officers and leading hands alike. Sparks intercepted a radio message which he passed on with unrestrained glee to the senior cadet. Apparently, Geoffrey's paramour of the last couple of voyages had become enamoured with the radio officer of a regular run British India Line passenger ship – one of two sister vessels on their India–Africa run. Sparks had been discussing the local state of love life in Durban and, in the way of coincidences internationally, mention was made of her name in such endearing tones that he investigated further. His *pièce de résistance* arose from mentioning to his fellow operator Geoff's long-standing interest in the same girl of such delightful charms. The ether doubtless resounded until our ship was in port – and (luckily) the radio station closed for the duration.

The *Earl of Guildford* was berthed just forward of our vessel on the usual Ellerton berths. I had served as a second trip cadet (somewhat ignominiously) aboard this vessel for what proved less than two days. In fact, my stay was for such a short period that I did not even have time to sign Articles. She was then brand new, and loading

Durban was probably the most popular port visited on the South African coast and
many deep-sea cargo ships berthed at the Ocean terminal (courtesy Tartan Studios (Pty) Ltd).

explosives for her maiden voyage to the Persian/Arabian Gulf from the River Thames Cliffe powder buoys when, at the end of my first day just as I had turned in, she was hit by an inward bound Red Star Line ship and sustained a hole that extended almost into number one hatch. She was removed to Tilbury dry dock for running repairs, whilst I was transferred to Ellerton's *Earl of Edinburgh* – the ship I had been due to join originally. I meandered gently aboard the following morning whilst the junior second was on cargo watch with Gary. It seemed strange to be padding along the deck officers' alleyway and passing the cadet's cabin wherein I had spent just one solitary night. Her cadets were busily engaged somewhere so I stopped outside the third mate's cabin, knocked on the jalousie, and hearing his response drew aside the door curtain and popped in my head. Glancing up from his desk, I immediately recognised the engaging smile of Peter Dathan who had been not only a fellow cadet from Keddleston navigation school, but also a close friend and mentor to me at the time when both were particularly welcome. His delight in seeing me was obvious and within a few moments we were supping ale and reminiscing about our days at nautical college whilst up for Second Mates'. His ship was closing cargo and due to sail for Indian ports a few days later. He had been aboard her since loading and we shared experiences over the previous months. I was due back on board to work overnight as duty officer so we agreed to meet later for an evening ashore.

Peter came aboard our ship the next evening when I was free of duties so following a few welcome starters, we embarked on what was becoming for me a regular pattern in Durban. The evening was spent initially at the Merchant Navy Officers' club, after which we went enthusiastically (and slightly sloshed) onto the XL Restaurant for a bottle or so of local wine – and a T-bone steak with all the trimmings. He had some news of ex-Keddleston cadets and staff, but that was even more than I could share. My divisional officer 'Fred' had apparently been dismissed from the college for alcohol offences. It seemed a number of parents had complained about his offensive behaviour towards cadets – which came as no surprise. My 'arch-enemy' Woodley had passed Second Mates', but then left the sea to work in a shipbroker's office, whilst Felsted was third officer aboard an 'ED ship' – or Elder Dempster Line – trading regularly to West African ports. It was good to hear about my old nautical Alma Mater and to know that Captain Mobbs remained in harness as captain-superintendent. We both agreed he was a good man. It was well past 0200 hours before we returned to our respective ships, both 'merry and shining brightly'.

Heaven only knows how Peter felt the next day – cargo watch for me was a complete nightmare. I did not have chance to enquire for by the time I had struggled onto the boat deck next morning, before going to our duty mess to take what passed for breakfast, the adjacent berth where *Guildford* was moored was now taken by a Union-Castle cargo ship – the *Tintagel Castle*, as I recall. Peter had mentioned his ship was working cargo late, in order to finish in time for the early morning tide, but had been rather vague about this. It had been good to touch base once more with him. Ever since leaving Keddleston we had each intended quite sincerely to write to the other but, in the manner of most nautical relationships, neither of us had actually got round to doing so.

During our homeward bound trip, commencing from Beira, Geoff was promoted fourth mate and placed on permanent watches with Andrew in the final stages of preparing for his Second Mates' examination. As I was the officer 'fresh from the press' – a worthy quote from Mr. Smart – we spent a lot of time in my cabin discussing 'finer points' regarding the written papers and particularly the dreaded oral examination. Quite early in his cadetship Geoff's parents had moved from Plymouth – following his father's advancement as principal executive officer in the Ministry of Defence, London – which meant he was now booked at the nautical college there for his three-month refresher course. My information regarding the lecturers and their important part-time role as examiners proved as useful to him as it had encouraged me during the final stages of my time as fourth mate.

Occasionally, when not turned-to with the bosun and working with the crew on deck, Gary also shared my deep-sea watches on a voluntary basis. I encouraged him to take and work celestial observations, and formulate decisions within the collision rules for proposed avoiding action, on occasions when we found ourselves approaching potential close-quarter situations with other ships. I discussed with him appropriate lights, sound and visual signals. These sessions were most interesting for me – and (I hoped) served equally as helpful to him. Mr Smart was in complete agreement. He actively encouraged this assistance as 'good for us both' and used my sessions to support those more intense meetings held with Gary every Saturday morning in his office, as well as the twice-weekly 'tutorials', as he called them, with Pete. The cadets aboard *Countess Elizabeth* had practical bridge experience 'coming out of their ear-holes' – but seemed to relish every minute of it!

Since leaving Cape Town the Commodore and Mate allowed me to keep watches alone, but on the strict understanding that 'if I were ever in the *slightest* doubt about *anything* then Mr Smart should be telephoned immediately.' These once again clear guidelines boosted my confidence and I had indeed called him, particularly when encountering fleets of fishing boats off the African coast, and on a couple of occasions when meeting deep-sea trawlers which I decided could result in potentially close-quarter situations. My response had in turn given both senior officers confidence to trust me and, although I often felt (probably rightly) that they were 'keeping an eye on me', the arrangement worked well.

Whilst crossing the Bay of Biscay, Commodore Browne popped into the wheelhouse for what had become an occasional chat. I had few direct dealings with him during the voyage, but those rare occasions were always marked by his courteous and friendly approach. On this occasion, after glancing automatically around the horizon and checking the radar, he informed me of the satisfaction both he and the Mate felt in the way I performed all of my duties and that they would like me to return for the next voyage 'if I felt this was what I wanted'. I agreed immediately. Certainly, being given responsibility whilst on watch, and helping train the cadets including during fire and boat drills was appreciated, but I was also well aware that there was still much for me to learn as a navigating officer. Now that I had become accustomed to the personality of Mr Smart, I felt little better opportunity for learning would be found aboard any other vessel in the Group. Commodore Browne advised that officers re-signing Articles intending to return deep-sea followed the practice of signing-off in the West India Dock and would then re-sign coastal Articles and do part of the ship's coastal and continental voyage before rejoining the *Countess* (as I had done nearly three months earlier) in the Royal Albert. On this occasion, I would do the entire coastal and continental trip, but would take some local leave in the UK both before and after this passage. It seemed a strange way of going about things, but I was quite happy to accept the idea – especially the welcome break of six days whilst the ship discharged, until the day she was due to sail for Middlesbrough.

Returning on board, I found a mixture of new and deep-sea officers. The Commodore was due the entire coastal trip for leave, whilst Mr Smart, Andrew and Gary were remaining until relieved in Hull. Geoff had gone for his study leave and was not replaced around the coast, so Gary enjoyed their double cabin alone for a couple of weeks. A Royal Naval Reserve sub-lieutenant from the London Division was also posted to our vessel. This was an unofficial arrangement that Ellertons sometimes allowed with individual units upon request from their commanding officer. The idea was to provide additional sea-going bridge training for younger officers and to cement relationships between the Royal and merchant navies. The RNR officers were not List One, but were employed in regular professions ashore and made a commitment to serve with the Royal Navy for a fortnight each year, interspersed between drill nights a couple of times per week. Howard was twenty-three years of age and had read law at Exeter University before becoming an articled clerk to a solicitor. A berth was found for him in a passenger cabin: there were enough of them spare, as no passengers were carried around the coast – and the Mate placed him on watches with Andrew. Inevitably, the senior second could not help making comparisons between the different standards of training and commented favourably on Howard's enthusiasm, but found numerous holes in his professional and academic knowledge. In fact, he stated our cadets were far more proficient and useful on the bridge. The thought crossed my mind concerning how any of us would cope with life in a solicitor's practice, but I then considered this an unfair comparison for each of us (to my knowledge) had chosen seafaring by choice – in the same way he had opted for law. It proved an interesting interlude and Howard fitted in with our social life extremely well, especially joining with the SODS operas that occurred occasionally to relieve boredom. I noted that even he gave an automatic 'sir' to Mr Smart, but otherwise used Christian names with us, including Gary.

I served for five continuous deep-sea voyages on the *Countess*, until sufficient sea-time had been accrued enabling me to attempt my Mates' (Foreign Going) Certificate of Competency. During these trips, I gained both experience and particularly confidence. It was a rare thing now for the chief officer to be on watch with me – unless I felt it expedient to ask his advice. Inevitably, this period saw a number of changes amongst all ranks, which brought different problems and many humorous incidents.

As anticipated after my second voyage, Mr Smart received his due promotion to Master of a cargo vessel. I was pleased for him, but astonished to find myself feeling quite sorry at his going. Following our initial meeting, he had proved friendly and supportive, but usually kept this within formal boundaries which would not allow any junior mate to 'come too close'. I had few difficulties with this but I knew his lack of familiarity rankled with some second mates. From an aside made by the Commodore on one occasion, it seemed that once he was certain of my reliability, he lowered his guard a little, accepting me more readily. I recalled an incident when he rejoined the vessel after his first leave before we sailed again for Africa. Apparently, he and his wife had purchased a new house just outside Liverpool and the first night in following the voyage, whilst happily settled, the roof had blown off in the teeth of a howling gale and torrential rain. They and their bedroom were drenched in a matter of minutes, leaving them to take refuge in the lounge downstairs and await the dawn. The ruefully dry humour he used to relate this made the incident appear hilarious and for a few days afterwards, he accepted (most surprisingly) the 'whooshing-noise' we made on encountering him, as relaxed fun. One of the reasons for his attitude of course, was although he had contacted builders and other appropriate agencies before his recall, it was Mrs Smart left ashore who had to sort out the mess. I reflected that the wives of merchant seamen, for mere survival, had to develop many practical attributes and work at many of the things shared by most married couples largely on their own – often for long periods. It was no wonder they developed into 'a meanly practical bunch of females', as Mr Smart described them.

I heard Mr Dawson, who replaced Richard as chief officer, carrying-on alarmingly during one inspection when he discovered that all four carbon tetrachloride extinguishers on the ship were empty. We all looked suitably amazed at this news, but as 'carbon tet' was one of the best agents for removing virtually any sort of stain from Number One doeskin uniforms, he should not have really been surprised – and certainly not fooled by our protestations of innocence. Whenever a mark appeared on a sleeve or elsewhere then a quick dash to the nearest extinguisher usually did the trick instantaneously, without the embarrassment of burning a hole in the uniform. It was universally popular amongst officers, especially (some would say, in the light of their 'mucky characters') our cadets. Being sworn to secrecy by the junior cadet on my third voyage it was even related to me that he had seen Mr Dawson himself (typical hypocrisy notwithstanding) tapping into this handy source conveniently situated outside their cabin. This occurred during an occasion when everyone else (apart from watch-keepers) should have been asleep. Bearing in mind that there are some occasions when silence is by far the best policy, I did not enquire what young Thomas was doing awake. This was more than true regarding this young man for, in the eyes of many, 'our Tom' was strongly suspected of being 'a little too closely associated' with Graham the assistant purser. This was the only occasion to date that I knew of of any deck officer carrying almost openly his label of being gay.

One of the junior engineers fell by the wayside. Following a festive Dinner Adieu, he was captured leaving a main deck passenger cabin by no less a person than the Commodore. The general opinion among his ex-colleagues, amidst customary laughter, was 'if you are going to fall, then you might as well make a damn good job of doing so'. He was up before the Master and chief engineer later the same day, and the agent instructed to arrange a seat on the next available flight from Cape Town to the United Kingdom. It appeared that he was dismissed from the Company, but subtlety reigned as ever, for a few weeks later he was reported (through the gossip of Sparky's the world over) as sailing on a Regal Steamship tramp-ship engaged on the iron ore trade from South America.

The European quartermasters aboard this class of ship had to insert a time clock into various points around the accommodation on a one-hour routine during the night watches. As this was the only duty about which I ever heard them complain, it came as no surprise one morning, shortly after leaving Lourenço Marques, to find that the clock had mysteriously disappeared. Mr Dawson called them into his cabin individually and threatened each with dismissal, courts martial and even castration, but failed either to budge their denials or find a culprit. 'It was just laid down, sir, whilst we entered readings in the book, and when we went to pick it up, sir we couldn't believe our eyes that it had vanished, sir.' Until arrival in London, there was little which could be done. The general agreement was that one of them had flung the thing over the side, but such an assertion failed to do justice to their subtlety. The night before arrival in the UK, the galley staff did their usual end-of-voyage cleaning of the stockpot. This apparently essential galley necessity was used to produce countless bowls of soup for all passengers, officers and leading hands when, lo and behold, the Goanese *yopass* found the much abused time clock amongst the debris remaining at the bottom – along with six odd socks and a pair of underpants. Life aboard the 'big four' certainly presented its own unique moments of enjoyment.

Countess Elizabeth carried in the purser's department about half-a-dozen leading hands who supervised the Goanese ratings. Most of these were far above the average 'run of the mill ratings', as Mr Smart (inevitably) described them. Over my voyages at different times, three of them – the writer, deck and saloon stewards, were all ex-navigating cadets who had fallen foul of the stringent Board of Trade (Marine Division) eyesight test. We did not have a great deal to do with them socially, although they and our cadets mixed quite well, and it was from the latter that we learnt of their varying misfortunes. One young man had failed the sight test when presenting himself for Second Mates' following four years completed sea-time with Shell Tankers. Of this chap, Mr Smart spoke for all of us: 'Gosh – if that had happened to me, I would have been devastated and as sick as the proverbial parrot. Where does he go from here?' Another young chap had his cadetship terminated after a couple of years with Blue Star Line, following a report from his captain expressing concern at the standard of his vision whilst on the bridge at sea. Another had not even made it to sea in the first place. He had a place with both a shipping company and at nautical college, but was unable to take these owing to a colour-defect fault. We sympathised considerably with each – 'there but for the grace of God, goes any one of us' being the epitaph, but there was little we could to assist practically. Certainly, nobody on board, not even the Commodore, had any suggestions. We believed they had taken these jobs at sea with Ellerton's whilst recapping their situation and deciding their next moves. It still came as no surprise to learn that two of them became alcoholics, whilst the other put on a stoically brave face, but became withdrawn and introverted. Their fate was one of those tragedies of the sea that rarely became news.

One of the cadets that was appointed had an unusual background, for he had recently enjoyed a six-month exchange trip with a German cadet. In an unaccustomed spirit of the German equivalent of *entente cordial,* Ellertons had agreed to take a Hansa Line's cadet and place a British boy aboard one of their ships. The German lad probably benefited professionally more from this as he came to the *Earl of Birkenhead* with an excellent knowledge of English, whilst his contemporary went to his ship without even a smattering of German. The officers refused to speak to him in English, forcing (but encouragingly helping) him to pick up a working knowledge of spoken German. This factor apart, the exchange seemed to have worked well and he enjoyed the experience. It seemed in many respects that German officers across all departments were just as wild as their British ones.

I enjoyed visiting all ports along the African coast but, after such a lengthy time, the trips began to pall in their familiarity and were becoming stale. Captain Gaskell's assessment proved quite true: my voyages indeed were turning into his proverbial bus route. Generally, at least initially, the time in foreign ports was enjoyable and significant only for innocent shore trips with either of the second mates or cadets, depending on duties, to the cinema and outlying districts. It was good merely to leave the ship for a while, stretch legs, see something of the scenery and capture local atmosphere. We followed the normal practice of keeping twelve-hour cargo watches between the three of us, which proved an admirable arrangement because it allowed a clear twenty-four hours free of duty giving time for a good run ashore and making possible visits of a more extended nature. In Cape Town, for instance, Sparks and I hired a car through the agent at a very reasonable rates and, taking the junior cadet, went on the seventy-minute drive past the Naval base at Simonstown to the Cape of Good Hope and onto Cape Point – prominent navigational marks often viewed from 'the other end'. We returned via the west coast north of the nature reserve. Sparky, on that particular trip, held an international driving licence and most officers took advantage to make visits whilst in all ports.

In Durban, the snake park with its collection of black and green mambas and other 'wriggling nasties' was visited, along with trips to the Addington nurse's home for dances and, for most of us engaged or married men, a quick escape afterwards from the more than generous hospitality offered by these enthusiastic young (and not so young) females. We went swimming frequently behind the safety of the shark nets, relaxing on the warm sands and enjoying a meal afterwards in our favourite XL Restaurant. I never failed to enjoy the sight of the larger than life Zulu rickshaw boys in their exotic plumes and colours taking passengers for tours around the city, although I was never tempted to try a ride.

One trip was, in a way, not so enjoyable. On a visit to the aquarium we watched in fascinated horror as ugly hammerhead and other particularly dangerous sharks swam aimlessly in circles. Our viewing was from all angles and it seemed quite frightening when standing on one particular level which allowed the sharks to approach alarmingly

*Beaded Zulu rickshaw boys added atmosphere for the tourists in Durban
(courtesy Constantia Greetings (PTY) Ltd).*

close. On one occasion one of these monsters had to be 'disposed of' because it started munching away happily at the other exhibits. These creatures filled most mariners with a fearful repulsion. This was emphasised for us following an experience further down the coast in East London. We often went swimming off a beach there until a shark decided to visit this popular area. For a reason that seemed without explanation, it swam on the surface between a group of about thirty swimmers and then singled out a young boy of about ten years old who was paddling quite near to the water's edge. A lifeguard raced into the sea and, in an extremely brave act, thrust repeatedly at the shark with a boat hook, eventually frightening it away, but not before it had bitten the lad twice on the back of the leg. Rushed into the local hospital, he sadly died a short while after admittance from shock and the loss of blood. This was the first recorded shark attack in this port and was widely reported. The views of other swimmers as they watched this monster swim past them apparently did not warrant mention, but I imagined most of them experienced a few nightmares for some time after the event. We heard about the tragedy whilst up the coast in Beira and all officers, even the most hard-bitten, were upset and visibly shocked at the news. The incident created an uneasy – and uncharacteristic – stillness in the atmosphere throughout the ship for a couple of days. None of us went swimming again in East London.

We all suffered from the irritation of mosquitoes in every port and simply took their sting in our stride. No preventative measures seemed to deter them. Spraying the cabin certainly helped – for a while – but all too soon one of the nuisances entered through the air ventilation system and it proved impossible to keep them out of the accommodation. They caused an incident when the ship was in Durban and our electrical engineer was stung just below the eye. This swelled considerably within a very short while and our surgeon advised hospitalisation. The electrician from the nearby *Earl of York* (another of the 'big four' homeward bound) was transferred, with a replacement for that ship being flown out to Cape Town. We heard later that 'Lecky' was flown home, and that he eventually lost his sight in that eye. Our surgeon explained his theory that the particular 'mozzy' was infected with some disease that then entered into the electrician's bloodstream.

My joy was unbounded when one morning in West India Docks a third officer reported on board stating he was my relief. He was indeed, and never had such a word coined my feelings so accurately! Mike Denton had served his cadetship with Ellertons – and Mr Dawson remembered him when Mike was in his third year and our chief officer was second mate aboard the old *Earl of Hull*. He spoke of him with a whimsical smile indicating that the cadet had 'been quite a character' – a nautical aphorism which spoke of many sins and unrecorded incidents. My final meeting with the Commodore was very positive as he handed me yet another in a line of watchkeeping certificates larded with a few brief but favourable comments. For some trips now, in efforts to further my training, I had been placed in charge of stand-by operations both on the fo'c'sle and aft, as well as taking more responsibility for duties normally undertaken by the second mates, but under their supervision.

The following day I reported to Captain Ford at the Kremlin and finalised arrangements for study leave. Sitting opposite him, I experienced feelings similar in many respects to those during final sea-time days during my cadetship when keeping my journal became little more than a chore. With amusement in his eyes he succinctly stated 'You are ready to leave the nest, young Jonathan, and fly towards greener pastures'. Other that that, he was very cordial and, hosting me to lunch, expressed his best wishes for my studying, stating how much he looked forward to reappointing me as second mate within the Group.

It was good to see so many familiar faces amongst the instructors at nautical college, many of whom remembered incidents from my time there taking Second Mates', but whether or not this was a good thing I did not think worth pursuing. I also met two contemporaries from Keddleston days, vaguely recognised but little known due to the almost fanatical emphasis on the rigid watch system operating there. I found much of the professional navigation papers quite straightforward, along with the maths, ship construction, ship maintenance, and meteorology. The separate magnetism, electricity and gyrocompass papers were very hard going and much night oil was spent prior to taking these. As it happened, I came very close to being referred in this paper and it was only following intensive questioning from the examiner during my oral that I was allowed to scrape a pass. For some reason I had thrown a total blank whilst attempting questions dealing with machinations of ferromagnetic materials. The oral itself was far more demanding than that encountered for Second Mates' and I really sweated over some of the questions. I passed, but to my mind not as convincingly as the examiner thought, and my confidence received a nasty knock.

Dathan was also up for Mates' but was taking this at Warsash out of Southampton, so it was not possible for us to meet until my parents invited him down for a short holiday before returning to sea. He also had passed, apparently without any problems, but I hesitatingly admitted my doubts and expressed fears already regarding taking Masters' certificate. He was his ever confidence-building self and stated that 'at least I had passed the thing, regardless of how close a call it may have seemed'. Putting that behind me, we enjoyed an excellent four days catching up on so much fragmented news about Keddleston, our cadet days and junior mate time – as well as information gleaned concerning some of our college contemporaries.

During a later interview with Captain Ford, he confirmed the Company wanted me to return aboard *Countess Elizabeth* for a sixth deep-sea voyage, but this time as junior second mate, upon her return in about ten days. I pointed out that a change in ship and scenery would be welcome and that I should like to experience his previously mentioned 'greener pastures'. His admonition was for me to return home and enjoy the remainder of a well-deserved leave. I felt a little disgruntled to put things mildly, but obedient as ever, made a compensatory visit to my beloved Potters, went home, and 'awaited the Company's heavenly summons'.

Chapter 3

CAVORTING WITH COMMUNISTS

———

I gradually came to at six o'clock in the morning, desperately wanting the loo following a hectic party the previous evening and wallowing in that delightful state between comatose and full awakening – fresh as the dawn, without a care in the world (how I wished) – when my ears were assailed by a strident ringing of the telephone. My feet caught in the sheet as I tumbled rapidly out of bed making (I think) towards the hall, causing me to stretch my length onto the bedroom floor. It was an inauspicious start to the day and I wondered who could be calling at such an unearthly hour. Reaching out a still sleepy hand, I came awake suddenly as the urgent voice of Captain Ford – it just had to be – apologised for the early arousal and informed me I was wanted immediately for a pier-head jump. He required me to fly out to Gibraltar and join one of the Group's associated dry cargo ships, the *King Joseph*. His 'if you would like to, that is,' added as a delightful afterthought, seemed more like an insult: he was clearly cashing-in on the fact that my contract still had a few months to go before expiry. He explained how, over the previous two days, her third officer had suffered acute stomach pain and following radio discussions with the surgeon aboard a distant Royal Navy frigate, professional advice recommended hospitalisation. The ship was shortly calling into Gib so, if I could leave that day, she would sail immediately without over-delaying her passage. It appeared any vessel calling into port for a medical emergency did not default her charter terms.

I was not too asleep to check the rank of my proposed appointment, being resolved firmly to turn it down if a drop to third mate was expected. Captain Ford's reassurance was immediate. It seemed I was the only available deck officer and so desperate was the ship's need that the superintendents had decided to place me aboard in paid second officer's rank whilst doing a third's job. Following two years on the African run visiting the same ports with the regularity of 'Captain Gaskell's bus route' – and becoming fed up with the monotony of routine – I secretly welcomed the change in plans. Therefore, I did not object too much, but merely offered an adenoidal grunt as a token show of disapproval and, rubbing a still smarting shoulder, accepted his kind offer. He compounded the sense of urgency accompanying my posting by urging me to take a taxi from home to office.

Circumstances had contrived my being alone in the house for a few days. Mum and dad were in Cornwall for their annual holiday, whilst Sue and her family had received an urgent and unexpected call to visit distant relations in Aberdeen. It seemed a much favourite elderly uncle had taken a fall down a flight of stairs with such intensity that doctors feared for his life. Knowing my recall to the *Countess Elizabeth* was due over the next few days prevented my joining either family, so our next door neighbours, aware I was alone kindly (if now I felt unwisely) had invited my participation in their wedding anniversary 'jolly' that previous evening. It was no good blaming them, for whilst they saw I never had an empty glass all evening, how much of it I drank (I ruefully admitted) was my responsibility.

Before 0900, the super faced me across his desk with usual apologies, but a much more welcome coffee. My flight was booked for noon from Heathrow and, as there was not a great deal of time for collecting tickets and the usual check-in, another taxi was summoned for the journey. The office had 'phoned airport reception clearing my anticipated late arrival and accepting their readily offered co-operation – as long as I could make the airport 30 minutes before the plane departed. *King Joseph* was on a Russia-Cuba/South America charter carrying flour outward-bound and assorted general cargo, such as varied tobaccos, cigars and sugar from Havana and San Diego – plus coffee beans from Santos in the other direction. Built at Swan Hunter's Newcastle yard just over two years previously, the ship was 7000 grt, with a 9500 shp diesel engine that gave a useful service speed of around 17 knots. She had an overall length of 445 feet, beam of 59 feet, and a summer draft of 27 feet. An assortment of ten and five-ton derricks served her five hatches – with one of 45 tons at number two hold.

The Group's agent met me at Gibraltar airport, whisked me down to a nearby jetty, and almost threw me into the launch in his enthusiasm to get me on board and the ship away. As we cast off, he left me wondering the reason for such undue haste – feeling an extra hours' delay would hardly add much to the ship's port account. He did find time to point out the vessel to me as we crossed rapidly the crowded anchorage, and we were plunging alongside in a moderate swell before I barely had time to blink. *King Joseph's* streamlined hull and accommodation block met with my approval, but clambering up a greasy pilot-ladder in neat civvies did not put me in the best of moods. My first indication that the ship was Asian-crewed came when I caught sight

The agent's launch provided a shuttle service for crews joining ships at anchorages worldwide (courtesy BP plc)

of my two holdalls passing me at a rate of knots as they were hauled up the side of the ship by an energetic Chinese quartermaster. Luckily, I arrived in time to take in my precious sextant and give this a much more gentle transit than had been afforded the gear. Leading me to a for'ard looking cabin on the boat deck, he left both bags by the table as I carefully placed the sextant on my bunk.

I then reported to the wheelhouse where the Old Man, Captain Michael Streatham, shook me warmly by the hand and introduced me to the Mate and another officer – Anthony Tilbury and Paul Wright. Exchanging greetings, I noticed Paul wore the rank of senior second mate. The Master interrupted further thoughts and discussion by suggesting 'we get this show on the road please, gentlemen,' upon which Anthony went forward whilst Paul remained as officer-of-the-watch. It was all something of a rush and hard to believe that just a few hours previously I had been enjoying my leave. Ruefully, whilst ringing FULL AHEAD, my thoughts strayed to the way in which I had joined originally the *Countess Elizabeth*. It seemed my more recent experiences of signing Articles to new vessels were becoming increasingly of the go–go–go variety, usually in the face of another's adversity.

It was no surprise to learn that I would keep the third officer's traditional 0800–2000 hours watches, which gave time beforehand to sign on, stow away my gear, and catch a brief snooze. Changing into working uniform, I glanced at ship's capacity and general arrangement plans before strolling around the main deck familiarising myself with our cargo equipment. The Chinese crew were working contentedly and I stopped off for a quick chat with their *serang*, finding out they were largely Hong Kong based. This led to an exchange of information about previous ports visited and shipping companies with whom we had previously sailed. With *bona fides* established, contact was made with this important chief petty officer.

Giving the Mate his half-hour meal relief later enabled familiarisation with the bridge gear operationally before taking my own watch. There were no surprises or shocks in the navigation department, although the radar was a more modern Marconi version than I had experienced previously. Remaining for a chat with Anthony upon his return filled in a few gaps concerning Chinese crew in general – with whom I had never previously sailed. Our deck crew were hard working, knowledgeable and uncomplicated – although their English was not too strong – in fact, some of them had very limited understanding. This meant nearly all commands needed channelling through their headman, which had created problems when attempting to work the crew in the absence of petty officers. Luckily, the quartermasters were all fluent. The Mate hinted though that a few difficulties were being experienced by the Second working his crowd in the engine-room. John had told him quietly that it seemed the recruiters had managed to find an agitator from further north

The comfort and privacy of a larger and better-furnished cabin went with any promotion to second officer (courtesy BP plc).

in mainland Communist China. Anthony offered also information concerning our cargo and voyage. The Russian ports were all in the Black Sea and were not very well administered – in more ways than one – a cryptic comment upon which he did not elaborate, suggesting I would soon find out for myself. We had a cargo of bagged sugar from Havana and coffee beans from Santos, bound for Odessa and other ports yet to be stipulated. The impression gained was this run was not a particularly popular one with either officers or ratings – apart from the South American port. On that sour note, I went below for my supper and then enjoyed a brief spell listening to a mixture of news and music broadcast on the World Service of the BBC until time for a return to the wheelhouse. Domestic listening at sea will ever remain in my memory for its varying flutter of volume increase/decrease (due to atmospherics), which was invariably 'enhanced' by the staccato song of Morse contributed by an enthusiastic Sparks.

Navigating the Greek archipelago and the Dardanelles was a fascinating experience, heightened by the Old Man explaining his adventures there following the First World War when anarchy seemed very much the way of life. His face grew extremely grave, reflecting quite severe pain, as he related some of the massacres witnessed in Black Sea ports and Turkey generally as opposing factions fought for power. It did not in those distant days sound a particularly healthy place to operate – not even for transient merchant mariners.

Twenty-one hours after leaving Istanbul, we arrived off Odessa for orders and joined a number of assorted cargo ships in the anchorage. Only an armed military launch came alongside us. Soldiers under an officer came aboard, billeting themselves on the Old Man for about 30 minutes. The only constructive note from this visit was a stern admonition that we were not to leave any rope ladders over the side, after reading the draught or whatever, and we should keep the gangway at least eight feet above the waterline, lowering this only for immediate use. We were kept wondering and waiting for a further three days until the harbour control launch visited. The Captain was promptly told we were in the wrong port and should steam across the Black Sea to Novorossiysk and there await further instructions regarding cargo discharge. None of these events raised the slightest surprise to our experienced officers, but still led to considerable conjecture and discussion at meal times.

The 355 miles from Odessa took over thirty hours after the ship experienced some of the most atrocious weather within my experience – even allowing for typhoons in the South China Sea. The ship pitched and rolled, at times quite alarmingly, as she met beam-to icy north-easterly winds emanating from Siberia which the Master told me was locally named the 'Bora'. When we thankfully arrived in one piece, our reward was to swing off the hook for four days in the Yuzhnaya Ozereika roads before being told we should have commenced discharging our sugar at Odessa. Whilst I glanced whimsically at the Mate, the Master merely grinned and rang down to the chief advising him of the change in orders and that we were to be despatched once more across the

Black Sea. So far, we had been in Russian waters for almost a fortnight and were no further advanced towards discharging. We spent two days at anchor off Odessa when, at 0530 hours on the third day without any warning, a pilot boarded and ordered the Captain to depart for a berth alongside. Fighting the momentary pandemonium caused by such an abrupt departure, rallying crew and starting the main engines took a while, and it was well after breakfast before we commenced weighing anchor – which was probably just as well as the tugs were late arriving alongside. I reported to the Master on our bridge for stations, to find both he and the pilot enjoying a meal on trays brought in by the Captain's tiger [personal steward]. The pilot was very friendly and spoke in heavily-accented English which it transpired had been learnt initially in Germany when a prisoner in the Second World War. It was interesting that he used a Russian navigation chart and, whilst keeping an eye on our position, using ship's gear and our own chart, I made a few comparisons. It seemed that the Russians, out of synchronisation with other maritime nations, did not use the British prime meridian, but had their own zero of longitude at Pulkowa Observatory in Petrograd – some 30°17'9 east of Greenwich. Other than that, the procedure for coming alongside was similar to any port in the world, with tugs taken fore and aft (eventually), and line boats and berthing parties available to receive our moorings.

Once the gangway was down procedures for clearance began in earnest. Even before the chief officer could commence opening hatches, local police supported by the military took over the saloon. Everyone from the Master to the lowest Chinese rating had to appear before this panel where their identity documents and the individual received scrutiny. The Chinese crew were not allowed ashore, but we officers were given passes and an official rubber stamp entry made in the back page of our Seaman's Identity Card – ironically under the page headed *Endorsements for use of Her Majesty's Government*. We were told we had to be in possession of both documents at all times when going ashore. An armed guard placed at the foot of the gangway made certain that no one, without exception, left the ship – even to read the draught – without showing passes to this soldier, and again on return. It was only then that Anthony, who was well familiar with the scheme of things, went on deck to liaise with shore officials, organise our deck crowd and commence discharging the sugar.

This was lamentably slow. Many of the sacks were of inferior reinforced paper, which was plainly not up to the job, and had consequently broken. These bags were ignored and slings made of the remainder deposited on the quayside where they were tallied by a shore-side clerk and the duty ship's officer. When figures for each sling were agreed, and the running total rechecked on each occasion, only then did forklift trucks deposit the load in a warehouse. The vast quantity of loose sugar remaining in each lower hold was shovelled into sacks and discharged for tallying – even though these sacks were much smaller than those from Cuba. It made a mockery of the time-consuming attention rigidly paid previously to the counting of each individual sack.

The dock scene was typical of that encountered at any maritime port. What was not the same were the working parties repairing and extending a jetty adjacent to our berth. These comprised women wielding pickaxes and shovels with the same ease as men who would normally perform such heavy manual work elsewhere.

Four berths along the quay another Regal Supreme Shipping vessel, the 15,000 grt *King Andrew*, was loading for Communist China. She was about four years old and, in the absence of little else to do, officers often wandered between the two ships paying social calls. It was interesting on one occasion when the Old Man brought his counterpart from their ship and, passing our smoke-room (where we were all lying around in varying attitudes of inebriation, total boredom and homesickness) introduced us to the bemusement of his guest as 'these gentlemen are my officers'. The look on the visiting captain's face was worth its own reward. It was surprising to learn that most of the *Andrew's* officers had employment contracts directly with Regal, rather than the Group, although their fourth engineer was also an Ellerton man who had been *shanghaied* from the *Earl of Chichester*. When we conferred, he spent the entire time moaning vociferously about the run, with its lack of facilities for shore leave, and the conditions on board. It was the first time he had been away from Ellertons (like myself) but he certainly made 'heavy weather of things', as we said on deck. Frankly, I was glad to see the back of him. Neither of us liked 'serving foreign' as we called it but, once there, it was advisable – for your own sake as well as that of those around you – to make the best of things. He impressed as 'a right little moaning Minnie', as our own third engineer politely called him.

There was little to do as far as shore leave was concerned. I wandered about locally, without any problems, but the constant attention of the black market touts, scrounging for cigarettes, American dollars, and offering phenomenal prices in roubles for items of clothing became very irritating. An old blue woollen sweater I was wearing attracted the equivalent of £15 – having been bought off the peg in Marks and Spencer for less than £2. A major problem of course was that it was illegal to take roubles out of the country – I had been warned about accepting these by all three senior officers – but there was no way in which they could be exchanged in the UK even if I had, because Russia was not a member of the international monetary exchange market. Items in the shops were sparse and expensive. I caught my Perspex protractor between the edge of the desk in my study and a wooden box of 'small stuff stores' brought in for investigation, and broke the thing. It was difficult to find a shop selling these and, when this proved successful, the cost was about £3. There was not much else upon which to spend money, so I bought it more for the curiosity value of its Russian inscription than its practical applications. Anthony and I went ashore for a meal one evening, but this also was not a success. We ended up eating some indefinable meat that arrived served with sauerkraut and black potatoes, but it was an effort to down the meal.

Among the Russian tally clerks was a young female who had quite a good working knowledge of English, so talking to her about our different ways of life, helped break the tedium of cargo watches. She was married and lived in a tall block of flats, the top of which we could see towering over distant sheds and warehouses. Apparently, loosely carpeted boards and naked electric light bulbs were accepted as the norm, whilst television was watched in a communal dormitory. Meeting the same cargo tally clerk during the long hours of night watches led to an interesting exchange of information about living conditions in our two countries. We varyingly, as watches changed, simply could not make her understand the way of life in Britain where a welfare state, and even the most modest accommodation, was luxurious in comparison. We got along very well together and, in an effort to convince me how superior their standard of living was over my home in England, she invited me to visit briefly their flat. I made certain that her husband would be present (not wishing any difficult involvement) but the trip was not a success. Her husband was highly suspicious of my intentions in calling and seemed to think it was at my arranging. A quick glance around the living room was sufficient to capture a flavour of their way of life, following which I made a quick exit and almost ran back to the ship. When next we met, she was extremely cool towards me. I think we both recognised my visit was a serious mistake, and one that could have been potentially explosive. The Old Man was completely horrified when he heard what had happened and told me so in far from unsubtle terms: 'Mr. Carridia. I have heard of officers doing some stupid things whilst in Russia, but feel you must have been out of your mind even to contemplate such a visit. Make certain you do not do anything so daft again.' In the face of such unreserved support, I made a quick retreat back on the jetty to continue the endless task of counting bags of sugar and coffee. As word got around the officers' smoke-room, my trip became interpreted in many different ways, and proved a substantial talking point until something more interesting replaced it in the idle chatter aboard 'our hooker'. The consensus matched the Old Man's opinion, so I wiped the considerable egg from my face, smiled, and put the event down to experience.

Odessa remains the capital of the Black Sea region and a popular holiday resort for Russians from most areas of the country, and a place of interest for foreign tourists. Because of these demands, the city possessed cultural and entertainment facilities not found in the other ports of Kherson, Novorossiysk and Batumi at which we called. Certainly, that paragon of seafaring welfare 'The Flying Angel' (Mission to Seamen) had seen a 'clipping of its wings' in Russian ports, for it was conspicuous by its absence. A state-run institute served the social needs of seamen covering all nationalities visiting Odessa and was set a short walk from the docks. The interior impressed as lavishly furnished Victoriana, with thick red carpets and huge drapes with heavy elaborate antique furniture. The entrance hall and lounge reminded me when I was a child of the home of a very distant (now long dead) aunt – and smelled similarly. Photographs of world ministers including Castro, Nasser and Nehru, vied for attention with national Russian leaders.

The staff were all 'volunteers' who, it seemed, were especially selected for their glibness of tongue, assortment of foreign languages and total inability to answer a direct question. By tacit mutual understanding, political questions never received an airing by either side, but whilst talking about the differing standards of living so obviously prevalent, it was inevitable that issues possessing political overtones became raised. The answers were not only elusive, but also contradictory when posed to another volunteer. They were, not surprisingly, completely unaware that I had visited the home of one of the dockers, and expressed bewildered astonishment when their descriptions of how lush were the living conditions of dock labourers was met by my cynically polite smiles. In fairness, we found that, as long as conversation was general and chatter limited to small talk, the helpers were very kind. They were hard-pressed to hide their envy of our standards of living and, from occasional glances, we could tell they secretly admired the quality of our dress and watches.

On the positive side, along with my fellow officers, I enjoyed organised complimentary visits laid on by the local version of Mission to Seamen. During one visit, invitations included a Saturday evening dance, which our junior engineers greeted with relish, showing a more than eager anticipation for what might pass as 'customary delights' afterwards. They could not have been more disappointed, much to the amusement of the mates, Sparks and me. The girls worked voluntarily following a day spent at their normal jobs, but personality or looks did not rate very highly in their selection process. I wrapped my meagre ten stone around a buxom – almost bovine – twenty-stone partner like a withering bough of Virginia creeper and, intimately linked, we endeavoured waltzing around the floor. It was akin to dancing with a cement mixer. During subsequent conversation, I discovered she was one of the lasses who spent her working hours happily wielding a pickaxe helping construct a new jetty, following a recent spell working on constructing a power station. It would be true to say she lacked more than a certain feminine finesse.

Other trips arranged were extremely enjoyable and well supported by officers from numerous ships. I enjoyed particularly one visit to a planetarium, which from a navigating officer's point of view was extremely absorbing, along with bus trips around the city centre observing modern buildings restored after the devastation from German bombing and occupation during the war. During our second call to Odessa, the itinerary included a trip to the State circus. The feats of the acrobats were truly spectacular and hair-raising, whilst the antics of the clowns had us rolling in our seats – much to the amusement of the rest of the somewhat sombre audience. In fact, I think they laughed more at us than at the clowns, which made something of a mockery of our so-called British reserve. We sat through (for want of a better description) a performance of *Swan Lake* at the State Opera House. However, philistine that I am (although thankfully not alone), my brother officers and I confess to sleeping through most of this – 'prancing around on the stage' being alien to our normal interests.

On our final evening in Odessa, officers of the three ships berthed in our particular section of the docks received invitations to share in a party. The other ships were German and a London–Greek bulk cargo vessel manned by British and Greek officers. The dinner, it transpired, celebrated an obscure Russian victory in some long-forgotten war, and our hosts were officers from a Russian tanker aided and abetted by

*The Museum of Western and Oriental Art epitomised the cultural visits arranged
by the Russian Sailors' Club in Odessa (courtesy PLAKAT Publishing.Moscow).*

ubiquitous institute volunteers. Conversations occurred through a genial combination
of interpreters, and that lingua franca of old-fashioned smiles and sign language. A
magnificent dinner was served as the main attraction of the party. It was truly a
sumptuous feast of five courses, including caviar, local wine and vodka. I still have no
idea of the meat in the main dish, but it tasted like roast pheasant, with vegetables
cooked for us in European style and with local cuisine for the Russians. The sight of
the table as we entered was impressive with silver plates and cutlery and a range of
glasses on a starched white tablecloth, the entire effect enhanced by cleverly placed
chandeliers of candles. It was an impressive but surprisingly informal evening.

Few complaints were heard from officers (a rarity indeed) over the lavish hospitality
and genuine efforts to please made on our behalf by the Russian authorities in Odessa.

In the middle of luncheon three days prior to sailing for Kherson, the Old Man's
tiger entered the saloon and handed the second mate a note requesting his presence
in the captain's cabin immediately. Taking a final fork of main course, and leaving the
remainder to grow cold on his plate, he obediently shoved back his chair and made for
the saloon door. All sorts of comments from his little friends in the engineers department
conjectured reasons for this summons but, in truth, we were all immediately interested
to learn what had clearly gone wrong. None of our accusations remotely approached
the truth, for when Paul returned in time for cheese, biscuits and coffee, he told the
world at large that he was leaving the ship immediately after lunch and transferring to
the *King Andrew* on promotion to chief officer. Although details were sparse, the mate

aboard her had gone ashore the previous evening and disappeared with no indication of where he might have gone. Our INFLOT agent [a local Russian shipping agency] had been notified earlier that day and had put enquiries into action with the local police but, so far, to no avail. The *Andrew* was due to sail later that afternoon, freeing the berth for another vessel all too eager to leave her queue in the anchorage and go alongside. As it seemed her need was greater than our own at this particular moment, Paul received 'his marching orders', as the chief succinctly expressed things.

I was called to the Captain's cabin after lunch and advised that if the mate from *King Andrew* returned, he would join us as first officer until we passed Istanbul, when a new third mate had been requested from (appropriately enough) our version of the Kremlin. Meanwhile, Tony and I were to share cargo watches between us – news we both greeted with unrestrained and unimaginable joy. The Old Man suggested six hours on and six off, but between us we modified the plot into twelve-hour watches each, so extending the time off duty for more solid sleep. It was certainly with mixed feelings that we watched *King Andrew* sail past our berth three hours later, and saw the diminutive figure of Paul waving sardonically from the fo'c'sle head. We were happy at his promotion and wished him well, but hoped also that our missing chief officer might appear from somewhere to take his due share of cargo watches. There remained between us a distinct sharing of concern for his welfare – even if motives were rather blurred.

The steward's cheery morning call next day with a cup of tea was not particularly welcome following, in the absence of cargo work, a particularly heavy night's drinking and wallowing in a SODS opera that lasted until almost 0400 hours that morning. Rousing from a deep sleep took all my willpower and, in the process, I knocked tea all over the bed linen. It was not a good start to the day but worse was to come. I decided to remove the board fitted to the side of the bunk to stop the occupant from being pitched onto the deck during heavy rolling – an essential piece of equipment during our recent severe weather, but clearly no longer necessary now we were alongside. Lifting this from its brass supports, I dropped the thing onto the big toe of my left foot. For a moment, I was too shocked to swear or do anything else, except go deathly pale as the pain shot though the foot and up my leg. Throwing the board across the cabin and cursing heartily, I staggered to my settee, rubbing the injured limb tenderly. I managed finally to slip on a sock and slippers and pop next door but one to the Old Man to report the injury and hope for 'tea and sympathy'.

There was certainly none of the former and not much of the latter as, examining the already swelling foot and darkening toenail, he told me to expect to 'part company with that nail' and that the swelling would take quite a while to subside. Meanwhile, I should 'slip on my deck shoes instead and relieve the Mate on deck, as exercise was bound to be good for both myself and my injury.' He also mentioned something impolite about 'being bloody careless' – which was perfectly true, but hardly helpful. Following a quick breakfast of dry toast and black coffee, I apologised to my steward for the mess on the bunk and ventured forth to see what the Mate was up to by number five hatch as there was still no sign of cargo being worked. He at least sympathised as I limped towards him, but was otherwise equally as disinterested as the Old Man – as were also the crew for that matter. I had reinforced once more during that trip the art of suffering in silence.

We eventually completed discharge and I prepared charts to cover the short 80-mile haul to Kherson. At the last moment, the agent from SOFRACT [a national ship agency having overall control of movements] cancelled our orders and instructed us instead to proceed the 575 miles across the Black Sea to Batumi, on the Caucasian coast, to load coal briquettes in numbers one, three and five lower holds. Neither the Old Man nor any of our officers had called previously at this port and the sailing directions on hand were sparse to say the least. We had taken the pilot on board, had tugs made fast fore and aft and I was just raising the gangway to venture out to the anchorage for the customary searching of the ship by military personnel for stowaways, when a car screeched to a halt on the jetty. I paused in my task and told the lads to re-lower the thing as I saw the INFLOT agent waving frantically from the passenger window to the Old Man on the bridge wing. He raced up the gangway, causing it to jump alarmingly in its traces and, ignoring me completely, literally flew up the internal staircase presumably to the wheelhouse. Just a few minutes later he returned at a more normal pace, muttering something about delivering 'importantly vital navigational warnings' and, in more sedate manner, walked down the long-suffering gangway to his car. Once safely anchored, I reported to the wheelhouse for my watch, relieving Anthony to look after the Russian soldiers, and learnt that the military authorities in Sevastapol had recently placed a minefield around a sector of the coast that included a length of our passage track. It seemed that they had something to hide in that region and took this drastic action of determining security, rather than resort to the less melodramatic recourse of issuing a more modest 'Notice to Mariners' indicating a prohibited area.

We went to the inevitable anchorage off Batumi before going alongside but, as the Master suspected at our time of the year for visiting, the strong south-westerly wind proved particularly troublesome. It created strong variable currents, with a series of surges known locally as 'Tyagon', which forced us into keeping the main engines turning and using both anchors. Neither hit the high spot as popular choices, even if here they proved a necessity, and the twice-daily swinging to the tide caused (to the unmitigated delight of the Mate) an entwining of our port and starboard anchor cables. It took us the best part of a day to rig a series of double 5-ton derrick runners between the links and, by placing a man via rope ladder onto the anchors, reeve the wires around the drum end of a winch. The Old Man was conversing with the Mate about the best method of effecting this, whilst I merely watched – and contributed where Anthony directed – and learnt a few more seamanship skills. I also added a few new words to my vocabulary, as the task was not an easy one to complete and leant itself to a flurry of minor frustrations.

Following the damage caused to our recently-painted hull and superstructure by loading coal, we returned to Odessa. Here, according to the prognosis of SOFRACT, we were to complete loading numbers two and four lower holds with flour, again for Cuba, following which we were to make the long-expected and threatened passage to Kherson, on the right-hand bank of the River Dnieper, and complete loading crated machinery in all five tween-decks.

It was during this passage that the situation in the engine room with the Chinese crew reached serious proportions. The engine room ratings were recruited from Hong Kong, but somehow an engine cleaner who joined the vessel from the shipping pool had travelled from further north and it seemed was a Communist-trained agitator. The chief's crowd were a close-knit bunch who preferred to deal with their own problems internally, which was fine while they did so, but in this instance, methods used by the senior ratings were clearly ineffective. It seemed the situation had been gradually increasing in intensity since the crew had joined *King Joseph* some seven months previously and, by now, everyone below considered it had gone on for long enough. Even we on deck had picked up vibrations that 'things were not well' with officers and ratings below, as Anthony had hinted when I joined the ship. We had four fitters in the engine-room whom the chief described as 'not only good people, but superb at their work', an accolade indeed from this rather dour man, but they passed occasional comments to the Second which let him know discreetly that the situation was far from resolved amongst the engine-room crowd. It seemed the agitator created problems of unrest by showing an attitude towards the officers that was close to insubordination,

The MV Athelempress *with crossed anchor cables due to swinging at an anchorage using both anchors during conditions of strong tides and wind (courtesy R W Weeks).*

but insufficient to justify a 'logging' – the way in which the merchant navy deals with offences of indiscipline. The *serang* had done his best, aided and abetted by his petty officers, but without any positive effect and it seemed that things were approaching a stage where the continuous wrangling created was causing unrest among the other men – like 'water dripping away at a stone', as the chief described the situation. The Old Man offered to have a timely word, but the chief was against this, preferring to wait until the cleaner did something for which severe action might be justified, and then take him to the bridge.

I never found out what really happened. My knowledge of the incident grew only from being turned-to after leaving my afternoon watch at 1600 hours just as I was preparing for a couple of hours rest before supper. Just as I settled on my day-bed, a rush of clumping footsteps stopped outside my curtained door, followed by a frantic banging and urgent shouts for me to come out. It appeared that one of the ratings had slipped down the main companionway and fallen heavily close by the main engine. It took only a few minutes for me to reach the cross-alleyway on the deck below and, treading carefully, descend to the lower levels. There I discovered the unpopular engine-room cleaner crumpled up and groaning. The Old Man had already found his way there, accompanied by the chief and second, and the former told me to bring the folding Neilson hospital stretcher and prepare the patient. It was the devil's own job to lash the man into the thing and get him up top. Fortunately, our Saturday

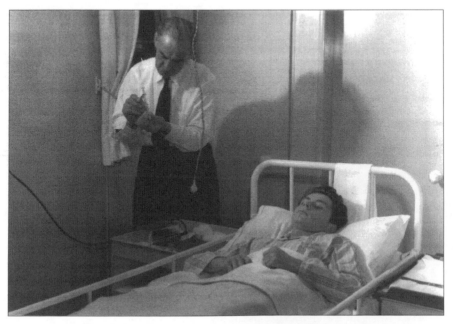

The second officer attends his patient in the ship's sick bay (courtesy BP plc).

afternoon drills paid off for we deck officers often took it in turns to use this stretcher and remove 'Fred the dummy' from a range of difficult places and situations devised by the Mate. As far as we could deduce, there was the possibility of a broken ankle – judging by the swelling, discolouration and pain – along with considerable bruising to the body, some of which looked very raw. All I could do, once the Old Man had left the hospital, was to make the chap as comfortable as possible and wait until we entered port the following day.

One thing the cleaner said that I found disturbing was his belief that someone had oiled the handrails and steps to the ladder for a middle portion of about five steps and this had caused his accident. Giving him a very direct look, I told him he should report this to the chief engineer and I would mention his accusation to the Master. Captain Streatham gave me an equally direct look in return and told me to ask the chief to come to his cabin. As the captain's quarters, including his office, were the next suite of cabins but one to my own I know the two were in conclave for quite a while. The situation certainly brought an element of light relief into the Mate's watch when I popped into the wheelhouse to recount all that had happened. Whilst his words were neutral, and couched in terms that would have created no suspicion in the minds of any subsequent police investigation once we were alongside, we both shared the unspoken and secret thought that (just possibly) there might have been 'a little enemy action down below'. The Old Man called upon me to make a statement of events as I had experienced them, which would be included with other written comments and, as I had suspected, submitted to the police in Kherson. The consensus at supper was to the effect 'that a certain viscous substance was about to hit the fan with an almighty vengeance'.

The Old Man radioed ahead and a port health launch came out with the military craft once we had brought up to anchor in Kherson roads. The cleaner was despatched to hospital ashore, but the officer stayed with the Old Man for sufficient time to deliver the customary warning about the gangway but showed no interest regarding what had happened to our rating. Then once alongside, the police arrived. They interviewed all involved and took their own statements, which were secured to those we had given the Old Man. Their findings, delivered a couple of days later in writing, were to the effect that there was no evidence to support the accusation made by the cleaner, and that rails and ladders in an engine-room were bound to be greasy, indicating that he should have exercised more care whilst using them. The Master inserted all documents in support of his entry in the Official Log Book. Subsequently, they would be handed to the appropriate authority when the crew signed-off and returned to Hong Kong.

The port of Kherson did not impress us at all, merely offering opportunities to stretch our legs and ignore the inevitable touts. It was interesting that although the swelling in my foot had disappeared, it continued to cause discomfort (rather than pain) and, true to forecasts from my illustrious captain, the toenail had indeed fallen by the wayside.

A typical series of ladders in the engine-room leading to the control platform (courtesy BP plc).

Whilst berthed in Kherson, the agent there informed us that the chief officer of the *King Andrew* had indeed been tracked down a couple of days before we left Odessa but, 'due to an oversight' the ship had not been immediately informed. Due apologies were expressed to the Old Man which he received in the spirit in which these were offered. It was all right for him to be magnanimous; he had not covered any of the extra extensive cargo watches. Apparently, our ill-fated mate-to-be had encountered the back end of a trolley bus, north of the city, and an ambulance had rushed him into a nearby hospital for an emergency operation and subsequent treatment. His identity documents indicated a ship not listed in the police records because it had already sailed. It took a few days to sort out the apparent muddle and, following his eventual recovery, the agent and Group decided to fly him home.

At breakfast that last morning in Kherson, I reported to the saloon at large the problems experienced with radio reception on my small portable. I had switched onto the BBC Overseas as usual but uncharacteristically, in the light of the reliability normally available from this service in any waters or port worldwide, the only sound received was a prolonged piercing whistle. All officers shared my experiences. It certainly served as an intense talking point until Sparks appeared and told us that this alien sound was the result of powerful signal jamming – presumably from the Russian authorities. This led to even more conjecture, which continued unabated as the Master walked into the saloon to take his place at the single table. We were so animated that no one even noticed he had appeared. He rapped on the table with his knife and called us all to order. His voice and face were severe and clearly reflected thoughts and feelings of some import. He paused, awaiting our attention, and then addressed the table at large:

'Gentlemen, I have to advise you that the international situation is extremely grave and it would appear that, because of our cargo charter, the ship and of course our good selves are directly involved.'

We all looked at him and each other blankly. Aware that he had our entire attention, he continued: 'It would seem that there is an almighty row brewing between Russia and the United States concerning Cuba. I am not entirely clear of the situation, but it seems that America is accusing the Russians of importing into Cuba by ship a number of missiles. Because the United States believes these not only exist, but also seem aimed at them, they feel their security is directly threatened and are obviously alarmed. As we are engaged immediately on this run, we may well find ourselves in the firing line but – hopefully – not literally. The situation gentlemen, is indeed very serious for a state of war could well be declared between the two countries – with us perhaps somewhere in the middle.'

He paused, as much for effect I suspected as to catch his breath leaving us, each one, occupied with our own thoughts. Certainly my mind was a whirlpool and all sorts of questions flowed backwards and forwards – each more frustrating than the last in the knowledge that our good Captain had no constructive answers.

The conversation around the table was reminiscent of the cacophony heard during the erection of the tower of Babel. It was a response directed towards hiding the fear of what might happen to us if war were declared. Inevitably, our animated talk automatically deliberated over the worse-case scenario. It seemed to be the collective agreement that, 'yes-man Britain', would blindly follow the lead of America and kill stone dead any possibility of our ship's neutrality, regardless of how our politicians might camouflage their actions. Poor old *King Joseph*, as a red ensign vessel, could be open to internment, with her innocent officers and crew gathered somewhere as prisoners of war. I was interested to see that the Old Man and chief were involved in as heated argument as the rest of us – and going nowhere equally quickly. In the middle of my own concerns, part of my mind was objectively observing those around me. Here we were, agitated, alarmed, concerned and bewildered, potentially facing imprisonment, firing squads at dawn and other 'nasties' reported luridly (and enthusiastically) by those who had served at sea during the Second World War. Having lived through the horrifying events of obscene Nazism as widely reported in the international press in the light of outcomes from the Nuremburg trials, they were adequately equipped to be expert commentators on our present situation.

The entrance of our Chinese chief steward interrupted our battery of immediate dilemmas – both real and imaginary. He paused alongside the Old Man announcing, to the table at large, that our stevedores wanted the duty officer to come to the jetty for continuation of our cargo discharge for the day. His entrance helped restore at least an element of normality and even sanity into the situation, for 'Father' advised he would keep us informed as he received information and that meanwhile we should continue with our duties and endeavour to remain calm. This seemed good advice to me, so I left the saloon and meandered on deck to 'do my bit' for England, Russia and presumably a grateful President Castro in Cuba.

Bitterly cold winds greeted me as I put a foot on deck and trudged through crispy snow towards the fo'c'sle head to check the forward moorings. The fresh fall on top of previous layers of the stuff looked romantic, but was not helpful as far as making progress was concerned. The main deck was little short of a skating rink. I passed one of the Chinese deckhands rigging a contactor box to carry a light cluster down number one hatch enabling the working of overnight cargo. As I passed, he glanced up and commented to the effect of 'how ****** cold it was, sir'. With my mind still revolving around recent international news I wholeheartedly concurred and then, a few steps later was brought up sharp, recalling that this particular deckhand had previously denied any knowledge of English when I had been working with him in the Bosun's store. I retraced my steps and queried whether or not I had heard correctly, and how had he managed to improve from a non-existent level to a reasonably fluent colloquialism within the space of a few days. He had the grace to look a little sheepish as he smiled and affirmed 'a very little knowledge, yes sir'. I could only cut my losses and agree with Somerset Maugham and Kipling that, in many respects of crew handling, 'east and west indeed shall never meet.' The short answer I was sufficiently astute to realise was simply that the crew did not like receiving orders, or even advice, from other than their own petty officers. I pigeon-holed this under the heading of progress for the days when as chief officer I might well find myself working Chinese crews.

I managed to fit into my time off cargo watches, the necessary voyage planning for our initial progress from Odessa through the Greek archipelago, and the early stages of our passage towards Gibraltar. Father seemed quite happy as we discussed my proposals. He offered little by way of amendment and consequently (in apparent default) much by way of encouragement. I felt confident in what I was doing regarding navigation, but often had to refer to either him or the Mate regarding running the sickbay, which had also landed on my lap along with the extra gold bar. With many British shipping companies, the chief steward found himself landed with this task, but throughout the Ellerton Group, traditionally it was added to the second officer's workload. During my recent leave, I had attended a Red Cross Society first aid course designed to provide at least some rudimentary knowledge, but running any ship's sickbay presented potential problems which would have tested the mettle of any general practitioner, let alone someone as new to the job as myself. The main problem confronting me regarding the ratings was 'a disinclination to work' and an amalgamation of imaginary illnesses that I felt had to be afforded some kind of preliminary investigation before arranging with the agent for the man to be examined professionally at the local hospital. Father was indeed a guiding light and it was instructional to hear the tone of voice he used with

*Conferring with the chief mate when passage planning for the first time a second officer
draws upon his colleague's wider experience and expertise (courtesy BP plc).*

suspected malingerers that managed to change their minds with a few astute questions.
I made mental notes and was pleasantly surprised later to detect successfully much of
the malingering, and to be able to confront the rue smiles of admission encountered
with considerable humour and aplomb.

There was no further news received concerning 'the Cuban crisis' as the world's
media were referring to the little débâcle into which we were apparently steaming, other
than an announcement that the Americans had imposed a blockade of Cuban waters.
There was still a considerable amount of hot air and waffle on the international scene,
as my trusty radio informed me – following departure from Russia, and leaving range
of their jamming stations.

On the positive side, we unexpectedly moored alongside at Istanbul. This allowed
us shore leave and it was good for me to wander the streets during a morning and
afternoon of idle sightseeing, which also enabled Anthony to go ashore for 'an overnight
of suspected debauchery' somewhere. We also picked up the promised third officer whom
Anthony and I greeted like a long lost brother. Having knowledge of how affairs worked
in the merchant navy generally, we had little hope of receiving a replacement. Already
visions of extra navigation watches had bedevilled conversations between us, whilst we
attempted working out ingenious preliminary overtures to our captain intended to induce
him (without it must be admitted much hope) to cover at least the 0800–1200 stint.
Terry Driscoll was also an ex-Ellerton man on a Group contract. The two of us had

Istanbul showing the Bosphorous and Topkapi Palace (courtesy Kartpostal ve Yavinlari).

sailed with mutual acquaintances and shared the same ship, although at different times. He was just out of his time – in fact, as he put the situation – 'so just out of it' that he had received his Second Mates' certificate only two weeks beforehand. It was a familiar story. The phone had rung early one morning and his enjoyment (and anticipation) of a thoroughly deserved leave had disappeared before his very eyes. Then followed the subsequent quick summons to Captain Ford for 'a cup of coffee', a delightfully disarming chat – and then an air-ticket to Istanbul, with an appropriate 'pier head jump'.

I was on watch as we approached 12 miles off the Havana coastline. Father had already warned us that we might be intercepted by an American warship – or two – or three – or even a fleet – and, in such eventually, he should immediately be informed. Such advice was not necessary because we three navigating officers had already decided upon such a course of action. It was very much a case we agreed, for 'a quick sloping of the shoulders' – with this responsibility cast firmly upon the man whose authority it seemed should take it. He also of course earned more than we did – not that this proved much of a major consideration.

It was about 1400 hours when I detected, on the 24-mile radar range, a number of echo returns. It seemed at least four unidentified vessels were rapidly closing our course-line. Subsequent plotting indicated their behaviour was out of the norm for ordinary merchant vessels for they appeared, from what I recalled of my Royal Naval Reserve training, to be idling on stand-by. It was interesting to note from the radar that two other ships were approaching in similar manner on our port side. As they closed us, I was able to positively identify them as warships, although their ensigns were indistinguishable through my binoculars. The Old Man disturbed from his post-luncheon 'zizz' by my 'phone call appeared on the wheelhouse simultaneously with an urgent Morse message flashed by Aldis lamp from what I rapidly identified as the lead ship of two American destroyers. Captain Streatham and I exchanged wry smiles, which broke any possible tension, because the signal from our American cousins (if not allies) was being transmitted at a rate almost beyond the capacity of the light. It came over to us as almost a blur and was quite incomprehensible. Receiving a nod from Father, I took the Aldis from its box, aimed it in the direction of the now almost adjacent bridge facing us and flashed, at a regulation merchant ship speed of five words per minute, the conventional calling-up sign.

As suspected, the destroyer took the hint and a message came from them requesting at almost insultingly slow speed, 'what ship, and from where and whence bound'. With the look of Christians entering a Roman arena faced by snarling and decidedly hungry lions, we supplied the required information – and in turn boldly enquired who they might be. The reply was hardly conducive to good relations. They immediately told us they were US warships operating (what they termed) 'a legal blockade of Cuba in the interests of United States security'. They also instructed us to heave-to as they wished to board us and examine our papers and cargo. Such a head-on approach hardly endeared them to us, so the Old Man instructed me to signal that 'we were in neutral waters and a non-belligerent ship engaged on peaceful trading'. We waited to see what response this might elicit, glancing at each other pensively. After a few minutes a further signal came requesting – we were pleased to note – that we heave-to and permit an officer to board us and examine our papers, asking our 'co-operative assistance as an ally' with their quest. In the face of such ultra politeness, we could only confirm our acceptance of their terms. Father then suggested I 'phone the chief engineer putting him in the picture and asking if he could advise his duty engineer. He then told me to phone the Mate asking him to pop up to the wheelhouse and afterwards to rig a pilot ladder on our starboard side. The Old Man told me he had already been in radio contact with our superintendents whilst we were still in the 'Meddy' confirming 'what the party line should be' in the event of being accosted (as he put it) by the American navy. After a few days' pause – we should have loved to know what machinations were going on behind the scenes – the Kremlin advised that we should offer any intercepting ships 'every assistance'.

It was some thirty minutes following our initial contact that a launch left the destroyer and closed us in a flurry of urgent movement. We took their forward mooring and a lieutenant commander clambered up our ladder – there having been no time to rig the gangway. He clearly lacked both the build and inclination necessary to board ships in such an undignified manner. By this time, both the chief and third officers had joined

Crew working on deck securing a guy rope to a derrick head (courtesy BP plc).

us awaiting developments in case their services were required. The officer introduced himself to us as 'a boarding officer' and, still breathless, examined our cargo documents and loading plan. He immediately focussed on the wooden crates, which we had loaded in all innocence at Kherson, requesting if we would be agreeable to opening these for inspection. They were in our 'tween-decks, but to get at them required rigging the derricks serving three randomly-selected hatches. Captain Streatham agreed to do this as long as their commanding officer issued our ship with a document – beforehand – certifying the American request, which we could show to the appropriate authorities upon arrival at Havana. This would justify, we supposed, the unofficial opening of these containers between ports, as the Master confirmed the incident was unprecedented in his experience at sea. Whilst all this was happening around us, the ship was proceeding on her course but at much reduced revolutions. I estimated we were doing around six knots.

It was quite a performance opening the hatches and then the wooden crates. When we had done so – everyone waiting with bated breath to see what they really contained – our sighs of relief must have been almost tangible, for the crates contained exactly what the cargo declaration and stencilled letters stated – namely an assortment of agricultural machinery in the form of ploughs and a very modern tractor. The American officer then thanked us for our co-operation. His expression indicated he was far from happy that, as a British ship, our charter covered this particular run. The best was yet to come for he took a copy of our crew list and advised that, were either the ship or any personnel to enter any United States ports in the immediate future, we could expect a hostile reception. After delivering this particular message, he left the ship, rejoined his launch and sailed out of our lives. The Master spoke for us all when he stated that, 'the incident had left something of a nasty taste in the mouth'.

We were delayed from picking up the Cuban pilot at Havana and spent 12 hours 'swinging off the hook' largely wondering what was going on as the pilot station seemed to ignore us. Following our experiences in every Russian port in this respect, none aboard expressed either surprise or exasperation, but I did wonder if any sinister enemy action resulting from intervention of some sort from the Americans might be working below the surface. The Old Man was non-committal regarding my suspicions although he clearly was not beyond doubting any possibilities. We were never to find out as the pilot acted quite in keeping with pilots worldwide, presenting a jovial and friendly personality. We could see no signs of positive evidence, at least in Havana, of the suspected missile sites.

Once we were alongside, the port authorities presented no difficulties and shore leave was granted to all crew without hindrance. Discharging cargo was as laborious a

Painting the hull invariably kept the crew out of mischief (courtesy BP plc).

process as loading had proved and led to many delays and frustrations. It proved an ideal opportunity in the hot sun for the Mate to rally the lads during daylight hours and paint the hull, superstructure main deck, and most other areas, so that by the time we eventually departed Cuba the ship looked immaculate. Going ashore in Havana left a great deal to be desired for there was not very much to do other than wander around the streets shopping and looking vague – much the same as in many other ports on this particular run.

A tragic incident occurred during the final stages of cargo discharge whilst Terry was keeping an eye on number three hatch and listening eagerly for the head stevedore's whistle indicating lunchtime. During this period all cargo stopped (in theory) for an hours' break. In practice, it was usual for the dockers to be away for anything up to twice this time. One of the workers at the bottom of number five hatch somehow trapped his ankle between the tank top and a few remaining sacks of flour, apparently spraining it sufficiently to prevent him climbing the ladder from the hold. A ganger came to the third officer who immediately grabbed the hospital key from the ship's office keyboard, went to the hospital, collected the stretcher and ran aft. He roped this to the cargo hook and lowered it by cargo runner to the bottom of the hatch. He reported this to the chief officer who was languishing in the officers' bar enjoying a chat and couple of pre-luncheon beers with myself, Sparks and some of the engineers. The Old Man and chief were presumably similarly engaged in his day-room. Looking at each other with shock, we were galvanised into action and all three of us rushed from the lounge simultaneously, becoming wedged in the door entrance until I backed off and followed Anthony and Terry as they rushed aft to number five. Sparks meanwhile reported to the Old Man advising him of the incident. Events in the hold had already gained their own momentum for, without waiting for us, the Cubans had taken charge of the situation themselves. The stevedore had arranged for his men to put their colleague into the stretcher, re-tie this to the cargo hook and begin the process of winching the man aloft. By the time we arrived, man and stretcher were being hoisted up the 40 feet separating hatch and tank top. There was nothing for us to do except watch as the stevedore directed his man at the winch controls.

When stretcher and burden were halfway up, I saw to my horror that the knot attaching rope and stretcher to cargo hook was gradually loosening. The Cuban stevedore, watching the scenario unfold before him, seemed frozen to the spot. I shouted a warning below to the dockers watching the operation, whilst the Mate simultaneously told the winch operator to lower the stretcher back down the hold as quickly as possible. He of course had to be one of the Cubans whose English was faulty and, by the time he understood what was required of him, it was too late. The rope parted and the stretcher dropped about 25 feet to land on top of the last layer of sacks. The event happened so quickly that the injured man could not have had time to realise what was happening – or so we tried to reassure ourselves later. Certainly, he did not cry out, but the sickening thump as he landed, with the sound magnified by the empty hold, remained impressed

Rescue operations from the bottom of a hold or tank were practised during weekly routine drills by officers and crew (courtesy Shell International Shipping and Transport).

on my memory for many years. The silence afterwards was oppressive, with the dockers at the bottom of the hatch standing around in a numbed tableau of disbelief.

Anthony climbed down the ladder and went to the man, announcing – not surprisingly – that he had died from the fall. Exchanging horrified looks with the bosun, my reactions were almost by autopilot. We watched the Mate make fast the stretcher – correctly this time – and we watched its ascent to the top of the coaming as the Mate came out of the inspection hatch –white and considerably shaken. Terry meanwhile had run into the ship's office where he reported the accident to the cargo supervisor and stood by as the latter 'phoned for an ambulance. By the time laborious telephone explanations had been made and the police notified, the dead man had been brought to the gangway, where his body was removed from the stretcher and covered with a tarpaulin to await arrival of police and ambulance.

Then, with cargo stopped for the day, we deck officers adjourned to the Old Man's day-room to begin an enquiry into events as witnessed from the mates' point of view. Initially, Captain Streatham made each of us adjourn to our own cabins and write independent versions of the events and our actions. These statements would serve as a basis of reports for the official logbook and the police. We then reassembled and began assessments to see if any negligence might be attributable to the ship. The only grey area discovered was the wisdom of Terry in failing to notify the Mate or Master before sending our stretcher to the hatch. Although it was a case of being wise after the event, the general verdict determined that there was little we could do about this – it was clearly an incident of a very young officer, just out of his cadetship, who acted as he thought appropriate in the light of his experience – or inexperience, whichever way the situation was considered. The Cuban authorities – much to our astonishment – agreed with our reports and processed the accident almost as a matter of course. Apart from the Master attending a local coroner's court to give evidence on behalf of his ship, nothing further developed, and the verdict returned attributed the tragic affair to 'accidental death'.

One evening Terry invited the third mate, Sparks and a junior engineer aboard a London–Greek cargo ship berthed forward to pop on board for a drink. They were the only British officers on board their hooker amongst a mixture of Greek and Italian officers – with Chinese crew – and he had met this opposite number whilst taking our draught fore and aft following yet another interminable day of discharging. They had arrived earlier that day from the Cuban port of Cienfuegos on the south coast and brought sobering news of clear evidence of buildings and constructions whose character indicated they could only serve as launching sites for missiles of some description. The Master and mates had attempted discussing these with the pilot and agent, but these representatives of officialdom were not only reluctant to talk but deliberately changed the subject as soon as it arose. The evidence seemed to indicate that both missiles and launching paraphernalia had somehow arrived in Cuba – presumably by Russian ships, and via other vessels flagged to Communist bloc countries. The launching pads seemed aimed in the direction of the USA – evidence that considerably modified our views of the situation into which we had unwittingly become involved.

Eventually, following a run of frustrating and inexplicable delays, we completed cargo discharge and, with sighs of relief all round, the agent received our order for pilot and tugs. The ship was prepared initially for departure to the oiling jetty to take on fuel and diesel oil, prior to following the current east of Point de Maisi towards the south coast port of Santiago de Cuba for loading. I prepared a passage plan and duly discussed my arrangements with Captain Streatham – receiving his complete approval for my efforts (something that did wonders for my self-confidence). There was no sign of life anywhere on the jetty as the time for departure arrived – and then passed – and the interval developed into two, and then four hours. The agent, linesmen, let alone pilot and tugs, were singularly conspicuous by their absence. When I took over as officer-of-the-watch, the Old Man asked me to 'phone the agent, but the fruits of my labours produced only the monotonous engaged tone. The chief was becoming increasingly agitated and I heard his curses long before I entered the Master's cabin to make yet another in a series of negative reports. There were more fumes emanating from his person than the main engine but, tactful as ever, I hid my amused smile on entering the day-cabin where both were drowning their frustrations by working systematically through a bottle of gin. It was interesting watching the level decrease as the pressure mounted – a sort of reversal of Boyle's Law I presumed. Certainly, Terry and Anthony shared the entertainment and each awaited my reports in the Mate's cabin with amused detachment.

It was with considerable relief that the watch was handed over to Terry but, just as I was settling down to a well-earned drink with Anthony in the smoke-room, the 'phone rang and a well-known, but slightly slurred voice, asked me to pop up to the Master's cabin. Father then suggested that whilst Terry remained on board he wanted me to wander along the jetty towards the agent's office in the main road to see if I could deduce news of a more positive nature. Even as I approached the main entrance, the empty building spoke its own message. The locked, barred and bolted door indicated an interior completely devoid of any signs of human life – although the office cat returned an equally glassy stare as we leered at each other over the CLOSED sign on the front window, before stretching luxuriously across a mass of papers deposited in a loaded (presumably) pending tray. Returning on board with my tidings the Master had no option really but to order a stand-down of all officers and crew.

It was two days later when the agent suddenly made his guest appearance on board bringing his cheerful countenance into the Old Man's cabin and with happy smiles dismissed lightly all responsibility for our enforced delay. It appeared that there had been 'a government instruction' that had temporarily prevented all port movements across the country – the reason for which was never explained (where had we heard that one before). The positive news was that orders had been booked for linesmen, pilot and tugs to attend the *King Joseph* at 1800 hours that day, and that we should prepare the vessel for departure to the oiling berth. By 1730 there was no sign of life on the jetty and, as we braced ourselves 20 minutes later for further delays, a lorry containing a fine body of linesmen drove onto the quay followed by a car that discharged an enthusiastic agent and pilot. There was still no evidence of the tugs. Pilot, agent and Father went into conclave in his day-cabin whilst we three deck officers drowned our mirth and awaited developments in the Mate's cabin. In the middle of yet another round of beers, the 'phone rang and the Old Man advised Anthony to call 'stand by' as the tugs had suddenly appeared, bustling energetically towards bow and stern. It seemed we were finally leaving our berth. Never had I been so pleased to shake off the dust of any port, and my sigh of relief must have been almost tangible as the ship slipped away from the jetty. From my docking bridge aft, I caught a final glimpse of that oft travelled hot and dusty road – shining romantically in dying rays from the setting sun.

All ships of all classes and size invariably took tugs to assist departing port or when coming alongside (courtesy BP plc).

Arrival alongside the oiling jetty saw no signs of life anywhere, much to the unbounded amusement of myself, the frustration of the pilot, and bafflement of Captain Streatham. To widen his experience, Terry had taken charge forward and I sensed the restrained humour in Anthony's voice as he discussed the situation with me over the wheelhouse telephone. My crew – holding fenders, preparing wires and ropes – looked at me with wondering trustful eyes, clearly expecting me to produce an answer. Although I had plenty of questions, the answers department was sadly lacking, so my only course was to smile at the leading hand and shrug my shoulders expressively. Between them, the crew caught the drift of my message and relaxed, recognising the humour in the situation. Our ship idled in gale force offshore winds that, working with a strong ebb tide, forced us off the quay and added considerably to the problem of our tug masters. Both tugs had to exert considerable power as they endeavoured to keep us parallel to the jetty. I could see my after tug master shaking his hands in anger and shouting at the pilot on the bridge through a bullhorn, whilst simultaneously struggling energetically with helm and engine-room telegraph to keep us on station. His visible actions seemed sufficiently effective, but his words became whisked away by the wind immediately following utterance. I caught sight of the pilot looking down at him from the starboard bridge wing waving his arms expressively in what seemed to be signals of ineffective encouragement. What should have been a straightforward operation, practised daily by ships worldwide without incident, had developed into a fiasco.

I waited, wondering what would transpire next, when suddenly the ship's whistle burst into life. The pilot was trying to arouse someone – anyone – from inside the building, at least to attend our moorings even if not to be more ambitious and pump some fuel. The sound emanating was far from impressive for what should have been a stentorian blast came out more as a half-hearted whimper. I could not fathom out what had happened to our electric whistle – usually so effective on the few occasions we had used it for collision avoidance whilst on watch, but the comparative squeak that emerged made us sound more like a diminutive railway engine than a 7000 grt ship. Either way, it had little effect. The buildings on the jetty, and the quay itself, remained completely deserted.

I was left for a while wondering what had happened ashore, what was happening on the bridge, and what we might end up doing in the immediate future. It was quite apparent (even to me) that we could not remain where we were and equally as obvious that for some reason the jetty had not been informed of our impending arrival. The strident ringing of the after telephone broke my reverie, as I mused idly over the docking bridge chuckling to myself. It was Anthony advising that the Master and pilot were exercising their only remaining options by turning the ship around to reach a position where the harbour-master could be contacted by Aldis lamp and advice sought regarding the next move. The outcome was that *King Joseph*, with main engines going half-ahead, sailed majestically back the way we had come, to return ignominiously alongside our berth – which fortunately had not yet been taken by another vessel.

In the smoke-room afterwards, in an hilarious monologue, Anthony related the atmosphere on the bridge between pilot and Father as they discussed the best way out of our nautical impasse. He wished fervently that a tape recorder had been available to capture the handling of exasperation, frustration and disbelief. He had found particularly hilarious the conflict emanating from the steadfast calm of our Master and the unbridled volatile histrionics from the pilot whose Latin temperament was at odds with the humour of the situation. The scenario of language, feelings and thoughts emerging in making decisions, countermanding these, and then reforming them was worth not only hearing but also preserving. Eventually the wisdom of Captain Streatham won the day as he wooed the pilot to his way of thinking. He finished his tale by relating thoughtfully how much he had learned from the incident for use when eventually he became master of his own ship. The officers in the lounge expressed a rarely held universal agreement that this unprecedented state of affairs was quite outside anyone's experience and we awaited the inevitable post mortem – once the agent again made his appearance.

This was not long in coming as our agent bounced up the gangway next day, exchanged a cheerful greeting with me and ran happily up the companionway towards Father's quarters. Anthony and the chief were both present in the Old Man's day-room as he asked for an explanation concerning the previous day's fiasco. Shrugging his shoulders expressively and shaking his hands dejectedly the agent confirmed that, due to a regrettable oversight, notification of our booking to the oil jetty staff had gone astray in the communication system, so they had consequently packed up work for the day and gone home. He vehemently denied any negative role in the proceedings, arguing that he had placed the booking as instructed simultaneously with that for tugs and pilot. Our senior officers decided quite adamantly that to attempt pinning down where the blame lay would be a futile exercise and result only in further denials – even if they could find someone who would do other than deny. The Master showed Anthony his report to our superintendents – who related that it had made interesting reading. The agent also told us we had a change in orders and should proceed to another berth in Havana for partial loading.

We were astounded next day to receive from the port authorities an invoice for tug and pilot fees which Captain Streatham promptly returned to our agent with instructions to investigate and have the account annulled. The change in orders necessitated another booking for tugs and pilot to take us to a nearby jetty where we were to part-load across all main lower holds iron ingots for Santos, sugar beet and tobacco leaf for Novorossiysk and Batumi. Our orders to visit the fuelling station prior to sailing for Santiago to complete loading still held – it was just a matter of 'the system' hopefully generating a more positive booking.

Painting the funnel was not merely good ship maintenance but Company publicity
(courtesy BP plc).

The second engineer discovered that reeds in our siren had somehow become dislodged (leaving us on deck with both questioning minds and open mouths) and that it was this defect that had caused the débâcle with our sound signals. In his quest for a cause, the mere hint that our deckhands might have been responsible during a recent painting around the funnel area went down like the proverbial lead balloon. Collectively we on deck could not possibly foresee how their actions around the horn could have caused this problem. Anthony argued the point vociferously with the second (to the secret delight of Terry and me) but eventually common sense prevailed and the defect was placed under the general heading of 'yet a further mystery of the sea' – of which we had experienced more than our fair share recently.

As it happened, our stay in Havana was without further incident. Even the Master and Mate, frequent visitors to Cuban ports, were favourably impressed to the point of astonishment at the speed of loading when compared to the abysmally tedious rate at which we had discharged. The sugar for example entered our holds manually at a rate not far short of 2000 bags in eight hours, whilst the ingots came aboard 80 to each chained sling. In around a week, we had taken our 2000-ton quota and, ever optimistic, booked pilot and tugs for a further visit to the ill-fated oiling berth and a hopefully uneventful short haul to Santiago. The one thing that did not disappear was the invoice for pilot and tugs as, just before we sailed, the agent returned and handed this again to the Old Man with the injunction that Havana port authorities insisted it was paid before clearance was granted allowing the ship to proceed to Santiago. I was resting in my cabin with Terry on cargo watch when I heard the howl of disbelief from Captain Streatham that brought me out of my cabin and along the alleyway wondering whatever next had happened. The agent was serious-faced but adamant. He had taken all action necessary – but in the absence of blaming anyone else – it seemed our ship was liable. The Master could only agree, but sent a strong protest with his signature for payment, requesting the port authorities to re-investigate and place the account with the department responsible.

To me, the incidents experienced were important, for I discovered that a new and unexpected approach of relaxed humour accompanied my attitude towards port authorities whom previously I had held in perhaps an over-sombre respect – if the thought had occurred at all. I was more than happy to place this, along with other things developing in my new posting as second mate, under the heading of progress.

The passage to Santiago was interesting for its delightful scenery as we passed the Cuban north coast, an inordinate number of fishing boats on every watch and, because we were close to shore, little interference from our esteemed American allies. We often caught sight on the radar of squadrons of ships that we deduced from their manoeuvring as US warships. We complete loading lignum vitae, cocoa, rum and cartons of wax for

Odessa, Kherson, and Zhdanov in the Sea of Azov, the latter being another port new to our senior officers. Loading passed with few problems and we experienced no further difficulties with pilot, tugs or linesmen. The port authorities and agent seemed far more relaxed and friendly in this southern port, something we deduced to being that much further removed from the capital city where undeniably firmer control seemed to be exercised over citizens as well as visiting merchant seamen. Without holding much hope, Captain Streatham asked our Santiago agent to investigate the long-running dispute regarding the invoice presented for the shifting ship fiasco in Havana. Much to everyone's surprise, he announced just before we sailed for Santos that the ship's account had been credited by Cuban port control for the full amount – less ten percent for administrative charges – although there was no mention concerning how these might have been incurred. I think the Old Man was more than pleased to have recovered the bulk of this payment and was happy to write-off the remainder.

A few miles off Cuban territorial waters we again encountered the American navy. Although communications were on this occasion conducted totally by Aldis the meeting (once again) could hardly be described as cordial. They were clearly glad to see the back of us from Cuba and confirmed that they retained our crew list taken by the incoming patrol and reassured us that should the ship or indeed any of us land at any later date in any American port we would be subjected to a cool reception. There was little we could comment on this, except to trust that the forecast event would not occur.

We sailed into Santos eleven days after leaving Santiago, having enjoyed one of the smoothest passages in the memory of our more seasoned officers. Even the Old Man sunbathed on the private patch of deck astern of his cabin on the starboard side of the boat deck and a cheerful atmosphere prevailed over the ship. Watches were informal to say the least for Father seemed to have no objections to his deck officers working in the wheelhouse clad only in swimming trunks and flip-flops. The Mate was able to catch up on considerable ship maintenance, the engineers sweated below and each junior downed at least an entire case of twenty-four cans of beer to compensate for liquid loss in the 120°F temperatures recorded below. *King Joseph* sailed serenely through the north Atlantic towards Cape de São Roque where we would continue passage towards Santos.

It was too good to last of course for otherwise, I asked myself rhetorically, where would reside the quirks of human nature? As we entered south Atlantic waters, the Chinese catering crew went on strike following a dispute regarding overtime payments between their chief steward or butler and the Old Man. A chain reaction set in as the engine-room ratings and our own deck crew decided to join in the fun and sent their respective *serangs* to negotiate for enhanced overtime payments with the Mate and second engineer. It was not long before Father became involved and threatened mass loggings for mutinous conduct. These received immediate rejection from an impassive sea of bland Chinese faces. The chief petty officers actually had the temerity to question

Radio officers kept the ship informed of a variety of interesting news items (courtesy BP plc).

the Master and senior officers regarding the further action they thought they could take. Once we realised that lunch would be non-existent (the crew held firmly onto storeroom keys), that the European galley was unmanned, and there would be no food that day, the Master and officers had little option but to back off and agree payment of the demands. Sparks informed us that cables had been winging backwards and forwards to the Kremlin in London but then (very wisely) refused to divulge further information.

The sequel to meeting our American friends came shortly after we left Santos and were heading again for Russia. Sparks gleefully informed us that the radio officer aboard the Company's ship *King Edward* had notified him of their experiences as a direct result of our unpatriotic trading and interception. She was on passage between African ports to the American gulf heading eventually for England and, quite unwittingly, had sailed directly into a maelstrom of American officialdom at its worst once she had berthed alongside Mobile. A veritable storm of port officials mustered all the crew in the officer's smoke-room. The health department subjected every member of the crew – master, officers and ratings alike – to an intimate medical examination. The Customs turned over all the crew accommodation, confiscating a lot of personal gear in the process, which they alleged was of sufficient nature to have warranted declaration on the manifest. It was quite impossible for any declaration to cover all effects and the authorities on this occasion instead of turning the customary blind eye had been ruthless in their efficiency. As a final thrust in the ultimate of American bureaucracy and spite, the police denied all shore leave. The same procedure occurred at every subsequent port called at by this ill-fated vessel. Sparks related how their crew cursed us 'up hill and down dale' – as his opposite number had stated things. Although we sympathised – to an extent – the merchant navy mind invariably finds considerable humour in the misfortunes landing in the laps of others, particularly when this derived (especially accidentally) from actions of our own ship. We – alas – were no exceptions, and even the Old Man looked me in the eye chuckling shamelessly over their fate.

Three days out of Santos we celebrated Christmas. This was not a major affair for our Chinese ratings, but they rose to the occasion and provided a feast of truly magnificent proportions for their officers. We had experienced complete peace following the overtime débâcle, but from occasional hints overheard between the Master, Mate, chief and second engineers, I rather gathered this incident had not been totally forgotten. What might transpire from those mutterings I did not know and Anthony was reluctant to discuss the matter – although a few direct looks in my direction indicated that 'something was indeed afoot'. Nevertheless, in both saloon and smoke-room, decorations abounded in festive fashion, but as these baubles had been accumulated from diverse parts of the globe, their exotic nature was very different to those normally draping English homes. I recall a preponderance of lanterns, along with streamers representing dragons, lions and other Chinese festivities of an unidentifiable nature, each doubtless related to the 'year of the whatever'. Before long we were replete with Christmas pudding and liberal glasses of Ellerton-donated wine.

We were all sober for our watches, but more from luck than judgement if the ribald laughter from fellow officers was any yardstick. This seemed particularly relevant as I tore myself away from a flourishing SOD's opera in the smoke-room, heading steadily for the bridge.

As a boredom breaker, we had sent occasional letters to the agony column of selected women's magazines purporting to be from some 'anguished soul'. It was great fun composing these whilst on watch in the middle of various oceans and our ingenuity knew no bounds – of either impossibly devious sexual situations or zealously complicated family affairs. We only had one letter published and that was an innocuous affair purporting to be from a troubled mother complaining that her son had 'recently failed the DTI Eyesight Test for potential mariners', and berating the fact that 'he had problems distinguishing between red and green lights' and asking why this particular attribute should be so essential to a navigation officer.

On that particular glorious Christmas Day, Anthony lost no time in handing over and rushing down to join in the fun, but Terry was decidedly merry four hours later when he came to relieve the watch. As we went through the handing-over procedures, I was relieved to see a more responsible attitude emerging from his seasonal fun.

As we cleared the Greek archipelago, a radio message directed us to call in at Istanbul for a crew change. It seemed that Ellertons were flying all of our Chinese home to Hong Kong, and we were to receive instead Indian ratings from Calcutta and Bombay. Of course, there were no hints verbally – but I gained a distinct impression that little bird mutterings overheard on passage had come home to roost. My quartermaster expressed feelings of shock and horror once he received the news from his *serang*. The Old Man's absence from the wheelhouse during my next watch certainly encouraged him to relate his feelings in very clear terms. He simply could not comprehend my carefully reasoned and tactful comments that perhaps somewhere along the line the entire crew had precipitated the Company's action – that by going on strike they had not exactly endeared themselves to any of their superiors either ashore or particularly on board. Once again, my experiences working with Chinese crew reached another (perhaps inevitable) impasse.

The same radio message notified us that I, the Master and Mate, and four engineering officers including the chief and second were to be relieved and flown back to the UK. In the absence of explanations, we assumed this directive to indicate voyage leave although the move came as a complete surprise to me as I had thought it would be my lot to remain on board for at least another return Russian/Cuban trip. This trip had certainly given me not only an insight into how Communist systems functioned but, more importantly, had allowed time for me to establish myself in my new rank and gain confidence in my ability to do the duties of second officer to a ship captain's satisfaction.

It was with a certain satisfaction (but no complacency) that I handed-over navigational stores and sick bay returns to my relief and signed-off Articles preparing for the long haul home by Trans-Orient express train via Bulgaria, Yugoslavia, Italy and France. The agent at Istanbul advised that our train trip would take four days and, during our crossing of the Communist bloc, neither food nor drinking water would be available even to work the toilets. Luckily, he equipped us with sufficient provisions for the journey. All kinds of diverse people joined the train en route, which led to some interesting exchanges in Pidgin English. Luckily, some of the more stalwart travellers were 'down to the gunwhales', as Anthony expressed their condition, with a very potent wine. This they were generous in sharing so aspects of the journey passed in a delightfully semi-conscious state of alcoholic euphoria. I left our cosy smoke-filled compartment in Belgrade searching for further food and on return was horrified to see the train departing the platform. A wave of cold sobering shock swept over me. I was stranded without identity papers, passport or seaman's card. Whilst wondering where the nearest police post might be located, I saw the train arriving again at a different platform. I did not stop to question what might have happened but ran down the concourse and, with feelings of unbridled relief, regained my compartment. Never, in the whole of my seven years Merchant Navy travelling experience, had the sight of my fellow travellers seemed so welcome. They were blissfully unaware of my predicament and were too fuddled with drink to understand the implications. When we eventually arrived at the Italian border *en ro*ute to Venice, Trieste and Milan, the toilets were in an appalling state, but we simply had to hold our noses to prevent nausea and use them – there was no alternative. Never had the Calais-Dover ferry appeared so inviting and luxurious, especially as we arrived just in time for that final day's sailing. My sighs of relief on landing in Dover might have been audible in distant London.

Even though we had been deeply involved with international affairs aboard *King Joseph,* it was only later as we read about our events from reports in saved newspapers that we realised the insularity of life at sea. As a generalisation, there was no doubt that any mariner's existence was akin to living on another planet. We had no idea of just how close the world had come to war or of the worry that our situation in the midst of these events had caused our families at home. There had been no hint of anxiety in the letters exchanged.

Being reunited with family and friends remained exciting – the very idea of going on leave never palled – but on this occasion, once I arrived home and was certain my leave was not to be cancelled – there was the added delight of cementing planned arrangements with church, reception caterers and family and organising my impending marriage to Sue.

Chapter 4

TEMPERAMENTS AND TEMPERATURES

––

The day before Sue and I were due to marry, amidst greetings cards and messages, a recall arrived from the Kremlin for me to join a ship. My father's comment 'This seems a slightly awkward moment' put the situation accurately – if mildly. I pondered with awe the administrative efficiency exhibited by my bosses, especially as Captain Ford, who was responsible for making this fateful telephone call, had invited me to the company's London local for a celebration lunch and drink shortly after I arrived home from the *King Joseph*. With church and hall booked, family and guests lined up in best 'bib and tucker' – doubtless with knives, forks and empty glasses at the ready – plus a honeymoon in Malta confirmed, my immediate reaction was to advise my esteemed superior that his summons was inappropriate. To give him due he immediately apologised, but then spoilt the effect by asking if I could join *Earl of Norfolk* anyway. It seemed she was loaded in Liverpool, bursting to go deep-sea, anxiously awaiting only the appointment of another deck officer to fill her legal complement before sailing. His suggestion that Sue and I could have our wedding during the next leave was met with a heavily negative response which he took quite well – almost as if it had been anticipated.

Anyway, wedding and honeymoon took place as planned so, allowing a few days for mutually contented wife and husband to recover after arrival home, I 'phoned the good captain acquainting him with my availability for further sea service. He looked a little sheepish (to put things mildly) as I sat opposite him next day sharing refreshments and discussing how the wedding had gone. My feelings were expressed again regarding his expectations to cancel our arrangements stressing that, although 'happy to remain a company man', I did not regard myself that much in love with the organisation he so enthusiastically represented. Surviving the pregnant pause introduced by this little homily he looked rather shamefaced and, shuffling around some papers, offered details of my proposed sea-going appointment. Some psychological advantage was taken by requesting posting to a tanker, but this attracted only a wry smile and little else by way of success. It appeared (once again) there were no vacancies as, on this occasion, most of their crude oil and product carriers were being sold or scrapped in preparation for a number of larger class 'supertankers', although he remained a little vague regarding the proposed tonnage of these. Once more patience was urged on my part and the promise made that he was well aware of my wishes.

Instead a renewed contract with appointment as second officer aboard the mv *Lady Vedera* was offered. She was the oldest ship in the Group's fleet – a little nautical gem some 27 years young with five hatches, 433 feet in length overall and a beam of 58 feet. The vessel was a steam-powered job of 5683 grt boasting a cruising speed of (an optimistic) 14 knots. Currently, she was lying in Queen Alexandra Dock, Cardiff, loading a full cargo of coal for South American ports, with a forecast return to the UK or Continent with iron ore from Brazil. The ship's shallow draft of 24½ feet made her ideally suited to working within the water restrictions prevalent down the Argentinian east coast.

After my experiences aboard *King Joseph* I expressed only vague surprise at this news. Although Ellerton's had never traded in any of these these waters, cargo inducments nowadays meant that increasingly the main fleet travelled all over the world, and its associates to a lesser extent. It seemed that the Group was branching more into near-tramping trades in addition to retaining their traditional regular runs servicing Far East, African, Indian, Australasian and North American and Gulf ports. I pointed out to him my 'thought for today' and he looked at me quite pensively. He paused and looked at me again, more directly on this occasion. Our relationship was quite strong and generally we got along well – notwithstanding a few 'knocks along the way' – so when he paused a third time, his brows thickened and face grew increasingly serious, it became apparent the interview was about to take a different slant to that anticipated upon first entering his office. I was left wondering what on earth was coming and – more importantly – how this might affect me. As he poured us both another coffee and passed me the plate of biscuits, I pondered both his sense of timing and build-up of suspense into what were hoped would prove something delightful. I took four biscuits anyway in case of the need for sustenance, sat back and prepared to receive a little homily from the captain: 'The shipping industry, Mr Caridia, with which I have been associated for over forty years – and you barely a decade – finds itself in a state of considerable transition in which I forecast monumental changes in ownership, cargo patterns and ship construction. You cannot have failed to notice, even within our company structures, how proposed amalgamations have forged mergers bringing together some previously unlikely maritime bedfellows. Ellertons have not been the only conglomerate formed from previously regular independent cargo liner owners who have swallowed tramp, tanker and (as you are frequently fond of telling me) even coastal operators, purely in order to survive. Even that august concern P&O Lines had, admittedly a few years ago now, to amalgamate with coastal and tramp companies – such as General Steam Navigation and Hain Steamship. This was doubtless a trauma to some officers (not that this would have done them any harm), but it represents additionally a move to the mutual benefit of all concerned, by offering expansive profits for their directors and shareholders, with additional job security for seafarers. Ellerton Group differs slightly perhaps in our far-sighted policy of hedging our bets regarding world-wide shortages of first-class officers by contracting directly to service anywhere within the Group – as indeed you have already discovered and are, I assure you, about to find again!'

Captain Ford shot an amused glance in my direction and continued to eye me inquisitively – clearly interested in assessing my reactions to his news. As I remained eating biscuits and pensively silent, he continued: 'The days of the traditional 'tween-deck cargo ships such as you have previously encountered within the Group, and are on the way to join, are numbered – although it will take a few years yet before they disappear completely to be superseded totally by new homogeneous bulk carriers and container ships. These will facilitate less time spent in port on cargo turn-around and almost certainly require fewer crew members. Already since you have been at sea these classes of ships have gradually been introduced – as well as roll-on/roll-off ferries, and colliers of increased size. Currently in service are specialised tankers, especially in the methane/butane gas trades and bulk ore-oil carriers. The size of crude oil carriers is increasing with 100,000 tonners already at sea for the past couple of years and plans being made for ships of even larger capacity.'

I interrupted him quickly: 'Sir. Are Ellerton's plans for larger crude tankers within that category?'

But he merely spread his hands sideways – and again would not be drawn. Instead he forecast appearances of other unspecified different types of ships with currently unknown functions although, in this area, he admitted lacking certainty. Of one thing he was very positive – the increased 'boxing of cargo into containers was definitely here to stay', as he put it.

I was aware that my total concentration on the super's words was creating a host of questions so, as he reached for the coffee pot, the opportunity was grabbed to place a few more queries of my own:

'Sir,' I responded, 'How do you see these forecast developments affecting officers serving within the Group? (I found myself using the term naturally). What do you think will be a possible effect on cargo handling? How will our own British ship-buidling industry be affected...?'

'Hold on a moment, young man!' he exploded, interrupting me quickly. 'I am not a maritime prophet so do not know the answers to your questions. However, I will tell you this much, taking your points in reverse order. German and Japanese builders will continue to increase their share of world orders. This is inevitable if you think things through. The Second World War has been over for nigh on twenty years remember. Their respective industries were devastated, determining that all new yards on rebuilding would become equipped with the most modern techniques. It is a totally separate question concerning in practical terms who exactly did win that particular conflict – one I do not wish to explore, but of another thing I am certain, British shipbuilding will have to produce new style ships at competetive prices – or they will go under. As "containerisation" takes off, ships will be constructed with "cellular holds" to carry boxes. These cargoes will almost certainly be less prone to pilfering (which can only be a good thing) and far easier to handle although, of course, certain commodoties will probably never be suitable for this means of transport – heavy logs, for instance, or the bulk carriage of coal, grain, ore, oil, phosphates and the like. All the time we remain an island, there will doubtless survive a merchant navy even if not in its present form. Officers and ratings in general will still find satisfying careers at sea, but will have to accept and become part of an entirely new state of affairs. You will have to learn new skills, be adaptable and accept different conditions of service.'

I glanced at the man who had caused me to reflect on my own ignorance of events taking place behind the scenes in my chosen profession. Of course, I had been vaguely aware that things were changing. I had recently, shortly after arriving home from the Russian run, gone to navigation school and taken my Radar Simulator certificate course. During my time there I had met other officers from container, and roll-on/roll-off ships – or ro-ros as they are inelegantly known – as well as a second mate from an Esso supertanker (much to my envy). Until this moment I had no real idea of the true situation happening around me. I experienced some difficulty taking in what this experienced master mariner was telling me, but his sincerity left me with a great deal to think about. It seemed winds of change were blowing with increasing momentum and could gust to gale force before I was much older.

As I shook his hand and he wished me a rather ambiguous 'good luck', my senses felt rather stunned and wandering out of his office on the way to join the *Lady Vedera* I assumed I was lucky to have a job at all. This may additionally have been at the back of Captain Ford's mind – on the other hand, such reflections might equally have resulted from my increasingly ingrained cynicism. I had to admit an irresistible urge to return to my chosen profession was the main reason for again 'signing on the dotted line'. At twenty-five years of age, my mind could cope more readily with such practicalities, but although grateful he had shared these confidences, the areas forecast seemed far too intangible. Although sufficiently realistic to recognise their reality, I was also quite happy to let this particular tide take me along – and simply enjoy life at sea as this was encountered.

*　　　*　　　*

Joining *Lady Vedera* focussed my mind directly on the present situation. I continued the multitude of onerous duties as second mate, including direct responsibility for navigating the vessel, following discussions of my various passage plans with Captain Malcolm, the Old Man. Of course, control of the sick bay; academic aspects of cadet training (when these were carried); and, during occasional survey periods, overseeing dry docking operations, were also dumped onto my specific plate. I felt quite capable to continue these: my entire training and watchkeeping certificates from previous ships had renewed my confidence in performing these roles. There were even more pressing concerns if I wished for anything to be concerned about. This was the first time I had sailed with European crew – especially one taken from the Shipping Pool in Hamburg. Of 44 officers and ratings there were eleven nationalities on board. The senior deck, radio and all engineer officers were British; the third mate Waclaw Joroski was Polish, fifty years of age and uncertificated. The ship boasted four nationalities in its engine-room ratings, including Spaniards, a Portuguese and a stray mid-European of indefinable origin whose papers purported him to be Armenian. There was a selection of Germans and Greeks on deck, plus a Norwegian chief cook, whilst Dutch galley and stewards 'completed the complement', as my humour led me to say to Pat Johnson the chief officer (who for some reason had given me a strange look). 'Heaven only knows,' I

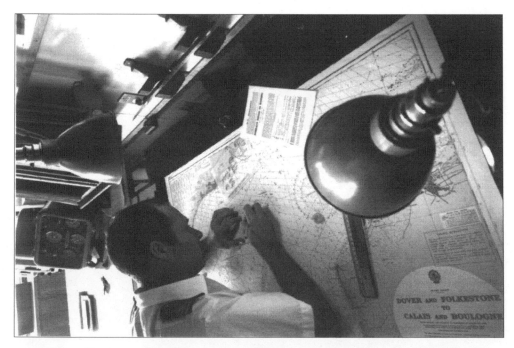

An endless process of chart correcting was always one of the more tedious if essential jobs in the second officer's brief (courtesy BP plc).

pondered, 'from where the authorities had managed to dredge this little lot'. Later, as we became better acquainted, Pat confided over a beer that an unexpected cargo inducement from Vitoria in Brasil to Hamburg had encouraged the previous British crew to take legal advantage of a visit to near-home ports to sign-off *en masse*. It appeared the lads, for some inexplicable reason, could not wait to leave their ship – not even remaining for Cardiff, the next port. This decision had encouraged the Pool to take a god-sent opportunity to clear what he termed 'an interesting crowd' from their books.

He also confided his opinion regarding the ship's name. I had never heard of a famous Vedera family and was idly conjecturing their origin during a change-over in watches shortly after we had sailed. Pat thought for a moment and then suggested she could have been 'a woman of ill-repute with whom the chairman of the Group had become enamoured' – an unlikely but, I supposed, possible explanation for her path to infamy. Certainly there was no plaque on this ship exhibited outside the officer's dining room that offered an alternative description of our ship's name.

We sailed at 0800 the following day. This was after an inordinate length of time the previous day battening down hatches, each fitted with two canvas covers, vertical and horizontal locking bars, and a host of wedges. The latter had to be driven home in a certain way using a large hammer wielded by a soon weary carpenter. My first duty was to turn-to the lads in order to cast off our moorings. They nearly all had

Responsible crew singling-up mooring ropes preparing for port departure (courtesy BP plc).

monumental hangovers from their previous night's indiscretions which, as my sickbay duties were to confirm a few days later, included also for some an unfortunate choice of female friends. Luckily, the Ministry of Transport (Marine) (recently renamed yet again from the Board of Trade) official, responsible for topping-up the ship's sickbay, had been well experienced in the 'ways of wayward sailors.' He had included generous supplies of penicillin injections (stored in the ship's vegetable room) as well as the other 'quick fixes' necessary as a holding operation until I could run sick-parade at our first (and doubtless subsequent) ports of call. Eventually an assortment of off-duty stewards and engine-room ratings was managed, but my eyes had to roam everywhere as this inexperienced and beffudled lot let-go stern ropes and backspring, and took a wire from the after tug. My main priority of course was the prevention of accidents − not least because I would doubtless have had to patch-up any casualties. This assumed they survived: after all (or so I had been regularly informed by numerous senior officers across many ships) nearly all deck accidents involving wires parting under stress from winches invariably proved either fatal or resulted in the loss of a limb. For the first time since becoming an officer I found myself lugging mooring wires and ropes, and leading by necessity as much as example − making certain the correct warps were actually slackened away and cast off. The Mate for'rard also experienced similar problems, but at least he boasted a reasonably sober German bosun and Greek chippy to assist. These key petty officers were luckily so experienced they could have worked the ship virtually half-asleep, which was probably just as well − seeing as they were. The Master later mentioned that the third mate had seemed competent enough in handling the wheelhouse stand-by. This also was fortuitous as the quartermaster steering the ship out of port clearly had difficulty deciding whether he was on a ship or the Royal Scot − 'completely legless' was the Old Man's view − which led to him being stood down and to Waclaw forsaking Movement Book and telegraphs for steering wheel. As I observed to Pat later, 'this stand-by had proved a most promising start'.

The Mate witnessed the logging of the quartermaster and all the deck crowd next morning, following a similar session earlier with the Old Man led by the chief engineer for most of his crowd − and the chief steward producing half of his department. They were still at it when I relieved the third officer at noon, providing at least some initial light relief for the first half-hour of my watch. Captain Malcolm closed the logbook with the sigh of one who had travelled this particular track frequently, after which he and the Mate adjourned to his cabin for what they doubtless regarded as a well-earned pre-luncheon tot. The Decca, usually so reliable upon departure of any voyage in UK waters, was playing up and recording a range of bizarre readings, with the crucial green decometer whizzing around happily on its own at a rate of knots which had to be seen to be believed. I suggested (perhaps tactlessly) to the Old Man we should fit the thing astern as it was a pity the ship did not go equally as fast. He smiled weakly at my joke, but his bland look was accompanied by a muttered comment about second mates who 'press their luck a little'.

During fine and calm days at sea, the crew were kept busy by the mate in duties which included deck scaling (courtesy BP plc).

The captain had already told Waclaw to take morning sights, and I managed to shoot a quick noon meridian altitude of the sun through a momentary break in heavy black clouds, crossing this with the uninspiring jumble of figures representing the Third's earlier Sight and run. 'In his case,' I reflected cynically, 'more a case of mourning Sights perhaps'. If his explorations were correct then we were somewhere in the middle of the Mediterranean whilst if our joint calculations were accurate, then the ship was slightly north of the course-line so, working optimistically, a couple of degrees was allowed on the automatic pilot to bring her back gradually onto track. We had made what the Old Man considered reasonable progress for an 'oldie' in the 28 hours since leaving Cardiff. My position put *Lady Vedera* less than 330 miles out of the UK, hinting at a steaming speed of under 12 knots, far removed from the chief engineer's adamantly proud boast of 14. I did not say anything to Captain Malcolm, but merely looked rather pointedly at the now dormant Decca. His smile, following my glance, portrayed what I was coming to recognise as one of continuous rueful mirth, especially as it was accompanied by his muttered 'Hmm...perhaps not so hot after all'.

In the long established custom of second mates worldwide, I had sprawled the words WIND CHRONOMETERS in gigantic letters across the mirror over my cabin wash-basin. Checking these against each other and giving the requisite number of daily turns was an essential duty and, normally whilst at sea out of sight of land, I would combine this job with taking a morning sight. In view of the *laissez-faire* approach to navigation exhibited by Waclaw – who would clearly never rise higher in his chosen profession than being what was known in the trade as a 'professional third mate' – this became an essential routine. The Mate's star-sights that evening and the following morning had confirmed we were slightly to the north, but my meridian noon did not put her so far as we thought – so we knocked off a degree. So much for Waclaw's mathematical marathon. The Old Man suggested he continue to make his calculations, but neither of us really had the available time to endeavour unravelling where he was making a variety of errors. The short answer was Waclaw had no idea of the theory supporting the practice of celestial observations. Pat reckoned he made a different range of errors according to a combination of the chief steward's menu and particular day of the week.

Captain Malcolm, the Mate, chief and second engineers had, in order to bring the ship home, joined her in Hamburg prior to loading at Cardiff. Before then they had served across a wide range of ships within the Group. The Master had spent years with Empress Shipping, who owned the prefixed *Lady* ships; Pat had sailed with Regal Supreme Line, owners of the *King* vessels; whilst the engineering officers had all come across from Ellertons, although our tracks had never previously crossed. Our radio officer was from a village near Chester – and was supplied to the ship by Marconi Marine, providers of much of his equipment. Waclaw had been recruited by Regal Line's Glasgow office from an 'unknown source' , a phrase which I considered a delightful euphemism.

We were due to bunker in the Canaries within a couple of days, so I set my passage plan and courses off the Cape Verde and St Paul's Islands, to clear San Fernando island then the South American coast off Recife, hence setting course for Cabo Frio in Brazil and the run down the coast to Beunos Aires. This was our destination for full discharge of what we were laconically referring to as 'our cargo of Welsh nuts'.

'Just take everything as it comes,' advised the Old Man genially, as he shared a pot of tea during my watch the following afternoon. He seemed quite happy with my passage proposals and, between disussing these, chatted amiably about the diversity of his petty officers and ratings. Directing my attention to the mixture of assorted names and nationalities on our crew list, he pointed to his own name at the top commenting, I assumed rhetorically: 'Bill Malcolm – what can be more straightforward than that?' What he made of my name, Jonathan Caridia, it seemed pertinent not to ask – so I did not. My Discharge Book had been lodged with him when signing-on so he was aware my previous sea experience had been only with Asian ratings. It was doubtless for this reason he continued acquainting me with a few of the idiosyncrasies to be expected from such a mixed European crowd. His comments did not leave me totally reassured but, fortunately, direct crew control was the problem collectively of the chief officer and his good self: my role was that of a simply more than interested observer – and student.

Our arrival at Las Palmas was totally uncomplicated and we were soon made fast alongside the eastern or Outer Quay with its oiling facilities. There was a large Norwegian tanker ballasting after discharging fuel oil – with the amazingly uninspired name of *Bergchief,* which she undoubtedly was (at least to my eyes), at nigh on 93,000 summer deadweight tons. There was also another cargo ship and ourselves equally as enthusistically taking the stuff out again. We were berthed about halfway along the one mile jetty which meant a considerable walk if a visit into town was being anticipated. I was duty officer anyway, continuing normal sea watches, and had arranged with the

Officers relax whilst on passage during a morning coffee break – or smoke-oh – in the duty mess (courtesy BP plc).

agent for a taxi to visit the port medical officer with one of the 'crew idiosyncrasies' (as the Old Man so joyfully used the expression) who had failed to respond in any way to my ministrations. This was a first medical run ashore in Spanish territory so, arranging for Waclaw to cover for me, I followed proceedings with the port hospital doctor with interest. He looked at the 'dripping seaman' (as it were) standing before him with trousers at half-mast and examined the offending member.

'Ahhhh,' he exclaimed intelligently, 'These sailors – they a-put-a their things where I would not a-put-a my walking stick, you understand?'

Yet once more in my seafaring career, 'I understood perfectly well', but on this occasion – uncharacteristically – could not think of anything in reply. The member attached to the cause of the problem just stood there looking a bit shamefaced, as well he might. Captain Malcolm roared with unrestrained laughter when I reported this maritime snippet saying something along the lines that 'your ignorance does you credit'.

Luckily, within the hour, the homeward-bound Union-Castle Line's *Edinburgh Castle* berthed just forward of us so, taking advantage of the local traders who flocked to any passenger ship, I went on board her and managed to purchase a small wooden, delicately-faced parquet-style trinket box, which seemed an ideal present for Sue. Pat exchanged some 'surplus stores' for a few cases of sherry which the two of us managed to share and taste enthusiastically, a transaction reminiscent of previous visits to this assortment of islands. It was encouraging to find old habits continuing to die hard. We were alongside only for the time necessary to take bunkers but, even in the space of these few hours, our deck and engine-room crews managed to find booze – whilst one of the stewards begat himself of a boy friend. So it was with a combination of both fuddled heads and passionate tears that the *Lady Vedera* set forth again on its voyage to Argentina.

Two days out, we received a change of orders instructing us to pop into Rio de Janeiro *en route*. It seemed our grade of coal was particularly desirable in Brazil and we were to discharge some fifty per cent of it there. How this conflicted – or became resolved – with our supposed charter terms remained beyond the comprehension of all on board.

'Hmmm, Mr. Caridia,' commented the Captain. 'I told you to take things as they came, didn't I?'

I could yet again only concur with events occurring totally outside my control or understanding. We could not have foreseen the circumstances deciding this change in orders, but reconciled ourselves to deciding such moves were certainly not our concern. I merely smiled in tolerant bemusement and, having already prepared the appropriate charts, ran off a few lines and pencilled in the new course for later use on the autopilot – after obtaining agreement from Captain Malcolm.

Three days out of Las Palmas we broke down. The ship swung-to and wallowed helplessly in a moderate beam swell, whilst pandemonium took place below as the engineers tried to sort something out with the ship's antiquated machinery. We hoisted 'Not Under Command' shapes and, being of a pessimistic nature, I rigged the appropriate red-above-red lights ready for hoisting in case ministrations of our 'ginger beers' developed into dusk – and perhaps beyond. It was never made quite clear what had caused the breakdown but Captain Malcolm, with a customary philosophical shrug, merely attributed this to old age, 'Something, you know Mr Caridia, which happens eventually to us all – so why not already ancient company ships?'

Yet again, I found myself rendered, if not exactly speechless, more resigned perhaps to keeping my thoughts unspoken. After all, I suspected he was secretly quite proud of his command, so saw little point in suggesting negative views which might prolong his hurt. As it happened, we were without power for six hours – on this first occasion.

For me, as we approached Rio and the compulsory visit to the clearing anchorage, there was a far more pressing problem. One of the deckhands fell off the hatch coaming whilst preparing to swing derricks out of the way in preparation for our coal discharge. He was unconscious and his laboured breathing was a major cause of concern. Once we were anchored, I tried for over an hour to raise port control by flashing the Aldis in their direction. All to no avail. I had previously, along with the customary flags, added the International Code 'W' to indicate requirements for medical assistance, whilst setting about the check of our anchor bearings – and waiting. Meantime, I reported my lack of success to the Master who indicated there was little more constructively we could do without clearance of the ship by respective health, customs, police and immigration authorities. We could only hope they would not be too long before visiting us.

Our signals were still not being acknowledged when Pat, my relief, arrived. While we were chatting about what further action we could take for the deckhand, we espied an odd-looking craft approaching. We could hardly have failed to notice because of the smoke being emitted from its long angular funnel and the weird coughing and choking sound emanating from its obviously antiquated engine, somewhat like a 'rheumatic suffering asthmatic'. Watching this vessel surging around its course-line we deduced that whilst it was not a port health launch (especially in its sorry state), it was making directly for our starboard side. Pat cast a lop-sided smile in my direction, left me an interested spectator on the bridge-wing, and shot down to the maindeck, grabbing his duty quartermaster and taking the offered paint encrusted and frayed forward mooring from our visitor. From the ensuing garbled conversation it appeared we had summoned this craft for, seemingly, local regulations in Rio overruled the International Code so that 'W' indicated a requirement for the port water boat. I saw Pat digesting this bizarre message and heard him point out our very urgent need for medical assistance. He requested the elderly skipper of this equally ancient craft to pass on our request to any port authority. As he returned to relieve me, we watched the boat creep painfully back towards port control and hoped that somehow it would actually make its destination and prove the Mate had been successful in his quest. Looking in again on my patient in the crew hospital there was no marked improvement or deteroration which I could detect so, before standing-down for a quick snooze on my day-bed, popped in to advise the Old Man accordingly.

But we hit the jackpot. Two hours later, just as I was enmeshed in delightful sleep, not only the port doctor arrived but the entire retinue of officials necessary to clear the ship before we could berth. It seemed our water boat had more than lived up to expectations and we expressed silent thanks to the ertswhile skipper and his craft. A quick stretcher-job saw the unfortunate sailor taken aboard the port health launch and on his way to the local hospital with what was diagnosed as quite severe concussion. With the port authorities came the welcome appearance of our pilot and, even before completion of formalities, two tugs came bristling across the intervening stretch of water to bring us alongside.

Roaming around the decks in a leisurely fashion at two o'clock the following morning, performing the purely functional duty required for discharging coal whilst on cargo watch, there was heard what could only be described as a slight fracas on the jetty. Cars were screeching to a halt, followed by heavy clumping footsteps up our gangway that caused this to rattle and sway in an alarming manner. Before I could register what was happening, by looking between the crane-legs from near number one hatch, my quartermaster came along the main-deck bursting with laughter and, in heavily accented English, attempted to inform me that the local police wished to interview the duty officer. Assuming correctly this was myself, I went back along the maindeck to the ship's office, wondering what could be amiss.

On arrival, I was confronted by the sight of four of our stewards, handcuffed and protesting violently, surrounded by six police officers. The sergeant in charge informed me that they had been arrested for their own protection whilst soliciting on Copocabana beach – that internationally famous tourist resort. Taking this news in the spirit it was clearly intended, I began negotiations for their release. It seemed the current price for police good intentions, in returning the miscreants on board ship instead of into the local jail, was 200 cigarettes and a bottle of Scotch to each police officer. As this bounty was plainly outside my ability – let alone jurisdiction – to provide, I suggested they leave the stewards on board and return next morning to receive their 'just demands'. From the volatile mixture of Portuguese busting amongst them, it seemed my idea was unacceptable: they wanted their reward neither in heaven nor later, but immediately. Not having faced this kind of situation before and finding no precedent in any area of my years at sea, caused me to pause a bit before determining the action to take. The stewards were of little use in this respect – they were still far too busy arguing (to my utter disbelief) with the police. The ensuing mixture of English oaths, supporting Dutch and Brazilian histrionics, created a bedlam in the customary calmness of our ship's office rarely heard or witnessed. In the end I banged the table trying to restore some sort of order and sufficient silence, to 'phone the purser/chief steward to pop along and sort out the ensuing mess. After all, I reasoned, the stewards were from his department as also was access to the bonded store. Even if the latter was customs-sealed, it was not unreasonable to assume – knowing the ingenuity of ships' chief stewards– that he had managed to acquire a more than reasonable 'float' *ex-officio* which would more than meet these demands. He finally turned up in a floral dressing gown which attracted open mouths from the police and a not so *sotto voce* 'Get you, dearie' from his crew. Following my explanations of the current situation to date, Perce trundled along to his cabin accompanied by these upstanding guardians of law and order, leaving the stewards still handcuffed standing dejectedly by the Mate's store lockers. I asked them what had been taking place: 'Oh Sir,' they cooed (for want of a more accurate description) 'it was truly wonderful. We were on this beach surrounded by hundreds of hunky men – until these beasts arrrived and manhandled us, but not in the way we wanted or expected.'

I could only grin, but did point out that 'these beasts' might well have saved them from a far more damaging fate than they had anticipated. Neither party however remained entirely convinced by my explanation. Eventually, the police returned clutching thinly-disguised boxes and bottles in an assortment of paper bags and – once the purser had managed to obtain a signature from each of the stewards, deducting the cost of their 'pay-off' from their 'pay-off', as it were – their handcuffs were removed. The police left the ship, Percy our steward returned to his bunk: his chagrined crew went below – and I thankfully made my way on deck to see how the discharge of our cargo was proceeding and to check gangway and moorings, simultaneously pondering on yet another unique contribution to my own seafaring experiences.

The idea of actually sailing with 'odd' stewards was itself a novel one. These situations rarely occurred with Asian crew – not, I suspected, because such gay seamen did not exist, but merely because they were more discreet than were their European counterparts – and, additionally, kept themselves to themselves far more. Admittedly, 'queens' had been encountered in dubious bars and hostelries shoreside, but never before had I been waited on by one in the guise of an officer's steward. It seemed to bring its own peculiar problems. Once the ground rules had been firmly established, with Sue's and my wedding photograph prominently displayed: 'Oh, what a diaBOLICal shame – and call me Dickie, you lovely second MATE, sir,' never caused any problems. Throughout the trip he continued to express severe disappointment that I was happily married, but seemed to accept this with aplomb. At least he never made too much of a nuisance of himself – but equally never completely gave up the idea of exhibiting at every opportunity the available goods. As he was one of the stewards arrested by the police I, not without justification (or inclination), considered him and his offer more than slightly shop-soiled, to say the least. His only indiscretion – so far as I was aware – was a propensity for nosing through every single private letter and piece of paper which crossed his eyes. After Las Palmas, I took all personal papers, bank statements and sundry documents and locked them in my navigation store abaft the bridge –

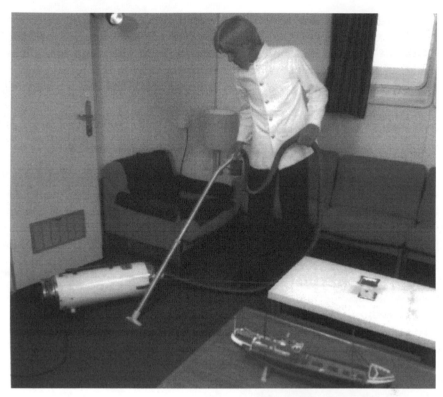

A steward sailing with a reputable company cleans an officer's cabin as part of his daily routines (courtesy BP plc).

managing to cope extremely well with the look of hurt cast in my direction for a few days afterwards. His powers of recuperation were admirable however for within a week the 'usual offer' was once again manifest.

One of the junior engineers received something of a more traumatic shock. On being called by the engineers' steward for his watch one morning, following a particularly heavy night of boozing, he dozed off to sleep. Ten minutes later 'Flossie' the steward called him again, advising him that if he was still in bed upon his return, he would 'jump in there with him'. That had the desired effect for he was out of his bunk within seconds – a somewhat rude awakening, in more ways than one.

We asked the agent, when he returned a few days later with our fully recovered deckhand, if he had any idea how our charter might have been compromised by diverting 50 per cent of our cargo. Whilst he denied any knowledge or could offer nothing particularly constructive by way of comment, Pat and I did wonder from something indefinable in his tone, whether or not something of a more financial explanation might be lurking somewhere below the surface. Either way, we gained no satisfaction and eventually stopped surmising, placing the incident under the heading 'yet another mystery of the sea'.

Sparks and I went ashore to visit the famous Sugar Loaf Mountain surmounted by its magnificent navigational aid of the statue of Christ. How such a city of unbelievable and unsubtle debauchery could boast such an eccelsiastical monument was beyond our comprehension. Things were sufficiently uninhibited during daylight hours but after dark it was certainly not safe to venture ashore in groups of less than three. Pat joined us on a couple of occasions when we visited a bar for a while, but the attentions of the local hostesses were frankly more trouble than they were worth – yet again, in more ways than one. It was fun for a while observing events little different from those witnessed in bars all over Africa and the Far East (or, for that matter, anywhere else in the 'civilised' world), but there was little by way of originality. I both treated and arranged with the agent to escort many of our crew (some twice over) suffering from a range of anti-social diseases to the long-suffering port health doctor, which kept me quite busy.

Our discharge of the coal was by grab-cranes, leading to a seemingly endless run of cargo watches, and unbelievable boredom. Pat could not have the crew doing any external painting or deck oiling and greasing because of wind-blown coal dust, so everything paintable internally was more than covered. We were frankly bored to distraction and even occasionally relieving the cargo watch from the nearest bar palled in

The statue of Christ at Rio de Janeiro proved an invaluable navigation mark whilst on passage or at anchor (courtesy Shell International Shipping and Transport).

And singularly impressive when viewed at close quarters (Author's collection).

its novelty. As Pat and I mournfully agreed, over a soapy South American beer or two, we could not wait for sailing day. Waclaw, although sociable enough, kept very much to his own company – even to the extent of going ashore alone during the day and mixing minimally in the officers' bar or smoke-room. We sensed a story or two being carried around with his gear, but being kept at a distance prevented the development of any kind of sufficiently deep relationship.

I discussed with both Pat and the Old Man the disturbing news received from Captain Ford concerning the future of merchant shipping and trading patterns. Neither could add much further information, although Pat had become aware of both the 'container-ship revolution', as he termed it, and the observed increase in bulk carriers. He had also witnessed some of the forecast crew and company changes. Captain Malcolm had passed one of 'those massive supertankers in the Persian Gulf' and suggested we should 'wait and see what transpired – and take things as they come,' which adequately reinforced what I by now plainly regarded as his total philosophy and put an abrupt end to further conversation in those areas. 'So much,' I reflected for 'my earnest quest for knowledge'.

The boredom of long sea passages or in ports offering limited opportunities for shore leave was often relieved by battles on the chessboard (courtesy BP plc).

When finally we completed cargo there was universal celebrations, and it was in almost holiday mood that we battened down hatches, took the draught and booked pilot and tugs. As if in sympathy with our departure, the heavens opened as the pilot boarded and we were washed out from Rio with hardly a dry eye or any other part of their anatomy for those of us who had to venture on deck. I was absolutely drenched whilst taking charge aft. Unusually – at least in my experience – the tug could not pass us a wire, so there was a considerable delay whilst we rustled a suitable towing length from the after deck store in the lazarrette. This was the first time since the old *Earl of Bath* that one of these delightful closets had been met aboard ship and, in that case, had been used by the purser (and engineers) as a general junk store and receptacle for old boxes of drink bottles (prior to landing these ashore) or drums of indefinable substances (either for eventual ditching or flogging). On the *Lady Vedera* the lazarrette was partially used for our deck stores. As it was originally fitted to house ammunition serving the after gun, during the Second World War, access was by means of a ladder extending down to a level below the steering gear flat. It was with considerable relief that my report to Waclaw on the bridge was made that we were now ready to proceed, but in the background the voices of both pilot and captain were reflecting a certain impatience. This was tough – but there was little that I could do to improve matters. I did reflect however how my skin was gradually becoming just that much thicker – something I felt pleased to put under the general heading of yet more personal and professional progress.

Our arrival in Buenos Aires coincided with a dock strike, a tug strike and, according to radio reports from the agent, considerable political unrest. I began to wonder if our voyage was really necessary, but hesitated to share this 'thought for today' with either Pat or the Old Man. As it was, we anchored off the pilot station at Recalada for three and a half weeks, by which time we were drastically short of food, water and patience and were even more demented than we had been in the final days of our stay in Rio. The catering department fortunately had been retro-fitted with more sophisticated refrigeration than the old traditional (for this class and age of ship) ice boxes – wherein slabs of ice had to be made and then used for chilling fresh vegetables and the freezing of sufficient stores of meat (as well of course for providing an essential to alchoholic drinks). Even so, we were almost 'schooner-rigged' (as Captain Malcolm expressed our situation) regarding food, and awaited pilot and tugs to take us alongside the coaling jetty with rumbling stomachs and eager anticipation. Inevitably, the engines broke down again as we steamed majestically up the Punto Indo channel blowing dense black smoke as we closed the resting place of a Royal Mail liner which had run aground some time previously, and the long-forsaken wreck of a certain German 'pocket battleship' forced to scuttle by a ridiculously small force of British warships. We passed both wrecks in apparent sympathetic mourning – and very nearly joined them – being rescued only at the last minute by the arrival of the two tugs necessary to bring us up and lug us reluctantly to our berth in the east-side coal wharf of the South Basin. As it was our little armada did its own dredging through the silt-laden sea bed.

We could not have chosen a better port from which to take on fresh meat, poultry, dry and general stores. We suspected that the chief steward made a fortune from his transactions, but were not too envious as Pat and the second engineer shared liberally good relations (through the agent), plus numerous quantities of 'surplus' ship's stores. The 'rake-off' for me alone came to a considerable amount of pesos.

Whilst the crew went off to assorted bordellos (and our stewards to their own delightful haunts of depravity) Pat, Sparks and I made a number of visits which were thoroughly enjoyable and unusual. One evening we ventured into the centre of Beunos Aires to a place remembered by Pat from previous trips where he had enjoyed

The wreck of the German pocket battleship Graf Spee *remained visible for many years following her demise (courtesy Montevideo Maritime Services).*

a lengthy display of gaucho dancing. This was truly memorable. I had wondered when he suggested this visit quite what we could anticipate, especially as we entered and saw the guitar and drum band rehearsing on the stage behind a barricade of barbed wire. The atmosphere was electric. We sat in a small hall, around rough wooden tables each with seating for up to six people, drinking locally-brewed beer – which was very strong and possessed a considerable kick. The lighting was very subdued. Each of some fifteen tables boasted a candle wedged precariously into an empty spirit bottle whose combined light contributed a series of flickering shadows around the place. We were joined by two local Argentinian businessmen (as it transpired) who expressed their gratitude at being allowed to share our table by treating us to a couple of bottles of local brandy, whose main consituent could have been anything from petroleum spirit to creosote. It was foul, but we felt compelled to go through the motions of drinking at least some of each glass, before despatching it very casually over the sawdust-strewn rough wooden floor. The gauchos were cowboys from the pampas, dressed in traditional gear set off with thick-soled heavy boots. Their dancing was very impressive, competing with the loud throbbing of seemingly discordant chords from a number of small drums and differently toned guitars. Somehow this cacophony managed to complement the intricate, flat-placed steps of each dance. Murmured explanations from our new companions, seen only indistinctly through the gloom, went largely unheard above the noise – even though we nodded polite enthusiastic agreement. The show lasted for over three hours at the end of which we staggered out of the place, following fond farewells from our newly-discovered friends. Pat invited them to an evening meal aboard the ship that he fixed for a couple of nights later after which, with heads strumming from music, stomping and alchohol, we managed to grab a taxi which took us back to the ship. As it happened that date was never kept by our potential guests. I suggested they had heard perhaps about our standard of catering and possessed more respect for their digestive system, rather than any reservations concerning the personalities of their prospective hosts.

Over a black coffee breakfast in the saloon next day, we all felt like death warmed up. Captain Malcolm expressed considerable interest in the dancing and said he would arrange a visit for himself and the chief engineer with the agent. But generally, breakfast was a very subdued meal. The waiters were conspicuous by their absence, leaving the minimal service required from the deck officers and Sparks to be performed by the chief and second stewards – the former cooking whilst the latter 'winged' the tables. As the engineers were collectively working all available hours coaxing life from our continuingly reluctant engines, they (and Waclaw) were the only ones able to face anything like a traditional meal. Our cabins were totally unattended for a couple of days leaving all officers – shock upon horror – making our own bunks. This was certainly something I had never done since my cadet days, Goanese stewards being totally reliable and first-class in performance of their duties. Those of us who had sailed with them only now fully appreciated their true worth having, like most things, taken them very much for granted.

Two days later the catering department was restored to its normal complement with yet another series of loggings taking place in the Old Man's office later in the day. Their descriptions of the missing days were hilariously recounted by them as they 'had found new friends, Second, some delightfully hunky cowboys, you know'. It seemed they also had enjoyed their own peculiar version of gaucho dancing – but Pat and I agreed that ours was preferable. Inevitably, a few days later, my sick parade to the Argentinian port doctor included the officers' cabin steward, Captain's tiger and engineers' messman. By that time, I was beyond expressing incredulity, shock, horror, or even disgust. Taking the words of my illustrious Captain to heart, I merely took it all as it came.

It was about 0400 hours the next morning that I was awakened by the sound of an enormous explosion and simultaneously felt the ship rolling extravagantly. Jumping from my bunk, I rolled in sympathy with the motion as *Lady Vedera* made a series of decreasingly impressive rolls before slowly regaining her equilibrium. Worried by what could have caused this hiatus (I could think only of some kind of shipboard explosion, probably in the engine-room) my dive out into the alleyway and up the companionway left me in collision with the Old Man as he left his quarters dressed only in a pair of uniform trousers. I backed away leaving him to rush up the stairs leading into the wheelhouse, closely followed by the Mate, who I think must have somehow jumped over me. Following their lead onto the port bridge wing, we noticed the ship had somehow parted her moorings and was slewed across the dock. We shared part of the dock with a Houlder Line cargo vessel and a Blue Star liner and noted that both of these, together with an assortment of foreign-flagged ships, were also adrift their moorings. On the quayside, there was spasmodic gun-fire as assorted troops attempted to settle some sort of differences with hot lead. With echoes in our ears of the sauve voice of our agent, advising 'civil unrest brewing' as he termed it soon after our arrival, mixing with further bursts of gunfire, we deduced that we had become involved in some kind of revolution. All too well aware of the volatile trigger-happy temperament of any South American soldiers – insurgents or national – we backed away from the wing and returned to the comparative safety of the wheelhouse. It seemed inappropriate to present too tempting a target. Once there we took stock of the situation – as far as we could determine this – by making a tentative plan of action. Frankly, there was little we could do. The smoke from a destroyed power station drifted slowly across the ship enveloping us in a pall which seemed symbolic as well as literal. Why on earth it was decided the generating plant serving the entire dock was a suitable target for destruction was beyond our comprehension, but that seemed to be the only observable damage.

By this time, the crew were stirring and the Old Man 'phoned the chief engineer and steward telling them the little we knew and advising them to inform their respective departments whilst urging the need for calm. Pat meanwhile had popped aft to tell the bosun and carpenter the same sparse news. Our after stern line still held, but the Captain felt it would be inadvisable to attempt reinforcing our warps – after all, as he reasoned 'we were unlikely to be going anywhere, and were probably better off without any access to or from the quay at this current moment'.

Following a pause, we suddenly heard the sound of approaching aircraft and shortly afterwards two jets zoomed into view firing cannon shells into a shed at the end of the dock into, or behind which, insurgents had apparently concealed themselves. Unfortunately, in order to reach the shed, they had to fire directly across our ship. It had to be then of course that Captain Malcolm suggested it would be appropriate for a deck officer to be with the crew housed in the after accommodation. Pat and I looked at each other with a suddenly increasing interest – and some speculation. We both privately decided – quite unashamedly – that we were not the stuff of which heroes were made for clearly, as we read in each other's glances, neither of us fancied making the trip along the after-deck in the face of live cannon shells.

The decision was made for us by the Master who suggested it should be me who ventured forth: 'You should you know, Mr Caridia, be able to pop down aft quite easily during intervals between bursts in the firing.' Thanking him very much for his timely advice, and pointedly ignoring Pat's best wishes of 'Good luck Jon, and be careful as you dodge,' I left the comfortable safety of the midships accommodation and ventured onto the after-deck. The shed at this time was still standing four-square and indomitable, even if the surrounding area was blitzed to destruction with a host of small fires burning acridly and well. It appeared the jet pilots were not the world's best marksmen. Even to my non-military eye, I was able to appreciate they had to come in very low at tremendous speed, and probably the concern foremost in the pilots' minds was for personal safety rather than the accurate aiming of their weapons. At least that factor would have been a predominant feature in my own mind were I in their invidious position. I can hardly say this thought was found particularly comforting though as, listening intently, I ran down the starboard side of number four hatch and sheltered behind the contactor house there serving both after holds. The jets came over in another run whilst I stayed put. Shells were seen hitting the cargo shed at last – as well as our own after accommodation house. Great chunks of paintwork magically disappeared in all directions, whilst the emergency compass and steering gear on the island top took a considerable bashing. Even more frightening was the previously unimagined noise of the jets as they completed their run just a few yards down our port side. I thought my eardrums were going to burst, wondered if the jets were about to crash, and felt the ship pounding wildly to the upthrust of the dock water, and its subsequent displacement prior to settling very gradually again after they had passed. Frankly, I had never been so scared in my life and wondered if my last hour was approaching.

Taking advantage of the distant sound of receding engines, I dashed in near panic to the accommodation entrance door only to find this stout wooden structure firmly locked from the inside. Even in my befuddled mental state, I realised that thumping the door would make little impression, so threw myself below the safety of number five hatch coaming, whilst thinking of my next possible course of action. It had to happen of course. Wedged below on the solid steel main-deck I heard again the sound of approaching jet aircraft. Making myself as small as possible, and stuffing my fingers into my ears, I cringed as the jets passed again above our ship and felt myself being covered in flecks of paint and shards of metal as these pilots once more missed the shed but hit our ship. I noticed, as my hands covered my head, the two gold bars on my sleeves in front of me were speckled with white paint, and wondered just what the hell I was doing serving at sea when I could (indeed should) have been safely at home working in a bank somewhere, securely married to my beloved Sue.

My thoughts lasted only as long as it took the noise of these blasted jets to fade away and I dashed aft of the deck house and, reaching for the solidity of the 'phone, sent a frantic call to the bridge hoping to ask the Master precisely what he intended me to do in the light of locked port and starboard entrance jalousies. The phone rang continuously and was totally ignored. Whilst I was wondering with increasing concern what might have happened up top, Waclaw answered and passed on my tale of woe to Captain Malcolm. There was little consolation in the voice of the latter as he suggested that a quick but careful return to the midships accommodation might be the most appropriate course of action. I did not enquire after the delay in responding, but simply replaced the 'phone and, in the absence of any sounds of returning planes, made the quickest dash along the after-deck on record, falling into the arms of our Norwegian chief cook as he came out of the galley commenting in a voice of unbridled astonishment 'I heard you clomping along the deck, second, and wondered what was happening'. It was perhaps significant that he made no mention of the jets and referred not at all to more recent events outside his little domain, leaving me wondering if he was deaf, drunk or dead - or in varying combinations of all three. It was at least a soft landing, even if the smell of his body odour did little to recommend our next meal. Clearly our ship's *contretemps* in the wider world had left such preparations uninterrupted.

Arriving back in the chart-room, I was confronted by the Master, Patrick and Waclaw looking pensively at shards of glass from shattered windows, covering the forward part of the bridge, together with cannon holes across the entire partition between wheelhouse and chart area. Apparently the second pilot's last burst had sent all three of my fellow navigating officers scattering in a frantic heap behind the chart-room working top. I took some perverse comfort from learning that they also had benefited from his appalling aim and reassured myself regarding the reason for the more than slight delay in responding to the 'phone.

Our pensive thoughts were interrupted by bursts of automatic firing from the jetty so, keeping well away from the port bridge wing, we glanced out of the starboard side wheelhouse windows. Troops were seen rushing into the thick acrid smoke from the still-burning shed astern, firing wildly. The fumes mingled with continued dark wisps from the smouldering power station, leading me to muse on the appropriateness of Beunos Aires' name – and its clean air policy. Once this concentrated outburst had subsided, there was a period of calm around the vicinity of South Dock, and even though spasmodic bursts of gunfire indicated the overall conflict was far from over elsewhere in the city, we were not troubled by further signs of inherent warfare. Captain Malcom felt it appropriate for an officer to remain on the bridge for the remainder of the day, and all next night, with orders to contact him immediately in the event of any movement – passive or active – which might happen to disturb our apparent period of calm. Inevitably, therefore, we reverted to standard sea watches of four hours on and eight off.

Our meal-times later were vaguely reminiscent of those aboard the *King Joseph* during the Russian–Cuban crisis, with officers heatedly debating points for and against the action and its possible causes. Conjecture was rife aboard *Lady Vedera* for, once again, no one on board had the remotest idea of what was occurring – not that this stopped us airing our views to all and sundry, whether or not they were listening. It must be noted that Captain Malcolm joined in as enthusiastically as the rest of us, which left me pondering yet once more the vagaries of the human mind.

It was two days later that the agent was seen wandering down the jetty towards our ship. By this time, we had drifted alongside once more even though the general atmosphere of uncertainty resulted in the gangway remaining raised. As I was duty officer the Old Man suggested, when I informed him by 'phone of this new development ashore, to lower the thing and escort Mr Corbena directly to his cabin, calling the Mate and chief engineer to his office as I proceeded below. The thought did cross my mind that he could just as easily have 'phoned these two seniors but, obedient as ever and not really caring one way or the other, I popped in and informed them of the latest developments and of course passed on the Old Man's instructions.

I felt quite honoured when Captain Malcolm invited me to remain and join the gathering for the general discussion concerning what had happened, was still happening, and events that might occur in the future. It seemed we were to have all damage to our ship repaired whilst alongside and a surveyor would attend the next day to assess the extent of this and then instruct the agent to arrange repairs. Meanwhile, we should reinstate our moorings and proceed with discharging our cargo. Of events on a wider political plane, Mr Corbena could contribute very little other than to say that the insurrection had been subdued and the leaders captured, and were in jail awaiting interrogation and trial. We were left to our varying levels of conjecture regarding their fate but (for once) totally agreed that their days on this earth might be limited, ruefully admitting, in the words of Long John Silver from Stevenson's *Treasure Island*, that 'those who had died would be the lucky ones'. The agent remained a silent partner regarding this aspect of the incident as he called it.

The long-suffering Lloyd's surveyor turned out to be an English ex-captain with Furness Withy, who lived in a very select part of Buenos Aires, although his immediate family remained (perhaps wisely) in the family home at Whitby in the UK. He assessed our damage as sufficiently serious to require the services of the local dry dock and promptly made arrangements through the agent for a suitable booking, either before – or even during – our cargo discharge. There would be some modest demand on the dry dock from other ships who had suffered from the aircraft, but our wheelhouse and poop structure particularly were deemed by far to be the most serious damage inflicted on any ship. We wondered how long it would take before the dry docking occurred – especially my good self who, by tradition, would be responsible for organising this. I was not too bothered by this aspect as Patrick, well aware I had not done this task before, and being ever helpful, undertook to guide me along the way. My first step was to catalogue the damage throughout the ship. This was comparatively straightforward as this report was based conveniently on that provided by Lloyd's surveyor. Meantime, we re-warped our ship alongside the jetty and next day resumed discharging the coal.

Whilst alongside, we heard the mother-and-father of a commotion coming from the ship astern. She was a red-ensigned London–Greek-owned bulk carrier and I had exchanged reminiscences and commiserations with her second officer when we met ashore whilst taking the draughts of our respective vessels. She had been away from the UK for over two years and showed no sign of returning 'probably within another two', if the bleak forecast of her second was anything to go by. It was shortly after our meeting that my watchman called attention to the presence of two car loads 'swarming with police, second,' as he described the situation. This was followed shortly by a van that screeched dramatically onto the jetty. The police made their way purposefully up the gangway of the tramp and, following a pause of about twenty minutes, we saw a number of crew handcuffed and escorted from ship to van and rapidly driven away. We of course were all agog to know what had happened – all ranks united for once by the prospect of maritime scandal. I met my opposite number on the jetty later that day as we continued our endless cycle of draught taking. Apparently, the bosun and two deck hands on his ship were seen with guns and ammunition on board, had become roaring drunk during the Old Man's inspection in their quarters and, following an altercation with him, the bosun had clouted his captain on the jaw. I was astonished – it seemed comparable to the dean of Canterbury Cathedral clumping his archbishop during a most solemn part of Holy Communion. Whilst the chief and second engineers restrained the deckhands, the chief steward had sensibly 'phoned for the police who, for once, responded with unaccustomed alacrity. We saw the results on the quayside and, a few of days later, heard that the three crew-members had been sentenced to three months in jail. What they intended to do with their armoury was never explained, but Captain Malcom told us weapons were easily available ashore in some of the local clip joints. These were clearly ones into which I would never have dreamed of entering – even assuming I could recognise them. He shrewdly suggested that the offer of guns and ammunition might have given the three an irresistible 'romantic' urge to purchase them. His explanation seemed reasonable, but I thought the price of residence in a South American jail a pretty high one to pay 'for mere romance'. Our Old Man offered his customary wan smile and hoped his crew would not acquire the same notion.

It was just over three weeks later, with considerable relief, that we heard a vacancy had been booked for our ship to enter dry dock the following day. 'Typical,' was Pat's comment. 'We are kept waiting for the best part of a month and then everything happens at once.' I kept my own counsel, but thought that by now he ought to have been all too familiar with the way things happen at sea.

We entered number two dry dock on top of a spring tide and remained there for about a fortnight whilst a collection of welders, shipwrights, carpenters and allied tradesmen sorted out our war wounds, preparing us to face again assorted rigours of the deep.

They also had a look at our antiquated engine, but merely grinned and suggested its transference to the local maritime museum – 'along with the ship itself,' Pat was heard to offer in what was intended to be a *sotto voce* comment. Unfortunately this was overheard by Captain Malcolm, whose uncharacteristic outburst showed it had gone down like the proverbial lead balloon. Our long-suffering chief was left to make the most of things below and rely on the ingenuity of the second and his minions. This was just as well for, as soon as we had left dry dock, luckily even before the tug had cast off our wire, the engines refused to function and, in response to the bridge command for SLOW AHEAD, remained obstinately unco-operative. Amidst great consternation up top and below, we were towed unceremoniously to the nearest vacant wharf and tied up, whilst all sorts of machinations occurred in the engine-room to 'mend the elastic bands,' as I remarked. My comment also earned from Father a more than bleak black look.

Once the agent found out where we were temporarily berthed and booked his launch to come alongside, our recalcitrant engines and the chief's staff signed yet another truce, indicating we were now ready to venture forth on the next leg of our voyage – to wherever that might be. Once more, great was the conjecture aboard as every crew-member played the guessing game concerning the ports to which we might be bound. Mr Corbena advised we were to proceed in ballast just over 220 miles up the River Plate from Beunos Aires to the port of Rosario. The company required us to clean hatches on the way and load bulk grain from San Lorenzo – a port 16 miles up the River Paraná that flowed into the Plate, for a possible return trip to Cardiff.

Coming onto the bridge to relieve Waclaw, I heard the Old Man carrying-on alarmingly, leaning over the chart and busily engaged with eraser, parallel rules and pencil. Our third mate was standing by watching the Master at work with a decidedly dejected look on his placid face. On seeing me, he made a quick exit from the chart-room whilst I approached father indicating my intention to relieve the watch. The captain looked up and explained that Waclaw had somehow misjudged shore marks as we were passing them and had put the ship some three miles ahead of her present position. My comments that 'he was something of an optimist' was received with a very jaundiced smile from the Old Man who, leaving his labour of love, went on the bridge wing to chat with the pilot, and left me to get on with things.

Before we could be passed by cargo inspectors to load grain, following a bulk coal cargo, called for a thorough cleaning of all hatches. This meant that 'tween-decks and lower holds including the difficult areas behind and between the spar ceiling (wooden struts that prevented the cargo coming into direct contact with the ship's sides) and limber boards at the lower part of the hold, would require concentrated attention. Mindful that we would have a pilot on board for the entire crossing and that the Master would be popping into the wheelhouse whilst on passage, Captain Malcolm decided to put the Mate on day work and leave Waclaw and I to do all bridge watches. There was certainly sufficient work to keep our happy crowd out of mischief and, as Perce the chief steward had signed (yet another) peace treaty with his erratic band, and the chief's crew were, as ever, speaking kindly to the equally as erratic engines, a period of tranquility prevailed throughout the ship. The 18-hour trip (assuming an estimated 12 knots could be coaxed from our machinery) was clearly inadequate for all five hatches to be washed and dried, so we proceeded up the River Plate at a leisurely seven knots. As even this period was insufficient to complete the work adequately, we agreed with the agent to anchor until the holds were dried and could be inspected.

A pilot with his helmsman discusses the passage plan with the ship's Master (courtesy BP plc).

We had to anchor in the Rosario Roads a few more days before the holds were ready for inspection, but afterwards went alongside immediately upon arrival at San Lorenzo. Our hopes that we could commence a quick loading were short-lived. We had to have shifting boards fitted to our hatches extending into the lower hold to prevent the grain from moving with the pitching (but particularly rolling) motion of the vessel once we were facing Atlantic gales and storms. The crowd of shore riggers designated to fit these timbers across our centre-line adopted a leisurely approach to their task - much to the frustration of Pat and virtually everyone else on board. As Captain Malcolm explained there was little which could be done about this, apart from making what proved to be an ineffective complaint to the agent. Once Numbers Two and Four hatches were fitted we commenced loading, moving along the ship as other hatches were completed, until the vessel was sitting evenly to correct draught-marks.

By the time cargo had been taken we had still not received final instructions for our destination from the Kremlin, but were advised to leave anyway and, as it was stated in the ship's logbook, proceed 'Towards Falmouth for Orders'. Captain Malcolm explained that the freight department were 'playing the spot market,' as he called it, before determining our destination. Following his explanations regarding what that might be, this navigating officer at least was left not much better informed. Either his explanations or my understanding of 'ship master's business' was at fault somewhere. As it was, we were approaching the Bay of Biscay before a lengthy cable was received informing us that we were to discharge all 'tween-deck grain in Cardiff and then sail to complete discharge at Southampton.

We also received instructions concerning deployments of our officers. The third mate – it came as no surprise to learn – was to be relieved and would not be offered further employment within the Group. Without putting too fine a point on things, he had been sacked. Waclaw received this news with little surprise, almost as if it had been expected (making me wonder where I had heard that expression before), and announced his intention of offering his dubious services to the pilot cutters and buoyage maintenance craft of Trinity House at Harwich. Both Pat and I were left open-mouthed at this news, but decided it was an occasion when our thoughts should remain very much unexpressed. The Master, Pat and myself were to remain with the ship, whilst all engineering officers were to be relieved – and 'doubtless sent to the nearest mental asylum to recover,' as I commented to the Old Man. As predictable as ever, he bit at my remark but, by way of originality added with a smile 'that it was not too late for a relief second officer to be organised,' thus leaving me facing my own version of a Waterloo, and chalking up this riposte to my endeared captain. It seemed our long-suffering chief and second were also to remain – 'probably as they represented the only members of the human race to understand their beloved machinery,' as Pat remarked to the Master – earning in return a veiled threat of his own relief. We were also to have a complete change of all petty officers and ratings.

Rather unwisely, Captain Malcolm left his voyage report to the company directors on the chart-room table. This was eagerly intercepted by his totally trustworthy senior navigating officers and perused with undisguised delight. We were both interested to see the glowing reports he had submitted concerning our integrity(?), sobriety, ability and conduct, but were totally bemused to note his conclusion that 'All is well, gentlemen, and having nothing further to report'. This was in the light of three engine breakdowns since departing Argentina, leaving us to conclude that these were now so commonplace that they barely deserved a mention in Father's annals. We both agreed that seeing the chief's report to our principals would make far more entertaining reading. Certainly, my discussions with him when I offered the daily run chit were nearly always moments of hilarity. These calculations compared our estimation of the miles run assessed from our astronomical observations, with the achievements of the ship in terms of miles deduced from machinery revolutions. On this vessel, there were only rarely heard complaints that the engines arrived at the next port far ahead of the remainder of the ship, so much the war cry of chief engineers on any other vessel upon which I had served.

Arrival at Cardiff saw the promised officer and crew changes. Dickie, our officers' steward, celebrated his departure in characteristic style with floods of tears and an outburst of histrionics that would have done any prima donna proud. It was a sterling performance. He crooned how 'lovely an experience it had been looking after us' – thanked us profusely for 'being so delightfully kind to him' – and vowed upon the names of various dubious gods that he would never forget us. Pat and I were left drained following this floor show but felt that the customary financial tip, given for somewhat dubious services rendered over what had proved a prolonged trip, might perhaps have been a little on the generous side. It was a small price to pay, for frankly we were both glad to see the back of him/her – and reasured ourselves with the possibly dangerous assumption that only better could follow with the new crowd. Mike Houghton, the relieving third mate, was an Empress man since his cadet days. He was a very experienced officer who was due up for Mates' at the end of this next voyage.

We were also blessed with a first trip deck cadet about whose arrival, of course, no one from either London or the local company office had bothered to inform the ship. Alcuin Blethwyd-Williams was not surprisingly a local lad who was 16 years old and had just completed his pre-sea training at Cardiff Navigation School. He lived at Llanelli further down the coast and was brought to the ship, with a surprising amount of gear, by his delightfully unaffected parents. Seeing him arriving in uniform with mum

The second officer discusses the day's run with the chief engineer – often a time of some hilarity as the observed position is compared with the daily run calculated from the engine revolutions (courtesy BP plc).

and dad was the first indication that a deck cadet had been appointed. Pat entertained them to a pot of tea, whilst I took 'young Alcuin B-W bach' as I was already thinking of him, to the cadet's quarters and stood back wallowing in the look of horrified shock which crossed his innocent young features. The reason for this was *Lady Vedera* had not been entrusted with deck or engineering cadets for about three years and their quarters had not even been aired during this period. As we opened the jalousie, a dense layer of dust and an even thicker smell of decay greeted us both, more to the chagrin of Alcuin seeing as he would be unfortunate enough to reside there. The study was a little more presentable, largely because it had been commandeered by an endless run of deck officers as an extension to the Mate's office. It was loaded with all those small desirables that the chief officer considered best kept under lock and key – for either immediate use or (more likely) later flogging. It also housed extra goodies, such as much of my navigational accessories which I had been too lazy to have transferred to my own locker four decks up. This was the hub of the problem. The self-contained cadets' quarters on this ship, consisting of two cabins, toilet/shower and study, was situated very conveniently on the main deck in the same alleyway as the mate's and engineer's offices. Inevitably, the study in particular was used as a general dumping ground. Afterwards, I returned him to the Mate and, following fond farewells with mum and dad and assurances ringing in everyone's ears that 'yes, we would look after him,' Pat took Alcuin and introduced him to an astonished Captain Malcolm. Taking pity on this mere slip of a lad moved me to suggest to Pat that the boy would be better dossing down in the ship's hospital to which, of course, I held the key. Mindful of emergencies, I had arranged with the voyage chief steward that this was kept clean and aired, with bunks being continually made up. This would give the boy a chance to make habitable his own quarters.

Our crew were nearly all local lads, with a few from Scotland (in the engine-room, of course), and various parts of England. On first impressions (always at sea rather dangerous assumptions) they seemed a reasonable lot. The new Sparks sent from Marconi was an Irishman, so we started with 'quite a cosmopolitan crowd that was at least home-grown and a far cry from the last lot,' as I remarked to the Old Man whilst discussing my voyage plan to Southampton. He just grunted in reply and, by way of retort, stated he had not the remotest idea where we would be proceeding from there.

Talking to the cadet in the smoke-room after supper the first evening following his arrival, in an effort to make him feel at home, was a fascinating experience. He impressed as painfully shy, but listening to his gently lilting Welsh accent was a delight. It was similar hearing those of the Welsh crew until, that is, they were in their cups when the seeming 'language of heaven' became strongly marked with harsher tones clearly emanting from that other place. I was able to report to Pat that 'once Alcuin-bach had settled, he showed promise of turning out quite well'.

Both the captain and Mate each had 'faithful wife' (as I termed them) to stay, until the ship sailed, whilst I was granted seven days local leave which was spent with

Sue and my family. This proved a very welcome and enjoyable time, not least because it was totally unexpected.

I returned on board happily contented and prepared for anything. This was just as well for, reporting back to Pat in time for lunch and enjoying coffee afterwards in the lounge, two bombshells were dropped that affected momentarily my indigestion. It appeared that we were now bound for Russia, and that the cadet would no longer be sailing with us. I had an inkling that perhaps something was wrong regarding the former news because, upon arrival at the dock gates in my taxi, we were diverted to another berth by the duty police constable and I saw us loading general cargo including bagged cement.

The news regarding Alcuin was sadder. He had been sent by the Master only the previous day to take some papers to our local company office and, whilst returning, had been knocked down by a car. Luckily, it appeared he had heard the vehicle as it lost control, mounting the pavement behind him, and had instinctively jumped out of the way. Unfortunately (not being a kangeroo) his hop had not been sufficient to avoid contact completely and the bumper had just caught his leg, breaking this in two places and sending him into a minor state of shock. My first job that afternoon, before relieving Mike on deck, was to pack and tally his gear for onward transmission to the agent who would despatch this back to his parents. It was quite a sombre task sorting out this mountain of stuff with its personal associations and, indeed, already fragmentary memories of this young lad. As I discussed with Father later, it was fortunate that his injuries were not more severe, for he could easily have been killed. His parents once again returned to the ship whilst I was on cargo watch. They collected his effects and told Pat that 'son and heir' had recovered from the shock of the accident but advised (not surprisingly) that he would be unable to commence his sea career for some weeks.

Regarding the change in orders, it seemed that we were now bound for Murmansk with both cargoes. I discussed provisional voyage plans with the Captain as neither he nor Pat had sailed previously in these waters. My experiences in the Black Sea would not prove particularly useful, other than to inform the Master about the battery of administrative problems which had beset us when attempting clearances inward and outwards from these ports. Needless to say, he said 'we would take things as they came' and promptly contacted our version of the Kremlin to ascertain weather routeing advice. From this it seemed the best passage for the time of year that we were voyaging would be off the Norwegian coast, rather than that through the White Sea–Baltic Canal. A few days later came the unexpected arrival of a supply of cold-weather gear for all hands whose duties took them even remotely on deck. This included fleece-lined boots (which covered to above the ankle), woollen sea-boot stockings reaching above the knee, balaclava, mittens and waterproofs.

About two hours after the arrival of our our clothing, a van came alongside containing assorted parcels which proved to be of charts, Admiralty Pilots and sundry sailing directions. As the Old Man commented: 'When head office decide to pull out their finger, they certainly make a damn good job of doing so.' Sorting the charts into new folios and reading through the pilots and sailing directions to select appropriate snippets, kept me off cargo watches for the remainder of our stay in Cardiff. Our loading programme was rapidly approaching completion and the Old Man suggested to Pat that I would be best employed preparing voyage plans, especially for the first leg of our trip which he and I agreed should be provisionally to a way point off the Outer Hebrides. As the gangs worked only from 0800 to 1700 hours and we were close to booking pilot and tugs, the Mate was quite happy to share the watches between Mike and himself.

Preparing my plan, discussing this with Captain Malcolm and then doing the necessary chartwork, proved inordinately interesting and kept me busy often far into late evening. It seemed Murmansk was situated on the eastern side of the Kola Inlet, 28 nautical miles from the Barents Sea. It was the final western part of the North Sea route that was ice-free for virtually all of the year, apart from exceptionally rare circumstances when ice-breakers (we were assured) would be available. The run from Cardiff to our destination was nearly 1850 nautical miles. We estimated if chiefy could keep our tired machinery going at 12 knots we could do the passage in around 6½ days. This was well within our bunker capacity and would allow us a safer than the 10 per cent extra mileage traditionally allowed for passage steaming. All officers were more concerned regarding the wisdom in sending us with our totally unreliable engines into areas renowned for gale force winds (that were often more severe) and accompanying wild seas. Apparently, discussing this with the local superintendent did little to reassure the Master. I came into his day cabin to discuss a routeing problem, and accidentally interrupted a chat clearly related to this topic. The expression on Captain Malcolm's face, as he waved me away with unaccustomed irritation, spoke volumes.

We sailed from Cardiff in foul weather and experienced storm-force south-westerlies complete with torrential rain. I was completely drenched after coming from my stand-by aft and had to strip off all clothes and take a hot shower. Our new catering crew were so far proving amenable and reliable, but I missed the ministrations of Goanese stewards who would have grabbed my gear from the deck, even whilst I was still showering and laid out clean uniform – complete with fitted shoulder straps. As it was, I had to put the whole lot into the washing machine, and then 'cook and iron' it myself. Life with a European crew was proving difficult in some respects!

Many of our deck and engine ratings were 'logged' for alcohol offences once we were at sea. Needless to say, the usual 'crop of the unwise' popped along to my sick parade a few days out with a selection of unsocial diseases. My visit to Father coincided with the Mate witnessing the recent spate of loggings in the Official logbook. He laid side-by-side the two catalogues of shame and shaking his head ruefully exclaimed that 'some things never change, do they, gentlemen?' We could only concur and accept cheerfully the (to me) totally unexpected tot that was offered, over which we chatted about the reception likely to be given them by a Russian port doctor when we finally arrived at our destination.

The foul weather continued whilst proceeding through St George's Channel. It abated slightly whilst navigating the North Channel between Ireland and Scotland, but soon made up for things as we cleared the Outer Hebrides and settled on our north-easterly course through the Norwegian Sea towards the Lofotens. Our engines protested a few times by producing some alarming 'shudders and jumps' – to use the chief's words whilst comparing chits during our third day's run – but at least they kept faithfully turning.

The density of shipping was about what we expected, but recently introduced Traffic Separation Zones reduced collision situations considerably along with much of the strain normally associated with the diverse crossing situations encountered in these waters. Fishing boats remained very much a problem on occasions – whether we were in Zones or not – and in the middle of one watch I considered it prudent to call the Master to the bridge in the light of three unenlightened trawlers who seemed to have a magnetic attraction for us. Whichever way I manoeuvred our ship at least one of these characters appeared on a collision course. Captain Malcolm asesssed what was happening and then, standing near the centre-line by the steering console, told me to continue handling the situation myself and see if it could be sorted out without his direct interference. This proved slightly nerve-racking especially with my quartermaster on the wheel (where I had placed him prior to calling Father) and the lookout watching closely everything that was occurring from his station on the starboard bridge wing. Presence of the Master gave me considerable confidence. I knew he would not permit a too dangerous close-quarter situation to occur, and so conned the ship into and out of a bowline (or at least that is what is seemed like to me) until our speed allowed us to steam ahead. It was then a question of straightening up on our course-line. I breathed a large sigh of relief and sent my two hands below for a twenty-minute smoke-oh, which allowed Captain Malcolm and I to discuss the situation over a well-earned cup of cocoa.

My duty quartermaster was quite one of the best European crew I ever encountered at sea – and a far cry from the QM aboard *Countess Elizabeth*. He was in his early sixties – a real old shellback – having served at sea all his life, including passages on Artic convoys during the Second World War. He related to the Master and myself many of his experiences in modest matter-of-fact tones which held a ring of authenticity. Captain Malcolm was able to vouch for these tales, not so much from his own experiences (he had been on Atlantic convoys and the Africa–Australia run in the war) but he had heard stories from officers who had also served on the Russia-run during these times. The QM's information about Murmansk was not of much help to us, as it was outdated by at least 20 years.

The weather remained stormy, cold and wet. We shipped solid green seas forward which extended to severe spraying port and starboard, the intensity of which often hit the wheelhouse windows and bridge wings. I do not recall having to use the Kent screens fitted to the wheelhouse windows so frequently on any previous ship or voyage. These were circular plates of glass, each operated by a powerful electric motor, that revolved at high speed throwing aside heavy rain and snow. They proved invaluable in offering a clear view ahead of the vessel, within the limits of visibilty, and were switched on almost continuously to the extent we worried about the motors burning out. The engines broke down just before we cleared the Norwegian coast in the face of a northerly-westerly gale. The Old Man reached the bridge before I even had time to 'phone for him and together we stood by helplessly as the ship pitched severely and rolled to alarming levels. The inclinometer, indicating rolling limits of the vessel at any time, thudded from port to starboard with considerable force. This told us in no uncertain terms the ship was rolling in excess of 45 degrees each way, and was becoming caught beam-to in the trough of an extremely heavy swell. There was not much we could do except 'roll out the barrel' as the Old Man stated the situation in a bland show of humour. I could tell the situation was quite serious, not only from my own experience but from the unexpected appearance in the wheelhouse of Pat and Mike. They were clearly concerned, as well as 'mildy interested in what was taking place,' as Pat stated – although a strained face and unaccustomed understatement belied his true feelings. Mike merely clung desperately to the now redundant telegraph and, like me, kept a restrained silence. After luckily only a brief spell, we received a 'phone call from the chief confirming 'all was well once more and we could proceed'. Never did Mike respond so thankfully to the Old Man's orders as he rung HALF AHEAD on the telegraph and we headed once more on course.

We cleared the Lofoten Islands in a snow storm which remained with us until just before we reached North Cape and entered the Barents Sea for the the run to Murmansk. I was disappointed that the appalling visibilty prevented us experiencing the aurora borealis – the northern lights. Apart from catching sparse glimpses of this phenomenon on occasions in Scottish and northern waters, I had only heard from others about its striking effects. Apparently it was caused by gases in the atmosphere becoming bombarded by particles from the sun. That we had not seen the lights was hardly surprising, for by this time, we were even doubting the existence of the sun itself. All navigation had been by dead reckoning or 'By Guess and by God' as I termed it to the Old Man. The heavens were kinder to us in later stages of the voyage and we were able to pick up visual navigational marks ashore off North Cape, from which we ascertained that our combined dead reckoning efforts had not proved too inaccurate.

I had not been proved too far wrong either in my estimate of clearance procedures in north Russia, for these were little different to those recalled in Black Sea regions. We were anchored four days before the pilot came out and, once alongside with the

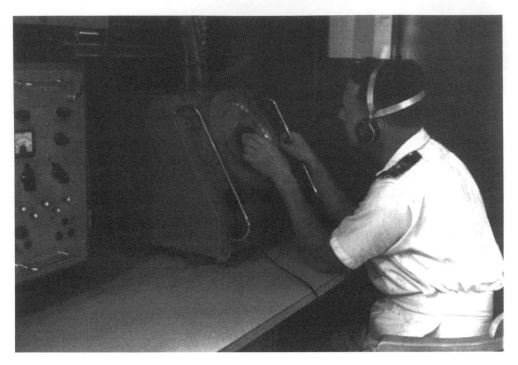

Navigating officers confirmed the ship's position by all available means, including using the services of the radio officer to take bearings from radio stations using the direction finder (courtesy BP plc).

gangway down, the port officials were abrupt and not overly helpful. We were allowed to bunker, but the chief and old man had to negotiate very delicately through the agent (for some reason) before the barge came alongside and transferred our coal. Stores were also difficult to obtain – the chief steward had to channel all requests through the Master instead of negotiating directly with the recommended chandler. The Mate 'cut his losses,' as he put it, regarding replacment deck stores. There was nothing urgent so he decided simply to go without until returning to the United Kingdom. It was all quite bizarre.

Perhaps something in our attitude was to blame and had been detected, although Father thought my prognosis as unlikely and put our reception down to sheer bloody-mindedness. It was true that we were ready for a break. Merely to have the ship as a stable platform on an even keel for more than a few seconds was in itself a physical relief. But I felt there was also a further ingredient that just *might* have come through and contributed towards our problems with shore-side contacts. The continuous unpredictable motion of such severity had caused tempers to become frayed amongst officers and crew alike so, perhaps the real problem was not so much personality clashes but that we were all extremely tired. It had proved difficult for anyone to experience deep sleep almost since departing Cardiff and the trip had taken two days beyond our estimation. No doubt fear also played a role. Even Captain Malcolm admitted the weather experienced was the amongst the worst he had ever known and that, at times – especially during the last engine breakdown – he had feared for the safety of his ship and our lives.

Life in the officer's saloon during mealtimes, with its atmosphere normally so relaxed and bursting with humour, could be 'cut with the proverbial knife' on the worst occasions during the severest motion. All chairs were linked to the deck and storm bars fitted to the edges of tables, with wet tablecloths holding utensils reasonably firmly to the table tops. These efforts however contributed little to keeping food and drink inside them, and our lunchtime and supper soup sloshed about alarmingly until most of the contents swilled over the plates. It was often easier to lift the plate from the table and swing it around almost like the gimbals in our compasses. Many of the junior engineers were violently seasick and absent from meals, which placed an extra burden on those who survived. This did little to help develop our social life. After-meals coffee in the lounge tended to be difficult, requiring immense effort just to hold the cup and saucer steady and remain in the armchair, let alone to exert the extra effort

Serving meals in the officers' dining saloon (courtesy BP plc).

required to be pleasant as well. There was nothing really I could do in my role as *ex-officio* ship's medical officer, except issue anti-seasick pills which themsleves were not kept down. Personally, I knew from early experiences when first at sea that these were rarely effective – at least for me. The side effects of very dry mouth and tightened stomach muscles were worse than being ill.

I found myself in danger of being caught up in the general mêlée for, a couple of times, I felt within me an unaccustomed aggravation that was frightening in its intensity simply to lash out with a few irritable side-swipes. I really wanted to hurt someone, but fortunately bit back any retorts before giving vent to these and causing damage. I remained in my cabin more often than usual when off watch. Mike was excellent value during the difficult times and remained cheerful and helpful. He admitted afterwards that he also had experienced the same feelings, but like myself, had worked really hard at making the effort to 'retain his civilised humanity' as he so aptly defined his situation. The experience was interesting and, to me, valuable lessons were brought home, not least that serving at sea could never be described either as predictable or boring. The ratings fared far worse and a number of black eyes and swollen noses indicated that a few ill-tempered fracas had occurred below.

Once discharging cargo started, we went onto 12-hour watches allowing all hands both to catch up on sleep and, once refreshed, to go ashore. There were hardly any problems encountered discharging. The removal of shifting boards in Cardiff (as the lower holds were each filled to maximum capacity to prevent shifting) had been performed quickly and efficiently, leaving the 'tween-deck areas clean and tidy. It appeared (for some reason) that the cement we carried from Wales was of a different and far superior quality than that available locally. I had noticed whilst supervising loading that it was in particularly strong reinforced bags which in itself was unusual, but had not really thought much about this, my mind being focussed more on passage planning.

Murmansk proved an interesting port. I was surprised to find the city so modern, but then memory recalled my quartermaster's stories of appalling damage inflicted here by German bombing. The port had been virtually rebuilt with wide roads and modern buildings that would have done credit to any western equivalent. We never caught sight of the promised ice-breakers zooming around the harbour as icing conditions remained below their optimum during our stay. We had occasional snow storms but, unlike southern Russia, these never settled, being quickly washed away by heavy rainfall as temperatures rose slightly above freezing. The winds remained bitterly cold, bringing their own version of 'chill factor' – and proved a source of irritation to all working on deck.

Most of our deckhands were disgruntled, not against their officers or the ship (for a change), but due to the resistance of local girls to 'do what the crew obviously expected'. It seemed that in this area also similarities existed between northern and southern Russia. I must confess a sense of relief for, after all, it was me who had

Shore-leave was always welcome giving an opportunity of stretching legs and seeing new sights – particularly comparing northern and southern Russian ports, such as Lenin Avenue in Murmansk (courtesy PLAKAT Publishing, Moscow).

to deal with this rather sordid aspect of my sickbay duties. Although the crew were comparitively speaking very good to work and be with, the usual symptoms of 'disinclination to work' experienced ever since I became second (and medical) officer abated little. It was often a case of psychological warfare reassuring malcontent ratings that 'the pain in the stomach sec that hurts summink awful' was nothing too serious and could be worked through literally without recourse to a bunk in the sickbay and hotel service from their long-suffering shipmates in the catering department. Anything looking too serious was dealt with by a dose of purgative the threat of which was miraculously suffcient to effect immediate cure. If temperature, skin effects and pulse rates indicated that perhaps there was 'something lurking' this was referred for discussion with the Master and Pat seeking a joint prognosis enabling a course of action to be determined. It gave perhaps a new interpretation to the expression 'a medical consultation'. I continued taking sick parades ashore in Murmansk to local port health doctors, but the experiences here were no different to those anywhere else in the world. I was fast becoming an expert on similarities and differences between international port doctors and wondered (luckily in a soon-passing uncharacterisically mad moment) whether or not a learned paper on this might be produced for submission to *The Lancet.* Mentioning this in passing (and again unwisely) to Captain Malcolm brought the expected response along with his observation that 'I was again winding him up'. This of course was perfectly true. I had been doing so in a subtle manner since joining the ship. It was just that he had taken a long time to comment on my ways of relieving boredom and making life more interesting. It probably showed to him also that I was perfectly relaxed in performing my duties – which (possibly) could have helped relax him.

Orders from our agent coincided with discharge of the final cases of general cargo from our holds. We were instructed to proceed in ballast towards the UK awaiting further orders whilst on passage. Tugs and pilot were taken without delay or problems and, following a rigid and abortive search of the ship for stowaways, we again ventured out into the Barents Sea heading probably for home – and whatever the elements could produce for our tantalisation.

The weather abated slightly during the initial stages of our homeward trip. We had just cleared North Cape, heading into gale-force sea, heavy rain and high swell when Sparks brought a radio message to the Old Man, who was busy spending a brief sojourn with me on the bridge talking about everything and nothing in general. In other words, we were enjoying a relaxing chat whilst I negotiated course changes with a generous portion of the Murmansk fishing fleet. Father read the cable and, without further comment, passed it for my perusal. I could hardly believe what was written. We were to alter course off Senja Island and head for Narvik to load a full cargo of iron ore for docks in the River Tees. The question prominent in our minds centred around Narvik as a loading port when we had just departed from Murmansk which was 'brimming over with the stuff,' as Father succintly put the situation. Anyway, ours not to reason why – if fact not at all – so, with a gentle sigh (more for effect than in anger), I reached for the next chart in our portfolio and scratched in a few additional lines.

The Norwegian pilot was quite a character whom, it seemed, liked working British ships and crews. He happily regaled us with lurid tales of his adventures gained whilst working for two years as second mate aboard a Bank Line ship, whilst simultaneously negotiating (with considerable aplomb) a mixture of rock outcrops, commercial shipping, yachts and fishing boats. The tugs were equally efficient and we were soon cleared by the port authorities. Narvik was accustomed to serving the newer large class of bulk carriers, about which Captain Ford had waxed so enthusiastically, and we commenced loading directly the ship was in position and made fast alongside. The Norwegian *Rimfonn* was nigh on 51,000 tons grt and had been delivered (we were pleased to learn) from Harland & Wolff's Belfast yard a few years previously. We were amazed, seeing her light in the water and so close up, by the sheer size of her. Her fo'c'sle towered over our stern and our coming alongside was witnessed, for the want of anything better to do, by her chief officer and what seemed to be half the deck crew. Fortunately, our engines had been behaving themselves since leaving Murmansk – a change in temperament which the chief ascribed to their 'liking the particular quality of Russian coal'. Pat and I wisely kept our own counsel, but secretly were convinced chiefy often went below to talk coaxingly to them and send them off at night with a gentle lullaby. Whatever the cause, they responded to the pilot's commmands without discord and played their part in allowing us to make a smooth berthing without incident.

The agent made clear why we had loaded ore from here and not Russia. It seemed that Narvik exported Kiruna ore which had a 65 per cent iron content and a density of 217 lb/cu.ft with a stowage factor of 10·3 feet per ton making it a mineral unique to Norway. We loaded by three conveyors in a surprisingly short space of time much to the chagrin of the crew who wanted to spend a longer period having, it seemed, found some 'delectable females, second, to make up for a lack of those in ***** Russia'. I could vouch for the efficacy of these unions a few days later when running my usual sick bay. The only surprise – I remained remarkably naïve – was when our first-trip deck boy became a patient at the tail end (I supposed, appropriately) of the usual throng of that 'surgery'. He was just seventeen and had been sent to the ship from Newcastle Federation shipping pool, following a particularly tough course aboard the Sharpness training vessel *Vindicatrix*. I was particularly interested in hearing of his adventures there when he was placed in the wheelhouse to polish brass and generally clean up the place, and also to complete the customary thirty hours at the wheel for his steering certificate. The '*Vindy*', as it was apparently known colloquially if not entirely affectionately, was the training establishment where I might have ended up when I was sixteen if a chance meeting with a senior marine superintendent, whilst working ashore in a shipping office, had led me to investigate and be accepted for pre-sea training at a navigation school. I am not so sure my career would have followed the same direction as this young man's. It seemed the more senior (and responsible?) deck crowd had treated him to 'savour the delights' as a seventeenth birthday treat. Pat's comment, when learning about the misfortunes of his most junior crew member, expressed surprise even to one hardened to the idiosyncrasies of European crews. He commented: 'This young man has not wasted much time. Newcomers to seafaring invariably leave "savouring the delights" until later voyages at least. I only hope the lad considers his shipmates treat a worthy present.'

Three days out of Narvik in customarily atrocious weather the engines stopped stone dead and we ground to a wallowing halt. It was clear that either the chief had changed his tune or our machinery decided it needed a new choirmaster. Either way, there was nothing we could do except (once again) hoist Not Under Command signals from their permanently rigged home in the locker abaft the wheelhouse and wait patiently for something positive to emerge from the nether regions of our trusty ship. Fortunately the seas were not so severe as previously encountered (but we still managed to roll quite convincingly) although the delay on this occasion ran well into the early hours of the morning. It was just towards the end of my watch whilst I was eagerly awaiting relief from Pat when the 'phone rang. It was chiefy asking me to inform the Old Man that we could now proceed, but only at reduced revolutions which would provide a steaming speed of 'an optimistic seven knots'. Captain Malcolm's reaction was something along the lines that 'at least this would keep us moving'. We had sufficient coal aboard to cover the extra steaming time this would add to our trip but I suspected Father was far from happy.

It was with a sigh of relief from all hands that we finally took the Tees pilot, entered the Fairway, and proceeded up river to our berth. As I put the finishing touches to our after moorings, and awaited the fixing of rat-guards to all mooring lines before dismissing my crew, I leaned over the docking bridge rail listening to ship noises around me. I reflected for a few moments on a voyage which had, so far as weather was concerned, been one of the worst in my experience. As if to make some sort of amends (or simply to 'take the mickey'), the sea was like the proverbial mill pond with a brilliant sun shining contentedly from a cloudless sky, and the wind wafting only the most gentle of breezes (termed 'light airs' in the logbook) across the tranquil scene. My reveries were broken by a 'phone call from Pat asking if I could look after the gangway as he was busy with the Old Man sorting out some paperwork. Meandering happily amidships, I found the bosun had virtually completed this task and glanced on the jetty below watching customs officers and sundry other officials, representing the paraphernalia of inward port clearance, waiting keenly to come aboard.

I was called to the saloon a little while later to discuss with the Customs my entries on the C142 clearance form, none of which caused too many problems. I had always found that if I was honest with the Customs then they immediately reciprocated (not that such virtue had prevented me in the past from indulging in bringing ashore the occasional undeclared bottle). I then signed-off before the shipping master and, once the Captain was free, proceeded to his cabin to enquire my fate. It was always a burning question whether or not I might be allowed to go for a well-deserved leave (at least in my opinion) or if I would be asked to remain for further trips. He soon put me out of my misery as he handed my Watchkeeping Certificate covering the entire voyage since Cardiff (almost light years behind me) and informed that my relief would be joining the ship next morning and, once he arrived, I could go home. He, the Mate, chief and second engineers were also to be relieved (in more ways than one I suspected regarding the latter two) and that, upon completing discharge, *Lady Vedera* was to be put out of her misery and towed round to Inverkeithing in Scotland for a well-earned scrapping.

Following this news, things seemed something of an anticlimax so I made my way to Mike's cabin and flopped onto his sofa, joining he and Pat for a relaxing drink. Even better news was that cargo would not be commencing until 0800 next day so we could all have a night in our bunks with Pat doing the duty officer stint − not that being on stand-by in case of an emergency would interfere too much with his rest. For a while we just sat around, absolutely shattered, discussing finer and wilder points of the voyage until the supper gong sounded calling us to a welcome meal. The highlight of the evening (needless to say) were my 'phone calls home and lengthy chats with Sue and then my parents – a subtle shift in emphasis of relationships. It appeared that everyone was well, looking forward to a 'tremendous reunion' and that all of my letters from South America and Russia had been safely received. I spent the remainder of the evening savouring the stillness and solitude of my cabin, gently reading, and feeling the generators throbbing quietly against my back whilst I unwound and relaxed in my bunk.

Jim Dewar came from Hull so did not have too far to travel and arrived around 1100 next day. He had served his cadetship with Clan Line before joining Empress Shipping and was on his second trip as second officer. Completing my hand-over of navigation gear and medical locker took us until lunch, following which I caught the 1430 London train and arrived home later that evening.

I was called to the Kremlin the following day and spent a pleasant hour or so with Captain Ford who intimated my leave could be as much as six months duration – if I wished to take all leave due, but the Group would be quite happy for me to liquidate some of this and then find me another ship 'as soon as I felt ready to go away again'. It seemed the demand for certificated officers had not diminished during my time away. I was more than pleased to hear this, knowing such a lengthy period of time at home would probably prove too much for my system. I was not yet ready for shore life as a regular hobby. He did mention the possibility of my doing Masters', but I killed that one stone dead by informing him I did not feel quite ready both academically and professionally, even though I had accrued more than adequate sea-time – which seemed to cover all options. I reminded him of my desire to serve aboard one of the Group's new 100,000-sdwt tankers, having learned from the house magazine that two of these were now in service, with a number of others in various stages of completion.

I took the opportunity of visiting again my favourite bookshop – Potter's in the Minories – not looking for anything specific, but merely browsing. The shop was quite busy with a number of obvious yachties seeking an assortment of maritime necessities (including, I hoped up-to-date books explaining the collision regulations). Suddenly I caught sight of a face which seemed familiar so crossed the shop towards its owner, greeting him casually. He glanced round but informed me he did not recognise me. I could read the thought in his face that this might be 'some form of pick-up' and felt the eyes of everyone burning into me as other customers watched and listened with increasing interest. Of course, I could not immediately place where our paths had crossed, nor remember his name. To say the situation was growing increasingly embarrassing was putting things mildly. I could not let the situation go at this point so asked him if he was in the Merchant Navy. He confirmed this was so, causing the tension within me to ease a little, but then said he still did not know me, which brought it on again. Suddenly, my guardian angel came to the rescue for I remembered, and confronted him, that his name was Derek McFay. He admitted this and asked in turn if I was with Ellertons which I was more than happy to confirm. We both racked our minds, and suddenly the penny dropped that we had indeed met previously. As the circumstances came flooding back, I recalled that as a newly-promoted third officer I had relieved him in Southampton Docks following his 19-month trip aboard the *Earl of Gourock*. I felt the atmosphere in the entire shop relax. I agreed with him that it was hardly surprising he did not recognise me for our meeting had been transitory, to put things mildly, at a time when he was anxious to leave the ship. I felt so relieved I suggested we had a drink in a nearby hostelry with me willingly – even eagerly – buying the first round. The incident was not a world-shattering event, but it became engrained indelibly on my memory bank as potentially one which could have been more than slightly awkward.

I lasted just under three months before getting again 'itchy feet' as my father – ever one with an appropriate phrase – described my situation. Sue was inevitably upset, which of course upset me, but the inevitable was precisely that, so shortly afterwards, I met up with Captain Ford to discuss my immediate future. Possible posting to a tanker was again off the agenda as, once again, they were all properly manned and at sea.

It appeared the vessel to which I would be assigned was presently unclear but, it was stressed that the Group was short of deck and engineering officers across all companies. I saw my noble employer glance directly at me and then reach for a thick folder. Opening this he begin sifting through assorted sheets containing seemingly endless lists of officer and ship names. I do not know what I detected in that brief glance, but some instinct made me take the opportunity of reminding him that, including leave periods, I had helped out the Group by serving aboard 'alien craft', as I termed Regal and Empress Line ships, for over two years and felt now that return to an Ellerton vessel would be appreciated. He paused in his paper shifting and, laying aside the current batch, reached for another wad from the other side of his desk. Catching my glance, he assured me that this could be arranged, leaving me with the distinct impression that it was indeed towards such another 'alien' he had been intending to assign me. I was glad to have nipped that action in the bud and thanked my personal maritime guardian angel for the prompt. Captain Ford pursed his lips in between his seeking, and stated how appreciative he had been of my assistance by serving aboard these ships, confirming that I would definitely be appointed as second officer to one of three Ellertons due to sail shortly. I listened in silence waiting for him to continue, determined to turn down any other offers – however tempting. He then promised my next appointment would be either the *Earl of Plymouth,* due out of Avonmouth and bound for South and East Africa and then towards India and the United States Gulf ports; the *Earl of Hereford* on the Liverpool,

India and Australasia run; or the *Earl of Nottingham,* sailing from Tilbury for the Far East. Most of these were familiar ports and destinations but, given a choice, the *Plymouth* with her United States Gulf ports had greatest appeal. Either way, I would be quite happy with any of these three ships, knowing it would be grand to sail again on an Asian-crewed vessel, and head for warmer waters. Meantime I was to return home, keep myself readily available, and await further instructions.

Chapter 5

PERSONALITIES, PAINT ... AND POETRY

———

Immediately on joining the *Earl of Nottingham,* lying at Ellerton's berth in Tilbury Docks, I detected a 'tense' atmosphere that left me feeling vaguely disturbed. The *secunny* on gangway duty who helped the taxi driver carry cases and gear to my cabin offered a customary warm greeting, but his look contained a guarded furtiveness that made me pause and study him more closely. Venturing to make myself known to Keith Harrison the chief officer, following the customary practice of reporting on board, offered little by way of reassurance. A galaxy of gold braid met me for he was in conclave with the chief and second engineers listening to Sparks ranting on alarmingly. Someone had clearly been tampering with his terminals. The scenario was definitely odd for, with such a disciplined company, it was unusual to find so many officers accumulated in the Mate's quarters at 1000 hours the day after return from coasting. Invariably far too much work required finalising before going deep-sea from this transit dock – usually within two or three weeks of arrival. They glanced up at my entry, looking (perish the thought) almost guilty. My face must have shown mystification. Keith leapt from his chair greeting me and simultaneously calling for the officers' steward and placing an order for coffee. I found at least some comfort in this observance of usual formalities. At his invitation, both engineers moved along the Mate's luxurious settee making room for me. Sparks sprawled glowering dejectedly in the armchair, leaving the Mate reseated alongside his blue Formica-topped table. Forestalling further introductions, and in an effort to filter this air of gloom, I greeted the chief warmly, reminding him we had sailed on the *Earl of Gloucester* some years previously. He was then a junior chief during an East African voyage just prior to my entering nautical college for Second Mates.

After a brief 'how are you – good to see you again' session we all chatted more widely, sharing small talk about company ships and officers, until the steward came in with a large tray of coffee and a plate of biscuits.

It was then down to business, for I was informed of the bizarre behaviour of the Master during the recent coastal trip and learnt how since then he had been acting alarmingly strangely. When my shadow crossed their doorway, they thought it was the Old Man. Only the previous day, immediately following berthing at Tilbury, the chief engineer received an unexpected summons to the Master's cabin. The latter demanded to examine the engine-room movement book and, in front of the chief, called in the third mate telling him to compare this with the one from the bridge to ascertain consistency of times. He had driven the Mate almost demented by wanting to see his cargo loading plans prior to arrival, and twice since then. As an additional pre-breakfast treat, the Captain sent for his purser wanting to know what stores were expected. Well-satiated with bacon and eggs, immediately upon returning to his office he 'phoned Sparks, insisting the ship's radio log covering the coastal voyage be bought to him forthwith. Then, poor old John faced an exhaustive examination on these routine entries. This third degree precipitated the explosive outburst greeting my arrival. Continuation of Captain Sawley's little catalogue of eccentricities was interrupted by a strident ringing of the desk telephone, which Keith jumped to answer. We watched his face cloud over, saw his features harden and, from the one-sided conversation repeated for our benefit, learned that the Master required an inspection of the ship arranged for 1200 that day. Gradually recognising the difficulties this would cause, across entire departments already frantically involved in a multitude of essential routines, caused us to look at each other aghast and in shocked amazement. Not only that, a full inspection would clash with lunch – and, after all, there was nothing to beat a satisfying meal in maintaining equilibrium – especially during times of maritime adversity. I felt the atmosphere was too tense to voice this aphorism: it might have given the impression that my treatment of the situation was a little too light. After coffee, still prepared to keep an open mind, I went to my cabin, changed into working gear of serge battle-dress drill jacket and trousers, then meandered along to the Master's cabin to report on board and sign Articles. In view of the fact Captain Sawley was doing the deep-sea trip I 'forgot' to bring with my Discharge Book the Mate's Certificate which, by law, he had to record before we entered into Agreement. In this purposeful way, my signing-on would have to be postponed which would give me further time to reassess the situation. It was a far from cordial meeting. Looking up in response to my knock, he called me from across the cabin suggesting I came over and stood *to attention* in front of his desk, offering a reminder of days both before and during my cadetship, when reasonably before a ship's Master this protocol was perfectly acceptable. That I was by now a second officer normally attracted a more relaxed reception with any captain. He enquired how long it had been since first I arrived on board his vessel. I told him a couple of hours and talked about meeting the Mate and then stowing away my gear. He immediately blasted forth his admonition that I should have reported to him before even going to my cabin, 'let alone having coffee with the chief officer'. There was not much to say in response to that, for technically he was correct, even though my action in seeing the Mate initially was perfectly correct and normal. Incidentally, although an unspoken thought, my pot of joining coffee and biscuits was far from a technical matter as far as I was concerned. I merely looked blank and shrugged my shoulders expressively. He broke the tense pause by telling me he wanted a complete and detailed voyage plan, accompanied by all relevant chart work, covering our Far Eastern trip to Singapore. This was to be ready for discussion before we sailed. His demands were so preposterously unacceptable (with the chances of success frankly impossible) that, although offering agreement purely for the sake of form, I simply refused to take his order seriously. My previously open mind soon closed. More disturbing was the distinctly far-away look in his eyes as he spoke. It was as if equally distant thoughts preoccupied him, although Heaven alone could guess what (or even where) these might have been. The situation did not prove particularly upsetting for there was clearly something wrong with him, leaving me thinking (not particularly optimistically) that the local marine superintendent ought to be informed and his advice sought.

I found Keith on the main deck by number two hatch discussing loading with Charles Day, the third officer on cargo watch. Smiling broadly, the events concerning

A weekly officers' conference in the captain's day room prior to sailing (courtesy BP plc).

my meeting with Father were briefly related enabling mutual sharing of mystification and sympathy. We talked further about the Old Man and what courses might be open to us. Before having an opportunity to moot my suggestion, Keith told me he had already approached Captain Bassey when he came on board earlier that morning, but had received little support and even less satisfaction. Local marine superintendent Bassey was a 'traditional Company servant' – an innocent nautical euphemism speaking volumes. Our paths had already crossed during previous voyages, which incorporated Tilbury within their itinerary, but I had never found him sympathetic to any opinion other than his own. This had been emphasised particularly during a débâcle concerning crew handling when I was a newly-promoted fourth officer. His treatment of that incident had left a clear impression that he and I were unlikely to become bosom friends. Before promotion ashore he had served deep-sea as a Master, originally in sail (no mean achievement), and was now close to retirement. He claimed a reputation for being a 'fire eater' (something of which I was well aware) and had apparently given his opinion to the Mate that Captain Sawley's behaviour, whilst '*possibly* a little fussy,' was certainly not extraordinary. With an apparent glint in his eye, he had confirmed they had known each other since early days as Ellerton junior officers, that each had a fine record during the last war (both complete irrelevances for the latter had ended over twenty years previously), and that the Mate should continue to do exactly as he was told. It was no wonder Keith appeared so jumpy.

Anyway, at 1200 precisely I stood-to at my inspection station, in a lonely deserted wheelhouse, preparing my voyage plan and initial charts for the forthcoming voyage. This was something I would have to do anyway. It seemed an action perfectly logical and consistent with such bizarrely uncharacteristic circumstances. The party consisting of captain, followed by the Mate with both senior engineers and purser in tow, finally entered and spread themselves around the chart table cluttered with my navigational paraphernalia. Seeing the frown crossing the Old Man's countenance, even before he halted and spoke, was similar to that lull before the proverbial storm. He glanced intently in my direction and without speaking directly to me said to the Mate that 'This officer is not wearing his cap. Ask him *why* he's not wearing his cap!'

Keith duly turned to me: 'The Captain wants to know why you are not wearing your cap.'

Looking at Keith casually I said, 'I never wear my cap when not on deck'.

Keith duly reported this verbatim to the Master. There was a pause: 'Tell this officer his cap is part of Company uniform and, as such, should be worn on all official inspections by the Captain whether or not these are on deck or internal.'

Barely masking his humour, he passed this information to me. I could see the chief and second exchanging amused glances behind the Old Man's back whilst the poor purser, standing in full view, had to exercise considerable restraint. Captain Sawley however had not finished. Still not speaking to me, he again turned to the Mate: 'Ask this officer why he is working. He should be waiting for my inspection party to arrive and then come to attention when we enter the wheelhouse. This he has omitted to do.'

It was like a scene from a stage farce, or the popular *Navy Lark* programme on the radio. Keith however dutifully turned to me and again repeated the Captain's words. Thoroughly fed up with this charade by now I pointedly threw my dividers onto the English Channel chart below me and cast a cold eye on Keith and with just a slight acerbity in my voice that was possibly lost on the Captain, but certainly not his retinue, said 'Tell the Captain wasting time is *not* one of *my* prerogatives and add please that I am due in the saloon for luncheon *soon* before relieving the third officer on deck. Having been out there for five hours, he is probably starving as well as needing a break.'

Following delivery, admittedly an edited version of this little love message, we all paused awaiting the reaction. Captain Sawley however ignored the repeated information, suggesting instead that Keith pass on to me that: 'This officer has not yet signed Articles. You should remind him I need to see his Certificate of Competency before he can be signed-on and accepted as a member of my wardroom.'

I refrained from the obvious comments. There are generally no wardrooms on merchant ships apart from P&O liners which, due to their adopted air of aloofness (some even said snobbishness), were universally recognised amongst the more placid Merchant Navy as mildly maritime eccentricities unique unto themselves. Wardrooms generally belong to Royal Navy officers, with the captain invited as a guest. I would willingly wear my cap when not on deck just to keep the peace, but had no intention of signing away my life for an unknown period to a ship's master who seemed in a deranged mental state. By the time these thoughts had grown the retinue had left the wheelhouse, but not before Keith turned backwards to me grinning widely, and passing what is known as the two-fingered 'Merchant Navy salute', which was heartedly reciprocated by my impenitent self.

Joining the other officers (without my cap) for a very late luncheon, the atmosphere in our saloon (appropriately, I thought) was as thick as the green pea soup of our first course. It was so uncharacteristically different from the relaxed ethos normally accompanying all meals aboard Ellerton ships.

My entry coincided with an exhibition on the Old Man's part concerning what seemed to be a complaint about food. Our poor purser was standing to attention in front of him receiving, to the embarrassment of all, a 'right dressing down'. Ellertons were an excellent company where food was concerned, with the purser's catering staff receiving generous rates per head for all meals, resulting in a varied and interesting menu providing good quality, well prepared and cooked food. That this affair took place, not in the privacy of the Master's cabin, its rightful place (assuming there was a rightful place for such antics), but in public before the purser's own ratings, was a complete effrontery. Taking my seat, and joining the muttered monosyllabic *sotto voce* conversations from the four non-centre tables, I ordered my next dishes from an immaculate Goanese steward. Eating these quickly, I went to relieve the long-suffering third mate by number two hatch. He was clearly wondering what was happening.

When I joined them, Benson the senior cadet was in a high state of dudgeon, and recounting something of the storm caused by the inspection party in their accommodation. Apparently nothing had been right and he and his junior had listened appalled as the Master told his chief officer to bring them to the captain's office that afternoon for disciplinary action which would entail their 'being logged'. This was a punishment of such severity that, if it were imposed on lads in a company such as Ellertons, could under normal circumstances lead to termination of their cadetships. I related all that had happened to me, amplifying reasons for the lengthy delay to their meals, and confirming the situation seemed far from normal, offering in my own way some minuscule reassurance to the cadet that *perhaps* their guest star appearance just might not be forthcoming after all. Charles and Benson took off for the duty mess muttering something mutual about feeling safer eating there than in the officers' saloon.

Whilst supervising the *serang's* deck crew as they prepared to close our MacGregor hatch covers in the face of perhaps a symbolic, but rapidly approaching deep black rain cloud, I thought on events concerning the captain. Sheltering behind his very privileged position with deck officers, the *serang* sidled over, mentioning cautiously the unrest that the recent inspection had caused not only with his department, but also with engine-room and catering staff. That this senior rating's men had noticed the Master's bizarre behaviour was quite apparent and accounted for the impression gained from the *secunny* on joining just five hours previously. I remained supportively noncommittal, but decided adamantly that this state of affairs was quite unacceptable. Whatever Bassey may or may not think of the situation facing us, my delicate temperament was definitely not prepared to be ravaged by sailing deep-sea with Captain 'Typhoon' Sawley, as I had privately named him. Firmly resolved, I decided to tell Keith of my intention to telephone Captain Ford at the Kremlin that very afternoon, advising him of the situation aboard this ship.

Whilst entering the accommodation, I saw two chauffeur-driven saloon cars coasting to a halt at the bottom of the gangway. Coincidental with the start of a heavy downpour, the deputy chief marine and radio superintendents emerged from one, followed by bosses of the engineering and pursers' departments from the other. It was clear the Seventh Cavalry had arrived. Entering our smoke-room, I saw what must have been the entire complement of officers assembled. Keith came over and updated me as he crossed the cabin. He, the chief, second engineers, and purser, together with Sparks, had chatted immediately following lunch and decided to overrule Bassey and contact their respective bosses in London directly. The telephone lines must have been positively humming. I had seen the outcome on the quay. At that moment, the posse of superintendents headed purposefully towards us requesting we form in our departments in various parts of the lounge. We were encouraged to speak freely and openly and, pointedly, to ignore Captain Bassey who (never one to miss an opportunity) had tagged himself on to this entourage and was standing by the lounge doors. It was our golden opportunity so, led by Keith we did precisely that, hearing across the room other raised voices, expressing (to be fair to them) mainly concern for this totally unprecedented situation.

After a while, the superintendents left us still looking determined, but heading this time in the direction of the Old Man's cabin. About an hour afterwards as we went about our respective duties they departed the ship, but not before the marine super stopped off to speak with Keith. As the latter reported to us the directors had decreed that, subject to their investigations, Captain Sawley should be relieved of his command and would depart the ship next day. Keith was to be temporarily in charge until the appointment of a new Master. The Mate suggested we return to our duties immediately, advising us he would inform the third officer, and speak to our *serang* and both deck cadets. He thought it would be a good idea for me to continue my chart work, and then relieve Charles when the shore gangs stopped work at 1700, after which I was to be duty officer until 0800 next morning.

After supper, I leaned on a dry part of the rail alongside the starboard side after lifeboat, glancing casually at the deserted quay below. It was so refreshingly quiet following the day's phenomenal events, and the heavy downpour that had terminated cargo well before the usual knocking-off time. The rain had only recently stopped. I watched the reflection of adjacent cranes and warehouse in a massive puddle over twenty feet below me on the jetty. Thinking back on the day's events I noticed absent-mindedly how it was dappled with occasional water drops and rainbow patterns from smudged grease. The sight recalled a line of Gerard Manley Hopkins, 'like the ooze of oil crushed,' and I trawled my mind trying to recall the poem from which these apposite words originated. Yes, that was it, I was certain – *God's Grandeur*. For a man who had never served anywhere near a ship he had certainly captured the essence of this sight before me. My literary reverie was broken by Benson coming alongside enquiring if there were specific duties for him to do. His was the 'glorious' task of duty cadet with me, not that either of us would be overworked unless a full-scale emergency occurred. I guessed we had experienced sufficient of those for one day (or even one, or more, voyages). Benson was clearly relieved at not being logged and wanted to talk about things concerning the Master so, thinking it best to let him get it off his chest, proffered him his opportunity. After all, it was not often a captain with Ellertons became relieved of command and, as it transpired, dismissed from the company. In fact, the only previous occasions when I had heard about any of such exalted rank meeting with disaster was initially during my cadetship on the *Earl of Melbourne*. This concerned Captain Thurlow who even then had not been sacked, but merely demoted from one of the larger passenger liners to master of a cargo ship. The second occasion was the incident related earlier that I heard about whilst third officer on *Countess Elizabeth*. Those direct actions had both occurred through overindulging in alcohol as enthusiastic contributions towards entertaining their passengers.

Suddenly, what sounded like a two-toned bugle or trumpet blowing peremptory blasts interrupted our chat. We looked at each other briefly in utter amazement and, totally bemused by such an alien sound, moved towards the after-end of the boatdeck, automatically following this to its apparent source. We might have guessed of course. Just across the main dock in Number 31 berth was P&O's *Himalaya* with the recently berthed Orient's *Oronsay* moored astern. They were each outdoing the other in conducting a ceremony of flags, during which both ships required half a dozen officers, cadets and quartermasters, stationed collectively in the bows, on the bridge and astern. At the bugle blast the forward Jack, midships House flag, and after Blue Ensign were simultaneously lowered. It was very impressive but, as General Bosquet was reputed to have observed concerning the magnificent Charge of the Light Brigade at Balaklava, 'certainly not the (Merchant Navy's kind of) war'. Eccentricities indeed! Openly grinning at each other, I suggested for Benson's first duty he take the watch *secunny*, together with the Mate's stand-by whistle, and go and do likewise to our limp and rain soaked ensign draped forlornly around our flag mast at the after part of our docking bridge. He looked at me a little blankly. Then the penny dropped that gently before his eyes had passed a joke – and then scooted down aft on his own to do the necessary with our own ensign. As our House flag (and indeed the ensign normally) customarily remained hoisted the whole of time in port, there being no need to lower these, my little missive had clearly fallen well short of target.

As the boy departed I reflected on our recent conversation. Our two deck cadets were in their third year, hence quite senior, with a couple of weeks in age between them and six months or so in sea-time, but then the difference of only a day was sufficient to decide seniority. Benson was a fairly new breed of company cadet, proficient enough practically and not afraid of hard dirty work but, alas, not overblessed with too many active brain cells. Keith confirmed he was 'a practical lad', who had survived an Outward Bound course for pre-sea training, having been at a minor public school prior to that. The Mate's heavily-loaded euphemism was his way of telling me, following careful observation of the cadets' journals, that Benson still displayed many weaknesses in academic aspects of his training which had caused problems on previous ships with his understanding of maths and basic theory across a range of subjects. Apparently the result slips of his last two Merchant Navy Training Board annual examinations had been a little too close to the borderline in most subjects for any complacency. As my direct dealings with cadets were precisely in this area, Keith was plainly warning me I might have extra work to do. Although my accelerated short Keddleston navigation college course had proved invaluable whilst serving at sea as a cadet, the deficiency in further in-depth training had left me doing considerable part-time study, most of it in my own time, additional to the generous off-duty allowance for cadets allowed by the company. We both hoped sincerely Benson would prove capable of working similarly hard voluntarily, but agreed he might need encouragement to knuckle down to sustained academic routines. Luckily Colin Ashby, the junior cadet, was in the more conventional Ellerton mode of recent years: an ex-grammar-school boy (like myself) followed (unlike me) by a year at Fleetwood School of Navigation. It was possible they might assist each other, but we both knew the success or otherwise of that venture would depend on how well they related. Ashby was ashore that evening with the third officer and Sparks 'making whoopee' amidst the fleshpots of Gravesend, doubtless living dangerously but I hoped not too much so, especially as running the ship's sick bay remained part of my duties.

I was on cargo watch when Captain Sawley left the ship after lunch next day. We had heard not a sound out of him prior to then as he busied himself packing his gear, and he had taken all meals in his cabin. Both cadets helped with his suitcases to the taxi and I watched as this suddenly aged figure in civilian clothes stooped forlornly down our gangway. It seemed poignantly moving that, as the car moved away both boys simultaneously and devoid of pretension, came to attention and saluted. Obviously, in keeping with most officers I wished him well, but remained adamant that sailing deep-sea with such an unpredictable man in command of ship, cargo and, not least importantly, our lives was a risk too far.

The new Master, Captain Chorley-Jones, joined the ship three days later thus ending Keith's 'moment of glory'. He was a senior Ellerton Master, whose name I had heard through the grapevine and from casual glances in the shipping pages of our Group house magazine. As a vacancy opened, rumour had it that he would command one of the *Countess*-class passenger ships. The Mate knew him from his own junior officer days, when they had sailed deep-sea on the Canadian (Montreal), Australian and New Zealand (MANZ) run for nineteen months, and spoke extremely highly of him. We met during signing-on in his cabin whilst discussing my first-stage voyage plans. I related to him immediately. The Captain possessed that ethos of authoritative self-assurance, emanating from years as Master, which attracted automatic respect. Keith, relieved of his more senior responsibilities, resorted to what I had previously suspected was a rather agitated manner in performing his duties as Mate. We got along extremely well, but I soon learnt to view his occasional energetic outbursts with detached humour. To give him his due, when he discovered Sue and I lived comparatively locally he suggested, as cargo was not being worked from 1700 that Friday until 0800 Monday, I should 'make myself scarce' over that period, before we sailed deep-sea later the following week. I was not backwards in shooting off and caught the Tilbury–Gravesend ferry in time for the semi-fast train to London. During this final stay with my parents, we incorporated pre-sailing Sunday luncheon that included my wife Sue and both sets of parents.

*　　　*　　　*

I had hardly entered the saloon for breakfast the following Monday before Keith caught sight of me from centre table and shot a hurried greeting. Even before I was seated, and without awaiting my reply, he continued by saying how much work there was to be done during the day, including completing 50 tons of general cargo in number three lower hold and finishing the 'tween-decks of two and four. Slightly liverish after a very early start to return on board from home, yet grateful to him for allowing my break, I gently interrupted his flow. Frankly, my immediate interest lay in feeding my face and having that first cup of breakfast coffee, rather than honing-in immediately to ship business. After all, Captain Chorley-Jones was still on board and there were no signs of any new emergencies or, for that matter, repercussions from the last. Glancing at the menu, I simultaneously took my seat. This action brought Keith up a little because, honing-in on my rather pointed non-verbal movements, he clearly recognised the importance of priorities from the broadness of my uniformed back. Before he could continue, I gave my order to the steward and slowly savoured my coffee. Only then did I turn to my boss, inviting him to continue.

The Old Man caught my eye and grinned across a welcome from his seat at the head of the senior officers' table. The exchange had mildly amused him for he was all too well aware of the urgent personality of his chief officer. Slightly raising my eyebrows heavenwards, I sent a sort of knowing half-grin back in response. Keith continued, only slightly abated, obviously assuming I had picked up his previous information. He informed me the third mate was on watch and he could get on with things accompanied by Benson. He meanwhile had to continue further work on an alteration caused to his cargo plan by a recent change in inducements. Taking on additional general for Singapore and Japanese ports meant rearranging our 'tween-decks stowage. He paused and looked at me meaningfully. I waited to see what was coming next as Keith was far from subtle. Although we had already taken the bulk of our deep-sea deck stores, some more had apparently just arrived. I offered to look after these, which was clearly Keith's intention, because he quickly nodded agreement and suggested I could have the junior cadet to help me, together with the deck petty officers and whatever ratings were available.

Focussing on the task ahead, I thought my initial action would be to contact the lorry driver. We usually placed such early casual visitors arriving unexpectedly during meal times in the duty mess for a cup of tea or coffee. Ashby could go there, rake him out, take his delivery notes, and start things moving by mustering the crew. Eating my final piece of toast, heavily laden with butter and favourite thick-cut marmalade, my mind was already working out the best methods for distributing the ratings. Keith looked up sharply and finished his coffee before adding, almost as an afterthought: 'Oh, by the way, Jonathan, these stores have not arrived by lorry, but are loaded in two covered railway wagons in sidings behind the shed. The railway people have already brought our consignment notes from their hut, along with appropriate keys, which are in my office.'

A typical (if rather dilapidated) 15-ton covered railway wagon showing the drop and step height from ground (Author's collection).

The cause for Keith's preoccupation became apparent. He was focussed more on making alterations to his cargo plan than worrying about twenty items outstanding on his deep-sea stores indents, so was quite happy to leave this job with me. The Second had told him previously he awaited some engine-room stores so we assumed the wagons held a mixture of their stuff and ours.

Interrupting our cross-talk, the Second chose that moment to come in and join the top table. The atmosphere in the saloon was back to normal (with a vengeance) for, after an exchange of preliminary greetings, considerable laughter arose from a 'late night ashore' which had clearly been enjoyed. This soon spread into considerable merriment with spontaneous exchanges of quick repartee (incorporating some ingenious punning) that involved Captain Chorley-Jones and most remaining officers. Still smiling, we left the saloon together working out a mutually-advantageous scheme for taking on board our respective stores. It was then the Second informed me that Keith had seconded most of our deck ratings to assist with an urgent repair job in the engine-room, which in turn he had clearly omitted to tell me. It was obvious aboard our 'schooner-run' hooker that an ability to read minds would prove useful and I wondered if the local chandler's store might run any natty lines in crystal balls.

The junior cadet was waiting outside the Mate's office for his orders. He gave me a cautious welcome. Both boys had kept an extremely wise and low profile during the recent débâcle concerning Captain Sawley. Apart from occasional cargo watches we had neither worked nor had many dealings together. Looking at him directly and smiling a response, I removed our indents from the bulkhead clip above Keith's desk. Noting our outstanding stores consisted of a few drums of silvering and other paints plus some assorted oils and varnishes with general small stuff, it was natural to assume the remainder of two large railway wagons must belong to the engineers.

I explained half of our deck crew were already below with the Second, 'helping' the engineering officers with their *serang* on an emergency pre-sailing job in the engine-room – busily taking something to pieces, or putting something back together, or something – so none of his crowd either were immediately available for storing. Ashby immediately linked into the dry tones of my sense of humour, for his response offered a sort of half-smile accompanied by a look from under his eyelids, as it were. Ever practical, I suggested he report to the deck *serang* and ask him to 'meander amiably along the wharf' with whatever members of our crowd would be joining us. Instead of coming empty-handed, they could live dangerously by grabbing a four-wheeled barrow from the cargo shed and meet me at the railway sidings behind the berth. Glancing again at our stores indents, I told him hopefully we could make an immediate start and might even get the job finished before smoke-oh.

Leaving Ashby to go aft and rally the *serang,* together with the ratings who remained from his happy crowd, I wandered over to the sidings thinking back to the plan decided with the Second. We had worked out that the best method would be for me to start by taking our deck stuff. I climbed the footholds and unlocked the first wagon, drew back the heavy wooden door and looked inside. It contained 'one hell of a lot of stores'. Moving over to the second one, I unlocked this and then stood back mystified, checking the labels on the outside of each. It was obvious that both vans were for our ship. There was a third wagon also, but no indication where this might belong as the tally space was helpfully devoid of its customary card. I dismissed this from my mind feeling unsympathetically it was British Rail's problem and not ours.

Waiting for the *serang* and ever-faithful Ashby to arrive, I reflected about our off-loading. It was just as well there were only a few willing workers for, if the Second's crowd were to join in the fun as well, juggling within close confines of two wagons would have led us to getting in each other's way, especially as the stores for both departments were clearly mixed. I decided the things should be locked-up and the keys handed to the Second if a delay occurred between the time when we finished and the engine-room crowd came over. Not, it seemed, there was much chance of that, looking at the amount of stuff that required shifting.

Over the squeaky wheels of the cargo barrow, I could hear the equally squeaky sounds of Ashby, the *tindal* (assistant bosun) and, as they clumped into sight round the corner of the shed, three of our *khalassis*. I cynically hoped that they would work as enthusiastically as they chattered, but then pulled-up sharply for after all that same remark had been made directly about me by a third officer in Africa when I, perhaps unwisely, had been 'an outwardly ruminating cadet', as it was known in the trade. I dismissed this embarrassment by reflecting we were lucky the weather was fine as rain was all we would need.

I glanced at Ashby asking where the *serang* might have disappeared. He advised the chief petty officer was working the remaining two hands on the main deck, whilst the *cassab* sensibly took the stores into his lockers for'ard. Both of us looked into the wagons as I told the cadet we were due to take a veritable 'bulk' of general deck stores, if that might be the correct collective term and if it was not, then surely it ought to be. He detected the questioning tone in my voice and agreed, then hesitatingly suggested another alternative could be, a 'mass' of deck stores. I smiled agreeably in response, telling him whether it was a bulk or a mass did not diminish the amount with which we had to deal. I called out some of the items immediately identifiable that were clearly not engineering stores: one six inch, three-stranded, manila mooring rope; two wire runners, one for each of the five and ten-ton derricks, and something approaching 100 gallons or more of voyage paint, at a quick guesstimate, plainly marked DECK DEPARTMENT. None of these items appeared on the Mate's outstanding indent.

It seemed good training for Ashby if he could get on with it, once I started the ball rolling and saw he had control. The *tindal* had excellent command of the crowd and I was not exactly going to be in Outer Mongolia. Suggesting this brought such alacrity of response that I gained the clear impression he would be well pleased with being in charge of things. Placing this under the general heading of progress and telling him, if he encountered problems, a short note via one of the junior sailors to me in the Mate's office would be the best way forward. By this time, the area outside the wagons looked like my proverbial chandler's locker, moving me to suggest the cadet always left a *khalassi* on guard when bringing over respective batches.

I returned on board, told Keith what was happening shore-side, and offered help with the stowage plan. Together we rearranged the cargo distribution arriving at something sufficiently workable so the ship would not capsize once we cast off our moorings. Keith left to take our joint ideas to the Old Man, keeping him in the picture, whilst I went onto the foredeck to see how Ashby was making out with the stores. It was pleasing to see how advanced he was with his task. Already, two truckloads had been off-loaded onto pallets, winched on board by the crane driver, and moved for'ard by the crowd under the *serang* to the Bosun's store. The lifting of the third coincided with my arrival.

'I hope you don't mind, sir.' The cadet approached me a little apprehensively, making me wonder what had gone wrong, and whether or not any potential 'flak' might be coming my way, in default as it were.

'Hmm…that depends really on what precisely it might be that I don't have to mind,' I replied cryptically – encouragingly, even if not very grammatically.

Ashby explained he had told the crane driver we would give him a case of beer for lifting our stores on board. I breathed a sigh of relief, putting all kinds of imaginary situations behind me, knowing all too well from my cadet days the kind of unbelievable chaos sometimes arising from simple tasks. Thus, happily relieved, I put the boy's mind at rest suggesting I would mention this to the Mate and draw a case from the ship's 'pool' of smokes and beer kept in a special 'bribery and corruption fund'. I suggested Ashby should come and collect it from our chief steward; he could then stow this in the office out of the way so he would know where it was and, as he had negotiated this deal, follow it through with his crane driver, apart of course from paying for it. I did not mention it had been my intention to negotiate such an arrangement, but had forgotten to do so. This must be old age or something I mused, trying some self-encouragement therapy.

Having sorted that out, Ashby went back with the *tindal* to his task, a decidedly contented little cadet. Whilst wandering over to the sidings, I felt warm and glowing inside, reflecting how good it was to spread a little happiness here and there. There might be little difference in seniority between both boys, but it seemed the Mate's forecast was correct: Ashby was by far the brightest star in this particular firmament. He had already launched into the second wagon, although a fair quantity remained for 'the ginger beers.' A thought occurred to me which seemed worth sharing so, suggesting the engineering job below seemed to be taking considerably longer than initially thought (probably because our lads were 'helping') we could lift on board their stores as well as our own, leaving them to check-off the stuff once they had stowed it below. The cadet agreed readily enough, not that I would have expected anything else.

Completion of the 'mutual assistance' storing operation coincided with commencement of our second luncheon sitting. We left those for our 'ginger beers' at the entrance to the engine-room under the watchful eye of the duty *secunny*, until a fireman (or *ag wallah* as our *serang* referred to them) from the engine-room could be detailed to relieve him, allowing his return to gangway duty. I then sent Charles to take his lunch in the saloon, allowing him time afterwards for coffee and a smoke, following which he returned to his cargo watch. Knowing Keith was wandering about keeping a general 'chief officer's' eye everywhere, I 'partook of my own repast' (as I had read in a book somewhere) and then went and got my head down for a short 'zizz', in preparation for a twelve-hour duty-officer stint, until relieved by Charles at 0800 next day.

It was coming up to eleven hundred when the captain's tiger popped along to the chartroom requesting my presence in the Old Man's cabin. Assuming he wished to discuss some aspect of our voyage plan, I straightened pencil and parallel rules on the Gibraltar chart, and popped along. He greeted me with customary pleasantness and charm, but my relaxed smile wavered when I noticed our shore superintendent standing by his desk drinking coffee.

'Captain Bassey tells me that you haven't unloaded all the stores, as he instructed the Mate yesterday.'

As if to reinforce Captain Chorley-Jones' words, Bassey shot me a look of daggers. He had lost considerable prestige over the Captain Sawley incident so was taking 'second wind' to regain the self-respect (at least in his own eyes) consistent with his reputation. Only the Old Man's presence stopped him exploding into a full-blown rage, which is why I suspected our captain handled this situation himself.

I managed to camouflage my racing thoughts: 'Oh?' was all I could utter intelligently, bouncing a look of total bewilderment between my senior officers. 'But I checked the two wagons after Ashby cleared them. I had to in order to sign the railway delivery notes. The fourth engineer took over the engine-room stores and, so far as I am aware, signed also for theirs,' I explained, wondering if the 'ginger beers' had dropped a clanger somewhere along the line.

'Well,' commented the super authoritatively, waving his empty cup in my direction and impatiently snatching the lead from the Old Man: 'There's still a complete van to be unloaded and the railways are becoming extremely agitated. They want to shunt these three wagons out to clear the track for further rolling stock off-loading a Palm Line ship, due this evening after you've sailed.' He accompanied this explanation with another glare.

'Fair enough, sir,' I said mildly to our ship's Captain, pointedly ignoring Bassey: 'I'll look into it with the Mate and follow it up.'

I went to Keith's cabin to tell him of this latest development. He was not there, but eventually I discovered him on the main deck speaking to our *serang*. Seeing me approach, he called in advance that we had now completed loading and advised he was just off to the Old Man confirming our previous booking for pilot and tugs, so we could hopefully catch the early evening tide. Before he could dash off too energetically, I explained we apparently still had another railway wagon of stores in the siding. His look clearly told its own tale, as he not only denied all knowledge of our ship being owed further deck or engineering stores, but suggested as I knew, both departments (and especially ours) were already well overindulged in that area. I suggested the best thing was for me to pop over to the railway office and sort it out – and without further ado off I popped.

After morning coffee and ample milk with my breakfast cereal made their own contributions to my discomfort as I meandered carefully over the railway lines towards the PLA's railway dock offices, so stepping into the nearest public lavatory seemed the most natural thing in the world. Immediately on entering, I caught sight of a dog-eared Jamaica Banana Steamship Company flyer pasted to the dusty wall, with the confident announcement: WE HANDLE YOUR GOODS WITH GREAT CARE. Underneath this some wag had scribbled, *and so do Blue Star Line stewards*. I took this on the chin and, aiming contentedly, glanced around at further missives pencilled across the flaking whitewash. It came as no surprise to learn that *Kilroy was here*. After all, he had made his guest appearance in every public toilet across the world. I recalled with wry amusement, on one occasion at the Mission in Osaka, trying to explain to a German second officer what this really meant. We gave up in the end, completely frustrated, recognising the Teutonic sense of humorous logic created too impenetrable a barrier. Warming to my task, I learnt next that crew members from the Irish Shipping Company had certainly never visited this salubrious establishment – they would hardly have approved of the riddle: 'Why is sperm white and urine yellow?' After a few moments blank reflection, I learnt it was so an Irishman would know whether he was coming or going. This was underneath the bold assertion (sign seen alongside an Irish railway line) NO OVERTAKING. Finishing my task, I observed the futility to fellow users against 'standing on the seat', in the light of some extremely acrobatic Essex crab lice which could allegedly 'jump ten feet'. Finally, whilst closing the zip, the heart-broken poetic lament of an impecunious sufferer arrested my eye. He apparently had 'paid a penny' and then managed only a generous out-bursting of wind in return. Leaving this hall of unmitigated knowledge, however dubious the quality, I reflected that the toilets in Tilbury Docks must represent the most eruditely creative in the world.

Thus refreshed, both physically and mentally (whilst probably diminished morally), my journey continued towards the railway shack where the traffic manager greeted me with mock horror, advising his two clerks 'Cross your legs, lads, the Merchant Navy has arrived'. He was clearly an ex-mariner, although I shuddered to think with what company he might have served. The thought entered my mind that perhaps here resided one of the bog-room artists whose handiwork had contributed so expansively to my ongoing cultural education. Smiling, he continued effusively to greet me like a long lost brother, clearly relating my second mates' battle-dress shoulder straps with the task bringing my august presence to his cabin, and doubtless glad that his wagon was about to be emptied. Reflecting how good it was to be loved, I explained my quandary regarding our stores situation. In turn, he pointed his grubby finger to a dog-eared desk ledger, directing my attention to a hand-scrawled four-lined entry. Being enthusiastically nosy by nature I deciphered, from the booking below, that the Palm Line ship due after us was the delightfully named 7275 grt *Badagry Palm*. He supported his tidings with a further consignment note, one I had not seen before, which he waved proudly in front of my eyes like a talisman. There was no arguing – the message was as large as life: 'Consigned to m.v *Earl of Nottingham* – Number 26 Berth, Tilbury East Branch Docks – Ship's DECK STORES – in Transit.'

Whilst admitting a certain level of defeat and taking the eagerly proffered keys, I went over to the siding, after delicately (but pointlessly) hinting that the lack of a label on this third wagon, and the sudden appearance of an additional consignment note, were not exactly the ship's fault. The previously unused key immediately released the lock and, sliding back the creaking door, there in front of me pasted on the immediate stack of paint drums, was clearly blazoned the stencilled words: DECK STORES. I re-locked the wagon and went back aboard. Keith was nowhere to be found so I took both cadets from the *serang's* happy band busily preparing the ship for sea and, giving Benson the wagon keys, told him to take Ashby and the trolley once again, go back to the third wagon and commence off-loading the thing, advising I would come over later. The cadets could muck-in afterwards with the *serang*. There was little option left to me. Meanwhile, still completely puzzled, I took yet another quick look at our stores indents in the Mate's office. This confirmed that we had in fact already generously exceeded our full quota.

I returned to the siding to find the boys well advanced with loading their trolley. An outraged Benson faced me and, in tones of absolute wonder (no mere phenomenon), he asked if I was aware the wagon was completely filled with paint and assorted oils. There was in fact 'bloody gallons of the stuff, sir,' as he put it. Telling him my preliminary look had seen *some* paint, my burrowing had not penetrated so deeply as theirs and so I had no idea what else 'might be there living dangerously'. Continuing, I explained we had already more than our full voyage consignment stowed safely on board and suggested he and Ashby had best take this lot to the cargo shed and dump it in a lock-up. Meantime I would go and see Captain Bassey, letting him know what we had done, so his office staff could sort out whatever had clearly gone wrong.

Without waiting for his reply, I shot off to see Bassey and organise the lock-up with the dock office. The long-suffering good captain had apparently gone home for his lunch (with a doubtless equally long-suffering wife) so, by the time I had drawn a key from the gaffer in charge, the cadets had arrived with the first squeaky trolley load and were waiting patiently for me. Unlocking the stiff padlock, I encouraged them for their efforts so far, told them they could be left to complete the job and should hand in both delivery note (following my signature) and keys to Bassey's secretary at the dock office, once all was safely gathered in. It seemed relevant to remind them that not everyone ashore had been converted by suggesting they remembered to lock-up the lock-up between trips, otherwise their first load of desirable paint might well have gone on walk-about before they could return with the next batch. Amidst an exchange of broad smiles, I gave Benson the keys and left them to get on with things.

It was at about 1600, whilst ashore taking the final draught, I thought I heard over the bustle of dockside noise someone calling my name. Glancing up to the ship's rail and seeing nobody leaning over, I continued jotting down the forward figures, before pausing and listening more carefully. This time there was no mistaking the blast of angry tones: 'Caridia, I am calling you. Come over here.'

I glanced up to see Captain Bassey waving at me wildly from a nearby shed exit. Placing the notebook into my battledress pocket, and wondering what might have caused this outburst of unrestrained love, the thought crossed my mind that perhaps the cadets had omitted to 'lock up the locker' after all. It was the only thing occurring to me that might have gone wrong.

He called again, in even more stentorian tones, causing passing dockers to glance in our direction with interest. My hackles started to rise – rapidly. Being the first to concede I was no gentleman, officer status had been conferred upon me for many years now and being called by my surname, without the courtesy of a title, had been alien since distant cadet days.

Going to the shed it soon became apparent what was biting him as he led me towards the lock-up and pointed at the paint: 'I told you to put those stores on board, didn't I? Not stow them in the bloody lock-up. They're no good there and you're sailing tonight.'

'Yes, but... ,' I tried to explain.

'Don't argue with me,' followed his explosively rude interruption, as he pressed keys and the wad of much abused delivery notes into my hand: 'You just do as you're told – get on with it. I'm not having the ship delayed by your inefficiency.'

'OK, if that's what you want I'll most certainly do it, with the greatest of lines in pleasure,' I responded, equally as ferociously, and pointedly ignoring our audience of amused dockers.

The thought of acknowledging such ignorance with that customary mark of respect appropriate to addressing an ex-ship's master and local super, rightly or wrongly, went by the board. Still livid, I stormed up the gangway and, much to the bemusement of the *serang*, once more grabbed the cadets from their ill-fated pre-sea duties, went to the shed lock-up and supervised personally taking on board these stores.

Cadets snake out an eight-inch mooring rope on the main deck in preparation for departure from port (courtesy BP plc).

We loaded paint in its appropriate locker, already bursting at its nautical seams. The residue was despatched to contactor houses serving every forward and after hatch, port and starboard...to the fo'c'sle head... inside our funnel... to my store abaft the wheelhouse, the carpenter's shop, gyro room...and wedged into the steering flat. I even stowed a few surplus tins under the table in the cadets' study.

There was paint everywhere.

As doors were open nothing was visible but a veritable sea of drums and cans. Five gallon, one gallon, even a forty-gallon drum of some unidentifiable oil whose label had fallen off. There were round tins, oblong and square, covering virtually every colour and shade imaginable. Paints for the hull, deck, funnel, derricks and masts jockeyed anxiously for position with colsa, raw and boiled oils, greases, varnishes, turpentine, and (appropriately enough) paint stripper. The gloriously endless tally read like a ship's chandler's delight. A complete cornucopia of containers.

Our Asian deck crew were happily rolling canisters everywhere in between sorting out mooring ropes, stoppers, rat-guards and warps, whilst the bemused *cassab* wrung his hands in abject mystification, wandering around the main deck in a trance, muttering in fragmented Hindustani something indefinable along the lines of 'Oh my goodness… these athings I no understand, Sahib'.

The Mate, busy finalising preparations on deck for sailing, watched in open-eyed wonder as even more sundry drums were swung on board. Using customary merchant naval language he queried, 'What the ******* hell's going on, Jon?'

Still bursting with frustrated anger, I momentarily forgot he knew little of recent events shore-side, so reassured him there was no major catastrophe and that our antics were caused directly by the irascible nature of Bassey, that he had actually ordered me to take this stuff on board so that was precisely what I was doing. He shrugged expressively and suggested we should chat later, as there was no time presently to sort things out in the hustle of pre-sailing, but could do so when we were at sea.

And so, with her *cassab* baffled now to the point of silence; her third mate, deck *serang,* crew and cadets creased uncontrollably with hysterical laughter; her second officer fuming; her Mate bewildered; her Master in apparent ignorance, and totally besotted with paint; the good ship *Earl of Nottingham* left Tilbury for Far Eastern ports.

As we cleared Gravesend Reach, I saw bustling tugs lining-up *Badagry Palm* for the dock entrance and wondered vaguely if her time alongside would prove as profitably entertaining as had been our lot.

Benson upset the captain just after leaving the Bay of Biscay. Keith had put the boys on afternoon watches following a morning's deck work with the crew – Benson with me on the twelve-to-four, and Ashby on his own four-to-eight. With customary beguiled sense of fun, Benson had spread the hood to the radar with boot polish hoping to catch out his erstwhile little companion Ashby. Unfortunately for him, Captain Chorley-

A ship's captain relaxing in his day cabin (courtesy BP plc).

The Captain looks into the radar hood ascertaining shipping in relation to his own vessel (courtesy BP plc).

Jones chose the moment of changing watches to discuss some aspect of cargo work with Keith and, passing the set had automatically glanced down the hood, ascertaining the shipping position in relation to his vessel. He looked up, blissfully unaware that across his forehead, bridge of his nose and around his face appeared the outline of the hood. Keith and I in the midst of routines for changing watch, completely unaware of Benson's venture into the artistic world, glanced casually across in the Old Man's direction as he came towards us. We saw the result of Benson's labours and restraining ourselves, at least partially, continued discussing gyro, magnetic compass courses, and the shipping situation with barely subdued chuckles. This made the Old Man look even more closely at us, clearly wondering what was happening to his two senior navigating officers, in the midst of such a normally serious exchange. Ashby had disappeared onto the port bridge wing and we could just catch occasional glimpses through the windows of his bottom bobbing up and down as he rolled around convulsed with hysterical laughter. Benson was standing by the telegraph, shooting alternative looks of malignant hatred towards Ashby, unrestrained shock in the direction of his Captain, and poignant hopelessly appealing glances at us. Of course, Sparks chose that moment to come along with the latest weather report, took an amused look at Ashby writhing around his legs, then saw the Master, and burst out laughing. This very traditional Captain then asked collectively the cause of such hilarity amongst his officers, to which no one was sufficiently brave to reply with honesty. We mumbled something about 'an internal joke', into which category perhaps this might fall. Bemused, Captain Chorley-Jones told me to remain on the bridge for a while longer and ordered Keith to his cabin, there to discuss the cargo question in a more befitting mood of sanity.

A few minutes later the 'phone rang. The Captain wished to see Benson in his day cabin IMMEDIATELY. Ashby meanwhile had joined Sparks and myself, and was contributing his own version of what might be brewing for his senior cadet. We watched as Benson went below to receive his just reward, passing Keith *en route*, who was returning to the wheelhouse. The Mate told us he could hear the blast of the Old Man's blistering to Benson through the closed door of the master's office. We all waited with interest as a very subdued Benson returned to do the cadet-watch hand-over with Ashby, surreptitiously trying to wipe his handiwork from the radar hood with an appallingly filthy handkerchief. Being a proverbial 'fifth columnist' on occasions, it fell to my little lot to inform the assembled company that Benson had at least managed to perform one job with unbridled success, receiving in return a myriad of varied and interesting reactions. It was with considerable relief, we suspected, that Benson received his stand-down to the cadets' cabin, as Keith and I exchanged further amused glances as we completed our changeover.

The next day, Benson and Ashby were taken to the Master by Keith who had caught them fighting furiously in their study that morning. 'They were knocking the seven bells of hell out of each other,' he nonchalantly told me concerning the situation. Benson sported a delightfully-coloured black eye and his junior was left with a split lip and blood-stricken nose. I of course, once the chronometers had been checked and wound, went to the sickbay to do my best to patch them up, before despatching them to the Captain to receive a verbal rocket (not a 'logging'). The hopes of Keith and me that Benson and Ashby could benefit from each other's experience had indeed witnessed fulfilment but, so often in keeping with seafaring life, not in the direction anticipated. It fell to my lot to attempt to fill the gaps lamentably existing in Benson's professional and academic knowledge.

Just as we had cleared the Suez Canal, Ashby experienced his own downfall, but with probably more humour than malice, much to the delight of Benson anyway. Keith set both boys the traditional cadet task of maintaining upkeep of the midships accommodation block. Ashby was chipping away at rust around the saloon windows a few moments before the senior officers' lunch sitting. Turning round to reply to something the *serang* asked him concerning some follow-up work relevant to his task, Ashby unwisely continued chipping. There was an almighty tingling crash as his hammer plunged through the ½ inch thick armoured plate glass of the saloon window. The Goanese stewards looked on with horror whilst the purser, hearing 'such an unmistakable sound' (as he later described it) hurried into his saloon. Both actions coincided with the grand entrance of Captain Chorely-Jones with the Mate and chief engineer each glowing brightly from a pre-lunch gin or two. All three took in the situation at a glance. Keith, with considerable laughter, left little time in relating to me this latest débâcle regarding his cadets. The Master stopped, surveying the tableau before him of stewards, cadet Ashby (complete with misplaced chipping hammer), the purple-faced purser and multitudinous shards of glass covering the starboard-side carpet. Keith stated his sense of timing was faultless: the Captain shot a look of devastating sternness at the scene, and with icy voice turned to a very white-faced cadet under his Red Sea tan, uttering these immortal words: 'Ashby. You are a very young cadet with quite limited knowledge. Suffice it to say even to one as inexperienced as yourself, glass does not corrode. There is, therefore, no reason for you to chip it.'

The comment broke the ice as certainly as the window for the captain's burst of laughter met its match in a ruefully relieved sickly grin on the face of the miscreant. The stewards cleaned up the mess with dustpan and brush and mealtime continued. The poor old purser however was not so forgiving, not that there was much he could do in the light of the Captain's attitude, apart from administering his own blistering admonition about carelessness, which did comparatively little harm to Ashby. The cadet took the correct view that he had got off pretty lightly in the face of things and, licking carefully a still healing lower lip, turned-to gratefully with the Asian carpenter that afternoon to replace the offending pane before going at 1600 to his bridge watch.

Our cadets on this trip seemed just a little fated. Benson (it had to be) was a railway fanatic. Keith often pondered that his talents and interests in 'Clara-chuffs', as he put it, might not have been better employed navigating a steam engine. Rubbing (yet again) my own handful of salt into the wound, I reminded them both that the cadet had already showed considerable dexterity in unloading wagons, adding I could visualise him waving a little green flag or shaking a black lantern from the stern of a guard's van attached to an endless run of paint wagons. It was somewhat incongruous, before supper on those (luckily rare) days when the sea was flat calm with low swell, to hear recordings of the Royal Scot trundling its way painfully up Shap Fell, or some other incredible incline, and had led to much laughter and gentle teasing, all of which Benson had taken in fairly good spirits. As he played the records at full volume, the sound of chugging trains and the shrieking penetrating pierce of frenetic engine whistles were audible virtually all over the accommodation.

His 'great train crash', as I termed it, happened shortly after we had left Aden and were ourselves chugging happily across a placid Indian Ocean towards Colombo. It was the morning of the Old Man's Saturday inspection and time for a visit to the cadets' quarters. Keith had allowed the boys to enjoy the privilege of a double-berthed cabin each, as much in an attempt to improve socially harmonious relations between the two as, with typically misplaced optimism, to enhance times of more intensely concentrated study. They had been turned-to since 0800 that morning with the *serang* oiling and greasing cargo gear so had no time to return to their quarters before the entourage began this weekly routine. The theory was cadets tidied and cleaned their suite in their own time between deck work and watches. Something had clearly upset this established pattern for, as the party entered Ashby's cabin they were amazed to find a hole neatly hewn out between the bulkhead separating this from the intervening study. They entered the latter only to find a similar hole on the after study bulkhead leading into Benson's cabin. Through the sections so removed ran a delightful little railway track, complete with electric engine and a few low open wagons (plus, of course, Benson's guard's van). The line commenced and terminated its journey alongside the bunks of the two boys during which, it transpired during 'good' days, they used to run cargoes of sweeties, cigarettes and matches to each other whilst in their 'snuggies'. I felt compelled to remark to Keith that this must be the only stretch of railway line in the civilised world that spent most of its time lifted and relaid, consistent with the moods of the train operators.

The Old Man's face was a picture of unbelievable horror as he realised the damage done to his ship. It would be untrue to say that I heard, from running morning sick parade in the dispensary, his roar for both cadets to report FORTHWITH to their cabins, but I am certain the vibrations re-echoed over the ship. Upon their appearance, both received a rocket that by rights should have landed them on top of the foremast without the bother of climbing there. Benson in particular was allotted the lion's share. They were both turned-to again that afternoon with a long-suffering chippy to replace the wedges, so carefully preserved, and make good the damage. Keith, in between bottling-up his laughter, stopped the shore leave of both cadets in Penang so depriving them of a much-favoured run ashore. He gave them instead the punishment of cleaning strum boxes, blocked lavatories in the crews' quarters and any other filthy job he could devise, discover or even ask the second engineer to supply. My own view was their 'engine-uity', as I termed it, should have received reward rather than punishment – an apparently singularly unacceptable verdict.

About three months into the voyage, with cargo dutifully discharged en route, we mooched gracefully up the China Sea towards Hong Kong. I meandered gently into Keith's office where he was puzzling over ships' papers and absent-mindedly singing what passed for a sea shanty that had clearly been extracted from a SODS Opera somewhere:

> *Twas in the China Seas,*
> *We met our great elation,*

he sung happily. I joined him, equally as joyfully, continuing the refrain concerning the fate of what was to prove, appropriately enough, a Chinese junk. We crooned into another verse, gleefully describing the peculiar antics of an amorous skipper and the ship's cabin boy.

Pausing for breath, we grinned at each other and I raised the question concerning what we should do about the extra paint loaded in Tilbury – simultaneously with a smile dropping on top of his paperwork the wad of delivery notes which, in the excitement of the moment, I had 'omitted' to return to Bassey. This meant there was no record in the dock office of this transaction that held an officer's signature. Glancing down at these vital papers, his reaction was prompt and without hesitation, for he said quite simply we should 'flog the lot'. I suggested that was foremost in my mind, but had not expected him to agree quite so promptly, pointing out that it seemed we sung in harmony a number of equally varied tunes. Smilingly, he acknowledged my humour, and queried in return 'what the hell else did I think we could do with it,' seeing how we were totally flooded out with the stuff. There was undoubtedly a 'hell of a lot of it', in fact excluding the engineers' stores, the best part of three 15-ton covered railway wagons. He thought it a wonder the combined 45 tons had not increased our load line by a foot or two, there was so much. He declared also that as 'it was undoubtedly in everyone's way so, obviously everyone would be glad to get shot of it'.

Following such penetrating logic, there was not much upon which I could comment. Keith had left shifting the stuff until Honkers, thinking a better price might be universally extracted there than in Singapore, and would discuss it with the agent upon arrival when cargo was being worked, and things would have quietened down a bit.

We reflected quietly. The extra ship's stores had been on board for the entire trip and there had not been even the hint of a cable from the office ashore concerning them. In fact, the only word for general consumption from the Kremlin, received with genuine sadness, was of Captain Sawley's sudden death in a nursing home. Pausing whilst the steward brought in his coffee, and telling him to return with another tray for myself, Keith offered the benefit of his immediate thoughts.

'You know what I think?' he asked cryptically.

'No, but I'm sure you're going to tell me.'

'Yeah…I reckon if we haven't heard by now, that bull-shitting devil Bassey will have forgotten about it. Making himself over-busy with other company ships inevitably creates an ill-wind unique unto itself. And he's getting well near his sell-by date now, with retirement looming over the sunny horizon.'

'Yes, I agree with that somewhat poetically expressed view. My opinion is someone at head office dropped a clanger and, in the absence of ship's receipts from the dock super, covered this up by losing his end of the paperwork so he'll not be in the "proverbial",' I surmised aloud.

'Yeh I agree. Disregarding the auditors' reports, in who knows how many months time when we are all dispersed between other ships, we'll not sit on it. See what else we can flog whilst we're at it. We might as well make a killing, if we're going to do anything at all.'

Hong Kong at night provided a number of interesting attractions for officers and crew (courtesy Shell International Shipping and Transport).

So, a few days later with cargo being discharged into Hong Kong junks alongside, Keith raised again the question of our paint. We were lying quietly at anchor in the Roads and our ship's agent had just brought some inducements covering extra cargo to be loaded for Kure and Shimotsu. We closed the office door and invited him to an after-lunch drink.

'Now, Mr Heng,' commenced the Mate, 'What's the market like ashore for top quality ship's paint?' he enquired as subtle as ever in his approach.

'Ha, Mr Mate, as ever, vely good,' was the equally blunt (if cautious) response. 'How much you have to make go?'

'Well, there's quite a lot of stuff actually,' Keith said, going enthusiastically into marine estate agent's mode. 'We've got well over one hundred and fifty assorted drums and cans, with a wide range of colours, some I might add are quite exotic, and some interesting lines in oils and varnishes. There are also a couple of brand-new cargo runners, a mooring wire and polypropylene warp. The second engineer's also got a load of stuff "surplus to requirements" whilst the purser wants to shift about a ton of rice with some meats and dry stores.'

'Hmmmm,' meditated the sanguine Mr Heng: 'Hucking he—.' (an indeterminate sound) Sounds like full yunk load.'

'I'd think all of that,' Keith confirmed.

'OK. You 'eave it me, for now. I get fings moving my end. Allange yunk come alongside in ea'hy hours one mo'hing. With ca'hgo yischa'ge, 'other yunk not out place harbo' police. I come back het you know day.'

'Who're we going to involve?' was the question I posed to Keith.

'It'll have to be virtually everybody, with a job this size,' he asserted firmly. 'We'll need all hands to the pumps in order to do things as quickly as possible.'

It was a few days later that honourable Mr Heng did the arranging trick for which he was renowned throughout the fleet. He invited the Old Man and chief engineer ashore for an evening's heavy drinking, eating and – whatever – to get them safely out of the way until well into next morning. After all, we reasoned, if they do not see what is happening, then they'll not know anything about it. He arranged also the 'yunk' and some extra Chinese members of his 'speciah chew' to assist with the heavy work.

For our part, we organised officers, cadets and both deck and engine-room *serangs* and the purser's *butler* so that, when the junk came alongside at 0220 hours the following morning, transferring the stores was soon undertaken. The harbour police launch came by on schedule, but barely cast us a glance. Storing ship, as they quite reasonably thought, was a regular undertaking at any time of the day or night at anchorages in which ships arrived and departed continuously.

Two days later Mr Heng returned on board with the proceeds. There was a lot of money for all officers, a cash bonus for the three petty officers and crew, plus the addition of a case of quality malt whisky each for the Old Man and chief. This would be a good idea for, as the Mate explained, if the 'proverbial' were to yet again hit the substantial fan, they also would have received a share in the spoils, even by proxy as it were, hence a generous portion of the guilt. Without further ado, Keith grabbed the cadets to do 'the whisky run', as he termed his pleasant task, and shot off to explain how the agent had kindly made for them a special delivery, without offering further explanation.

Of course, the Old Man had been Mate himself for some years, prior to his promotion, and could not have but failed to appreciate, during his weekly inspections that his chief officer had apparently been more than generously liberal whilst painting ship, even if his efforts had hardly dented the remains. After we had sailed from Tilbury, Keith told me quietly in the manner of 'all crooks together', that the Old Man (contrary to my belief) had indeed noticed me actively supervising onboard net loads (appropriately) of paint, oils and greases and had wondered what had been occurring. On inspections, he had of course seen something to the order of two voyages' consignment spread delicately around his ship, with the unusual appearance of 30 gallons of boot-topping-black in the already ill-fated cadets' study. He had mentioned these observations to his chief officer only in passing and was doubtless well aware what would be its eventual fate.

There was also an additional 'goodie' for the Mate and myself, as chief organisers, in the form of a quarter-pound of gold dust each. I had never seen this stuff before and let it flow freely over my hands in its pliable plastic bag. It glowed disappointedly dull in the cabin lights and felt viscous to my touch. I wondered how the hell to get rid of it ashore, so hid it carefully away in a little used part of a lamp locker which incorporated my surplus navigational store abaft the wheelhouse, deciding to worry about that a little nearer the end of our voyage. If found by port Customs, or whoever, wherever, the key was not restricted entirely to use by myself, even though I made darn sure no one else had immediate access to it. It would be just my luck for the cadets to find this little nest egg whilst nosing around in the manner universal of apprentices worldwide. Suddenly another thought crossed my mind leading me to remind Keith of the importance of all officers continuing to draw subs, as it would look extremely suspicious to the Kremlin's accounts staff if, in the midst of a Far Eastern voyage of all things, everyone suddenly stopped receiving cash. He agreed the wisdom of this move and confirmed initiating it over coffee in the lounge, after lunch.

Whilst doing chart corrections, during on afternoon watch bound for Taiwan, my gaze focussed suddenly on what appeared to be smoke emanating from the fo'c'sle head. As it was Saturday afternoon, the crew were granted their customary 'make and mend' and, with all off-duty officers tucked in for their afternoon 'zizz', the area was deserted. I immediately sent Benson to investigate, suggesting he call the chief officer on the way. That he did was obvious, for I caught sight of them doubling along the foredeck at a rate of knots. A few minutes later Benson went hotfooting into the fo'c'sle head store locker, whilst Keith 'phoned me informing me that a small fire had occurred outside the Bosun's store below the ladder on the port side. I then saw the cadet return lugging a large fire extinguisher which he proceeded to spray in all directions – with some of the content managing to hit the base of the fire. It was a small blaze and, being outside on deck, was not in itself over-serious. Then an investigation began into its occurrence. It transpired Ashby had spilt a quantity of oil whilst doing deck work before lunch and, in all ignorance – but not very wisely, had spread a very liberal wad of sawdust to dry up the resulting mess. He had then been called away by the *serang* to do another job and consequently forgot about reporting his accident or going back to complete the mopping-up. Another visit to the Captain ensued, with far more serious implications on this occasion, resulting in a very subdued cadet. As he explained, whilst we were having a navigational theory session in my cabin next morning, he had no idea that spontaneous combustion was a probable result of such a volatile mixture but, very ruefully 'certainly knew now'. He had his shore leave stopped in Kaioshiung, but this was not too severe a punishment. There was little to do in that port apart from visiting the Mission, although the curtailment reflected sufficiently his crime.

I took the opportunity whilst on watch, after we left Taiwan, to service the gyro repeater on the monkey island. Nothing too exotic floated around my mind, but merely to give the gubbins a thin coating of oil. Benson was lounging around, supposedly on lookout duties, so it seemed sensible to take him with me: after all, I ruminated, I might as well make some constructive contribution towards practical aspects of his professional education. We took off the repeater and up-ended the thing, balancing it on the edge of the binnacle. Of course, the little berk dropped one of the locking nuts inside the casing. 'That blasted boy is absolutely useless where practical things are concerned,' I found myself thinking, only to be brought up sharply as I remembered the same thing being said about me by the chief officer on *Earl of Bath*, following an unfortunate smoke-bomb incident when I was a cadet and had nearly asphyxiated all the officers. It was amazing how history repeats itself, even with variations. Nevertheless, I must confess to not feeling over-sympathetic towards Benson.

We made one or two futile attempts to retrieve the nut. The problem was the binnacle stood about chest high. It was impossible to get a clear view down inside because the thin cables to the repeater prevented lifting it off completely. To say I was 'not well pleased' is putting it very mildly, but the incident was not sufficiently high on my personal Richter scale to blister him, at least not over-much. I made him support the thing whilst 'fishing' with a length of bent wire. We became quite engrossed in this task, too much so, because Benson suddenly went white and directed my attention to the Dutch ship *Mississippi Lloyd*, that was dead ahead and that we were rapidly overtaking. Well, *undertaking* might perhaps be more accurate, seeing as we were directly in line for her stern. There was no time to panic. I dived off the monkey island down the starboard ladder and into the wheelhouse. With unaccustomed sense

Cadet applying Brasso to the binnacle of a magnetic compass fitted on the monkey island of a deep-sea ship, with gyro compass binnacle on the left-hand side (courtesy Shell International Shipping and Transport).

of urgency I rushed to the steering control and knocked Mad Mike from automatic to manual, simultaneously swinging the ship hard a starboard to take the Dutchman down our port side. Benson, to give him credit, carefully lowered the repeater on top of the binnacle and followed me into the wheelhouse. As we swung over, I told him to sound one short blast on the siren. I thought we might as well let the Dutchman know we had not completely forgotten (even if we had slightly neglected) him.

As we passed quite closely, but sufficiently far away to avoid interaction, no sign of life manifested itself on their bridge. Strangely, I experienced one of those occasional flashbacks which occur in moments of stress, as thoughts flitted across my mind of the video seen when a cadet during pre-sea training, which had illustrated the effects of that particular nautical phenomenon. I could almost hear again the broad tones of that elderly Scots pilot whilst reflecting simultaneously the incongruity of that particular thought.

Our ship however was far more aware. The violence of swinging hard to starboard at full speed caused us to heel considerably, ejecting Benson across the wheelhouse to cannon into the telegraph. Shortly afterwards came an insistent ringing from one of the telephones, which I waved Benson to answer. It was the purser/chief steward informing us that the violence of our swing had dislodged plates, drinking glasses and sundry crockery from his five saloon tables beautifully set up for supper, into an unholy muddle on deck, breaking the lot. The heeling and sound of the whistle also caught the Old Man rather indelicately balancing on one leg in the heads, and threw Keith across his day-room. They both came hot-foot to the wheelhouse, clearly wondering what was happening aboard our hooker – Keith up the port side ladder and the Old Man through the internal companionway.

In the middle of what is known in the trade as 'an intriguing three-way conversation' the 'phone rang. It was the purser again, informing us that the severity of our swing had caused additional damage. The entire midships Asian catering crew accommodation had been flooded through their open portholes, drenching bunks and cabins equally, with personal gear left floating around their cabins. They were berthed on the deck immediately below our officers' cabins and, normally, sufficiently high for ports to be fitted with windshields and left open without any problem. It was clearly not the stewards' day. Keith, after assuring himself that neither heatstroke nor total insanity had struck me, left the verbal clearing-up to the Captain. An impression, in a roundabout way, delicately dawned on me that Father was not particularly overawed by my watchkeeping proficiency on this occasion. Mind you, he would have been even less impressed if his ship had run into the stern of that accursed Dutchman. Benson stood by 'all agog' as his esteemed second officer received a blistering from 'Daddy'. Had I been a cadet under these circumstances, 'making myself scarce' would have been very much my byword, mindful of a nautical law dictating that 'when the substance is flying around the bridge, anyone (especially a vulnerable cadet) is certain to receive some residue'. Still, we knew Benson to be rather insensitive at times. Uncharitably some might even call him 'more than a little thick'.

After the Old Man had blown himself out and reassured himself his second officer had not entirely taken leave of what senses were remaining, he left us to it. Giving Benson a thoroughly deserved baleful look, which would have liquidised any other mortal, I despatched him to Sparks to enquire if he could pop along and help us out. Just at that precise moment, I could not face returning to the monkey island. In fact, I could not do anything remotely useful (except, of course, keeping a typically conscientious lookout) because reaction had set in. My mouth went completely dry, my stomach felt constricted, and I experienced a severe attack of the shakes. Anyone suddenly coming in at that moment could have been excused for thinking I was suffering from an extreme form of DTs – or similar.

By the time Jim and Benson made their guest appearance my equanimity had returned. Refraining from any obvious comment or even subtle sideswipe, they pottered off to the monkey island where Sparks soon took stock of the situation and, from his toolbox, managed to find a suitable spare nut (he assured me with no pun intended) that he fitted to the offending repeater. Ten minutes with a pair of pliers soon had the thing sorted out. The incident was one of those momentary occasions (albeit intent in their appearances) when working ashore in the NatWest Bank seemed suddenly (but luckily briefly) desirable.

The 'life of Riley' for many officers amongst the variegated fleshpots in virtually all Japanese ports took its inevitable toll with baggy eyes and haggardly worn expressions. Their bold non-verbal announcement flashed a message that spoke of an excessive sampling of delights that for some would never become intimacies within the family circle upon arrival home. One of the junior engineers became involved in a fracas that brought him literally into contact with the Kure police. They carried him back on board after giving him a beating sufficiently severe to leave him in the sickbay for three days. Chats with the agent, chief engineer and Captain failed to ascertain details of the incident, but they believed firmly that it had occurred in some seedy bar-cum-brothel. Even his colleagues apparently failed to unravel the conundrum, whilst eyebrows were raised interrogatively and ears listened intently every time I entered the smoke-room, in the hope – vainly as it happened – that he might have imparted something to his ministering angel. I told the Master it was clearly 'a mystery of the sea, on par with the *Flying Dutchman*'. An unwise comparison, in the light of my recent adventures,

Shipping in Kobe in the 1960s – a port possessing many attractions to seafarers (Fukui Asahido Kyoto).

which could well have rebounded. His smile and charitable response confirmed my forgiveness for that slight mishap.

Benson fell by the wayside at the notorious *Cherry Club* in Kobe when, under the influence of the ship's engineers, he celebrated his twentieth birthday in what I termed to the Old Man as 'commendably lamentable style'. I was always annoyed when this happened because it was avoidable. All any officer had to do was to see me privately in the sickbay before going ashore when various protective measures could be provided. I was after all a second mate, not a vicar. It was with a certain sadistic satisfaction that I added his name and weeping body to my sick-parade visit shared eagerly amongst a number of enthusiastic port medical officers. Ashby's celebrations of attaining the same years of wisdom were affairs of a more sombre nature. The engineers treated him to a generous round of drinks in the lounge after supper, whilst the third officer, Sparks and I, took him for a modest wining and dining in Yokohama. We returned him safely to his cabin on the right side of midnight – but only just.

It was nevertheless (in certain quarters) with considerable relief that we completed discharging the last of our general cargo in Otaru. The questions always raised at this stage of the trip were invariably a little agitated and the visit of the agent became eagerly anticipated. Whilst we conjectured what might be our next port of call, and how many months this could add to the trip he, in his tacky little briefcase, held the hopes and fears germane to nearly all of us. I knew from bitter experience (not always my own) that a ship beginning the loading cycle in Otaru could be sent anywhere in the world for a prolonged voyage. The early morning sighting of Mr Motiyama next day carried its own element of suspense, bated breath, and a certain anxiety, as he headed purposefully from his car towards the Old Man's cabin, with his arms on this occasion full of sheaves of papers.

Watching his arrival from the main deck, I wondered what had happened to the famous holdall, and quietly ruminated why most merchant navy crews ever bothered going to sea at all, considering that what this quotient really wanted was to be ashore. That most crew members could not wait to get home again – even after a few weeks away – was a phenomenon that defied psychological assessment. My situation was little different. When ashore I yearned for the life at sea, and when away more or less contentedly seafaring, part of me whilst fulfilled, yearned to be ashore with Sue, my home and surroundings. It was a paradoxical situation and one seemingly with little chance of satisfactory explanation.

The Mate and chief eventually received 'their heavenly summonses' to Father's cabin. We could tell when Keith came out wearing a beaming smile that we were in for something positive. His grin was not merely 'that on the face of a tiger' for he bore grand news. We were to commence loading Honda motor cycles and a multitude of assorted goods, including toys and clothing, from four Japanese ports, and precede homeward bound for Britain and the Continent. It was certainly something of a bonus to be returning after probably just seven months away and, inevitably, great jubilation abounded at this news. It was rare for the entire officer-complement on any trip to begin quite so early a serious attack of 'the Channels'.

It was at this stage of the voyage that the cadets exchanged duties. They retained their normal work pattern, but Ashby became blessed with my watch now whilst, with sighs of relief from us both, Benson was turned-to with the Mate. I must say young Ashby's style impressed as quite appealing. He was highly intelligent (a refreshing change from the almost bovine Benson) with a quick turn of humour and grasp of academic principles that he readily transformed into professional practices. His recent end-of-year correspondence course results had been extremely encouraging and boded well for his forthcoming Department of Trade (Marine) Second Mates' examinations. The *serang* spoke highly of his ability on deck and he related well with most officers. Although not professionally important, he still had moments of crises with his fellow cadet. I sometimes overheard such altercations whilst passing their accommodation, but wisely left them to sort out such things. At least they never again came to blows, but the sight of Ashby walking frustrated on the boat deck – quietly cursing and blistering imprecations presumably upon the head of his fellow cadet – became quite familiar. Ashby neither complained to anyone directly nor, for one of such tender years, indulged in 'snide remarks and side-swipes'.

Whilst on diverted passage towards the Philippines to complete loading, a novel and surprisingly unexpected cultural side became uncovered in Ashby's make-up. On the runs between Japanese ports, I noticed the cadet would occasionally spout a poetic quip that, although largely ignored, registered with me as being often quite apposite, sufficient to attract from me an occasionally absent-minded smile. As the trip continued so did the quotations. The climax came shortly after we had left the uninspiring port

The port of Masinloc in the Philippines offered little in the way of light relief (Author's collection).

of Masinloc whilst I was in typically relaxed mode, with very little shipping around all of which was behaving itself by passing well down, clear and open: 'Tell me, Mr and Mrs. Ashby's little bundle of fun, why are you always so poetic? And, before you answer, explain if you ever burdened the chief officer similarly with such little gems whilst whiling away smouldering darkened hours of deep ocean watches with him?'

He paused, but his response took me slightly by surprise: 'No sir. You are quite correct. I never mentioned poetry to Mr Harrison on any occasion. But your reply and, sir, the very way you uttered this leads me to think you might be more appreciative, and would certainly not blow my head off if you are not!'

I found myself smiling. Whatever this young man lacked it was certainly not courage, and I could always admire a bit of cheek, being blessed myself with an abundance of that quality. Nevertheless his reply was sufficiently intriguing so, like the mad man my Sue said I could sometimes be, I asked him to elaborate. Pausing a moment, he shot me that infamous look from underneath his eyelids and, taking a deep breath, replied, 'Sir, I should like to quote to you a poem which I believe is completely relevant to the work you are doing at this precise moment at sea, and if you cannot see this relevance, sir, then I shall never quote poetry on the bridge again.'

Being naturally gullible in some respects, I fell for this sally. In fact, I walked right into it: 'All right, my son, fire away, and then hold your peace, so we can have a chunk of that commodity up here for the remainder of the trip. It seems to me that you might be better engaged committing to memory every aspect of the Collision Regulations, which would be of far more practical use to you up here, than spouting poetry.'

Suitably encouraged, whilst pointing out very politely that he knew the Regs intimately (as I was well aware), he did so. It transpired therefore that I found myself listening to the six stanzas of Rudyard Kipling's *Sestina of the Tramp Royal*:

> *Speakin' in general, I 'ave tried them all,*
> *The 'appy roads that take you o'er the world.*
> *Speakin' in general, I 'ave found them good*
> *For such as cannot use one bed too long,*
> *But must get 'ence, the same as I 'ave done.*
> *And go observin' matters till they die.*

He paused, clearly awaiting my response. I liked what was heard, very much so, particularly the idea associated with changing ships and living in different cabins. But still – a little against my better judgement, and standing on my dignity as second officer – I waved him on for more, being almost compelled to listen with increased attention and mixed emotions as the boy continued:

But, Gawd, what things are they I 'aven't done?
I've turned my 'and to most, and turned it good,
In various situations round the world –
For 'im that doth not work must surely die;
But that's no reason man should labour all
'is life on one same shift; life's none so long.

Therefore from job to job I've moved along.
Pay couldn't 'old me when my time was done,
For something in my 'ead upset me all,
Till I 'ad dropped whatever 'twas for good,
An', out at sea, be'eld the dock lights die,
An' met my mate – the wind that tramps the world.

It's like a book I think this bloomin' world,
Which you can only read and care for just so long.
But presently you feel that you will die
Unless you get the page you're reading done,
And turn another – likely not so good;
But what you're after is to turn 'em all.

Gawd bless this world! Whatever she 'ath done –
Excep' when awful long – I've found it good.
So write, before I die. 'E liked it all!

The silence after he had finished was virtually tangible. I was acutely conscious of the gyro clicking quietly, of soft swishing sounds of the passing sea; the gentle vibration from engines, and muffled laughter and voices of our *lascars* working on the boat deck. I was only vaguely aware of the cadet standing by the telegraph – hardly daring to breathe it seemed, and looking at me quizzically – clearly wondering what reaction he might have provoked. He need not have worried, at least not too much, for my thoughts were continuing a frantic scurry around the poem; examining the emotions aroused by sentiments expressed through such profundity of words – whilst of course continuing conflicts with my professional dignity. My life until this moment had properly been concentrated upon professional and academic development, but some deep compulsion within led to an inevitable submission. I paused, for in Kipling's verse (as with Hopkins whilst we were in Tilbury) was discovered another poet who felt and wrote with empathy, expressing exactly my precise feelings about aspects entailed in my job as a marine navigating officer.

The words of *Sestina* appealed considerably, to the extent that I found myself asking Ashby for a copy, but the lines, 'Turning my 'and in various situations around the world' jumped out at me as I considered the variety of duties entailed in a deck officers' work. Whilst the thoughts contained in the line, 'Must get 'ence the same as I 'ave done,' were singularly appropriate to, 'something in my head upset me all'. They spoke volumes about that indefinably disturbing aspect of seafaring upon which my thoughts had recently dwelt whilst in Japan. I found myself automatically replacing 'from job to job I've moved along' with the words 'ship to ship'. It seemed a natural transition to make. It was not the only transition for, during that same watch I submitted, relented and admitted, 'to being completely sold'.

In such casual way came the birth of my introduction to a poet who immediately became a firm favourite. The cadet however had not finished with me for when we were below he came to my cabin, to loan his T. S. Eliot edition of Kipling's *Selected Verse*. After turning-in and before dropping off to a well-earned sleep I found myself literally wallowing in such gems as *The Sea and the Hills, McAndrew's Hymn, The Last Chantey, The Mary Gloster, The Long Trail,* and numerous other poems that began speaking deeply to my inner instincts. It was true to say new horizons became open that were to contribute another dimension to my life. Even at the time this experience seemed more than merely escapism (whatever that might be) for Ashby had reawoken within me the poetic muse and love of words which my English master in grammar school had identified years previously and played his part by inspiring. For the first time I understood Mr Harber's frustration on learning my decision to leave school prematurely, effectively smashing his hopes of leading me through a certain A-level subject. It was a combination of circumstances and my own dedication to professional study that had cast this into dormant mode. I began to develop a long neglected part of my make-up, a love of language. It was not long before Ashby's subtle machinations added selected works by Robert Browning to my repertoire, for here abounded another solid 'good leg of mutton' poet, something you could get your teeth into and relish. He explained this quotation emanated not from his learned self, but came from works of the Victorian writer Dixon Scott – and so opened my yearning to read an assortment of prose.

My literary aspirations received further impetus one drowsy evening when, again completely unexpectedly, I heard Benjamin Britten's *War Requiem* transmitted on a perfectly clear BBC programme in, of all places, the Sunda Strait. I liked the music, which was different to anything heard before, but this oratorio contained half a dozen poems by Wilfred Owen that appealed to me even more. Owen, it appeared, was a First World War poet who tragically received a fatal wound in the throat just a few days before the ending of that conflict.

In the manner to which seafaring inevitably accustomed me, the ship was diverted unexpectedly to Singapore to collect an interesting, and to me at least unusual, 'tween-deck cargo of nutmeg and assorted spices, mother-of-pearl and a batch of postage stamps. The comparatively small tonnage, but combined value of this cargo, had clearly made it worthwhile for the company to divert us and fill what would otherwise have been wasted payload space. It certainly answered a few questions for Keith who had rightly wondered why some of number two 'tween-deck had been reserved when (to his mind) it could easily have been filled in Japan. In fact, he had actually been forced by the agent to turn away a shipment of electrical goods from Nagoya for what was then no apparent reason. As the Mate with full responsibility for loading the vessel, he was the last person to be informed of plans resident in the minds of the inward cargo department at 'the Kremlin'.

The stamps were of particular interest, especially to Captain Chorley-Jones who was a keen philatelist. A famous manufacturer based in the United Kingdom had printed the original blocks but, on this occasion, someone's 'quality control' (I used the unaccustomed Americanism quite naturally) had been questionable, because a previously undetected flaw existed in the finished product. They arrived on board in a package under an armed guard, which aroused the interest of everyone down to the lowest *topass*, and attracted attention to what otherwise would have passed without knowledge or comment. This sealed package directly and dramatically was passed to the Old Man, who promptly locked it in the ship's safe in his office. In keeping with everyone else aboard, I also was intrigued by the mystery attached to the handling of this consignment and was agog to know what the fuss was about. It speaks volumes for the parochial nature of the seafaring mind that such a trite incident should quickly become a major talking point. In an effort to diffuse the situation, the Captain, apparently drooling at the mouth at having such an unattainable gift so closely within his grasp, informed Keith that 'Simply because of this defect, if these stamps landed in the wrong hands, such as the wider philatelist market, they would be worth a small fortune'. I wondered if he had told the Mate 'simply' in the knowledge that every officer aboard would learn the true facts within an hour, but then thought charitably (but without too much conviction) that I might have been doing Keith an injustice.

Our stay in Singapore saw a serious accident that could easily have led to the death of Ashby, and the loss of my poetic mentor. He was detailed by the Mate to work on deck and open number two hatch in readiness for this all-important loading. All hatch covers on this ship were of the multi-folding type, which are generally easy to operate and used aboard ships internationally, virtually without incident. It is a cardinal rule that the tracks along which the covers roll needed checking carefully for any obstructions. This apparently the cadet had done and Charles the duty mate satisfied himself everything was clear. Opening and closing hatches was a job familiar to every deck officer and cadet on board which we all took turns to do, pretty much without conscious worry, as the occasion arose. Certainly, Ashby had done this job numerous times before without incident, but on this occasion something went drastically wrong. Operation of the hatches was by a single bull wire attached to a cargo runner at the end of the topped derrick arm. A shackle joined the bull wire to an eye in the centre of the first hatch section. Somehow, the leading panel slewed across the hatch coping, at which point an officer with more experience would have immediately stopped the operation. Ashby however continued the opening process and put undue strain on the bull wire which, not surprisingly, parted with a resounding crack. The free end with all tension released flew backwards viciously behind the winch where the boy was working, and then swung forward to become entangled with the runner, so that the pair of wires jammed themselves at the block on the derrick head. As the forward hatch section started to slew, Charles had called Ashby to stop the winch, whilst simultaneously diving below the coping. His cry became drowned in other shipboard and jetty noises, for later (and probably quite reasonably) the cadet denied hearing anything. The first Ashby knew how close he had come to being struck by the free flying wire was when he felt the wind of it rushing over his back and head. Afterwards, he spoke of wondering what the noise was to which Keith, wiping sweat and anxiety from his brow, bluntly told him. Colin was in considerable shock for a couple of days but, with that resilience of youth so very much a guardian of all cadets, soon recovered. Sorting out the mess however delayed us on the berth for a few hours. The derrick had to be lowered and crowbars, plus a considerable convolution of wires ingeniously woven around winch drum ends and dollies, used to lever the panel back onto its track. Keith took the two cadets aside to explain how such dangers could arise. Clearly, there was necessity for this, but I did wonder if by then that particular stable door no longer required bolting. Such salutary an incident focussed all minds in the deck department to the possibility of an accident, which previously had not been other than remotely considered.

I was free from duties that afternoon whilst Keith and the crowd sorted out a certain bundle of knitting around number two so took an unexpected chance to go ashore alone. Shivering simultaneously at the thought of what might have happened to Ashby, I enjoyed once again the sights and 'busyness' of this rapidly growing commercial city. I always enjoyed the ethos of being anywhere on the Malaysian continent, of wandering around savouring the combined smells of spices, openly-cooked foods and assorted fruits from wayside stalls. The occasional whiff from open monsoon drains carried its own detraction, but seemed strangely indicative of the contrasts within this country. The assortment of different Races, Chinese, Malays and Indians, each with its unique individualism, personalities and colour schemes and largely smiling friendliness, lived on the whole in harmony, contributing a unique kaleidoscope of interaction not found in similar dimensions anywhere else in the world.

After enjoying a civilised afternoon tea in the famous Raffles Hotel I passed a dingy second-hand bookshop and popped in to browse 'for what exactly I did not know, but looking hopefully anyway'. Lounging on the shelves, a copy of Owen's collected works reposed anxiously awaiting a literary mariner. Also discovered was a dusty paperback gem by Archibald Wavell, entitled *Other Men's Flowers*. The anthology looked rather interesting, to put things mildly, and glancing through I noticed a number of poems by Kipling and Browning. It seemed a crime to leave it gathering further ungrateful dirt, so the volume rapidly joined my Owen to become as essential to my personal travelling library as *Nicholl's Concise Guide – Volume Two,* and that other navigators' bible *Norie's Nautical Tables.*

Returning to the ship, on the way back to the docks, I noticed the pure white stone of St Andrew's Anglican cathedral near the waterfront. I had sung in a church choir whilst a boy and retained a love of sacred music in the English tradition, especially as occasionally we were invited to sing in the diocesan cathedral at Southwark in south London. My musical interests however, like poetry, had also 'gone the way of all culture', having been restricted to the deeper recesses of my mind by the immediacy of professional examinations. Acting upon impulse, I crossed the contrasting lush green lawns of the purlieus and passed through the large doors that to me suggested antiquity. The nave proved a refreshingly cool refuge after the heat of the sun and, entering the main aisle, the unexpected atmosphere of peacefulness resident in this suddenly sombre setting struck me forcibly. After a few moments savouring total solitude in near-sepulchral silence, distant sounds reached my ears from what was obviously a choir practice taking place in preparation for the late afternoon service. I paused, feeling very much an intruder, and listened as powerful tones from the organ were replaced after an unobtrusive pause by the beautifully modulated voices of the choristers as they reached into the very depths of a perfectly composed motet. Gradually the work unfolded into the *Ave Verum Corpus* in its setting by William Byrd and I froze, frightened to draw breath, in case of missing even a single note. Utterly transfixed, I listened as fragile thin threads of innocent voices broke into the powerfully poignant finale of this beautiful composition. The moment proved an emotional epiphany of tremendous import and in the ensuing silence, interspersed by low tones from the director of music quietly complimenting his boys on their efforts, I felt an overpoweringly choking desire to howl.

It was not surprising, perhaps, that memories flooded into my mind from well over a decade previously. These were not particularly sad, because my days at Saint George's parish church had been thoroughly enjoyable, at least for me. How far those adults responsible for my training and welfare shared this view was a different matter, for I recalled overhearing my choirmaster on one occasion describing me in evangelical terms to one of the lay clerks: '…young Carridia undoubtedly possesses a veritable pearl of a voice and is very quick on the uptake, particularly when learning quite difficult psalm and canticle chants. It is unfortunate that he is otherwise a right and proper little sod.'

The exasperated tone in his voice I could still hear and I smiled in whimsical agreement with his sentiment as a series of past incidents flooded my mind. The time when I had organised the choir boys into a strike for more pay following attendance at weddings and funerals; of filling the vestry full of leaves one autumn after practice when the men remained whilst we boys were dismissed; of singing the words 'four pence' after the refrain '*and io…io…io….*' in the middle of *Ding Dong, Merrily on High!* This had happened during a Christmas Eve service with a packed congregation that included my parents. My voluntary contribution was picked up by microphones and resounded around the church, leaving my fellow choristers struck with awed laughter, and my being struck with a suspension for three weeks by the vicar. My *pièce de résistance* occurred when I removed screws supporting the top of the choir-stall book supports. The director of music came out front to direct us in the anthem during evensong so, following his usual practice, he lent upon the top form. As I was fond later of telling my cadets, 'physics does work, you know lads'. It certainly did on that auspicious occasion, for the entire board not surprisingly crashed to the ground with papers, books and hymn sheets cascading across the aisle. The ensuing chaos detracted from the mood of evensong, and attracted from our long-suffering vicar additional far from ecclesiastical looks in my direction. Supported by the head boy on the decani side, we blamed the incident upon a group of Boy Scouts who had visited that morning. The determined yet frustrated enquiries of church authorities, clearly out for my blood, remained far from convinced as they searched for evidence supporting their suspicions. I do not think my innocent protestations did very much to pacify them, but with the lack of anything conclusive to the contrary, I recalled getting away with that one. The problem of course was quite simple; the choir lacked that sense of discipline other than towards music, practised strongly by my grammar school, which was the one reason why there I had always been such a model pupil.

A suddenly bursting beam of sunlight, blazing gloriously through large narrow windows and creating enormous shadows from long columns and small pews, broke further reveries. It threw a rich, almost spectral, beam upon the gilded cross of the high altar. I felt sufficient ethereally spiritual damage had resulted from my visit to this haven of peace, so gently retired, to battle again hot sun and the sticky atmosphere of monsoon-laden Singapore.

My return up the gangway coincided with pilot, tugs, and the crew working under Benson, who lost little time in bringing the thing in board. Nonchalantly casting aside a distant black look, thrown in my direction from the bridge wing by Captain Chorley-Jones, I grabbed the long suffering cadet even before the gangway was made fast and, still in civilian shorts and shirt, supervised my stand-by on the after deck.

It was with unrestrained interest and pleasure that the enthusiastically envious Ashby examined my purchases. How he wished he had been with me, instead of 'playing with wires on the foredeck'. He assured me of his certainty that he would have entered the bookshop first. This proved the only occasion when I heard the cadet mention anything remotely detrimental about his time on deck. As it was, the books broke new poetic boundaries between us and were exclaimed about, minutely dissected – shared and explored – in a welter of literary delight. I felt a certain English master would have approved without question.

During the long ocean passage home an interesting hiatus occurred between us deck officers which proved typical of the manner in which we found relief from the

Part of the training of the third officer was to take noon sights in preparation
for his next Certificate of Competency (courtesy BP plc).

potential boredom resident in long ocean passages whilst still prematurely 'chirping with the Channels'. Like most things at sea, the incident arose quite innocently. Charles came up to take and work a noon sight, developing his own professional training, whilst *Earl of Nottingham* headed towards Aden for bunkers. I had of course been well aware that he used Burton's edition of *Nautical Tables* and reflected how each mariner without question developed into either 'Burton's or Norie's men'. The Mate and Ashby joined Charles by swearing to the efficacy of the former, whilst the Old Man, Benson and me thumped equally as vociferously for the latter. It was dependent, I presumed, upon which one of the two collections of nautical tables cadets had received whilst undergoing pre-sea training. As a matter of interest I decided to test if, as suspected, any fundamental differences resided between the two volumes. Charles and I used a common sextant altitude, resolved our workings independently, and compared results. Ashby followed suit using his *Norie's* tables. Benson entered into the spirit of the thing, clutching the ship's trusty gun with customary aplomb but, alas the workings of any sight remained as alien to him as the machinations involved in devising a railway timetable would have been to the rest of us. The Old Man and Keith, chancing upon the way whilst discussing ship maintenance, enquired what we were up to. They took an immediate interest, collected their nautical tables and joined in the fun. We found collectively that calculations differed minutely leading to slightly different results and deduced these came from one set of tables rounding down the sixth logarithmic figure, whilst the other set rounded up. The result was negligible, but the interest factor resounded around the wheelhouse quite heatedly, with each contender swearing to the accuracy of his 'little book' and damning the other edition to purgatory. Even the cadets became quite carried away, but more circumspectly than their example-setting superiors.

We bunkered as usual in Aden and, as we were proceeding through the Suez Canal with our pilot on board and at peace with the world, Captain Chorley-Jones asked my opinion regarding Benson's academic and professional studies.

'Sir, he is very practical: the things Ashby got up to earlier in the trip regarding the fire and chipping hammer job would simply not have happened with Benson. Frankly, I suspect he regards me as something of a tormentor – one, because for my dutiful sins I have to help him – secondly, because I keep his nose to his studies, and

Relieving officers were frequently pressed for time of handing-over equipment and records, with the deep-sea man anxious to go on leave, but occasionally the process was more leisurely, with time to share refreshments (courtesy BP plc).

thirdly because he is something of an uphill struggle – another suggestion for the "—tor". He has just failed all of his end-of-year examination subjects, which frankly takes some doing, and is nowhere near ready for Second Mates' nor indeed any other examination at present, nautical or otherwise.'

The Master shot me a very hard look and confirmed that everything said had received confirmatory support from the Mate – and he would cable the Kremlin accordingly.

We arrived eventually in the West India Docks, after a voyage of just under eight months duration, 'virtually a coastal passage' as Keith was to remark with a touch of almost prophetic gloom. This was because relief officers arrived next day for all of us, except the Mate, and we went for a well-deserved leave, and then awaited further appointments. Poor Keith, much to his chagrin, received orders to remain for the coastal and continental trip. I had helped Charles throughout the voyage, upon request, and he had finally mastered the complex arithmetical marathon known as the Great Circle Sailing and felt confident, having accrued his necessary sea-time, to enter nautical college for Mate's, 'up North in Liverpool'.

The cadets also went on leave. Ashby, as predicted, had fared exceptionally well in his end-of-year examination (which had been supervised totally by Keith) so, pending a further few months deep-sea acquiring requisite 'time', he would then be ready for nautical college and Second Mates'. Benson (presumably complete with train-set) was summoned for interview by the senior marine superintendent at Ellerton's head office to which, he was informed, his parents would be present. This intimate (but timely) discussion would lead to the decision whether or not it was worthwhile sending him for further sea-time, or if it might prove mutually beneficial simply to terminate his cadetship.

The next day, filled to capacity with poetry and laden with gifts for all, I grabbed my taxi and headed for home, Sue, sanity and a well-earned leave. I felt however that my debt to a certain cadet Colin Ashby was perhaps too great to receive adequate repayment. I did wonder if, in the manner of seafaring internationally, our paths might again cross at some distant time in the future, but then remembered I had pondered similar thoughts concerning Peter Dathan after we had left Keddleston, many years previously.

It came to me, whilst clumping down the gangway that my bag of gold dust remained tucked away safely in the store locker, necessitating my return quickly on board to retrieve it. The look of amazement on the face of some unknown officer finding this when next clearing-out the locker would hardly have matched the chagrin crossing my features when, once ensconced safely at home with the ship en route for 'Heaven knows where', the realisation had come that my nest egg was still aboard. I stuffed it underneath the seat out of the way of the taxi driver's prying eyes, but more importantly, those of the dock entrance police constable. Were contraband discovered during a gate search, as sometimes happened, how it came into my possession would necessitate a raft of ingenious explanations and confiscation, combined with all manner of unsavoury investigations, and possible police prosecution and dismissal from the company. It was a risk virtually all officers and crew seemed willing to take. On this occasion, custom ran true to form, for my dock pass (with its £1 note tucked discreetly beneath) proved acceptable and, with an equally customary salute from an upstanding guardian of law and order, my taxi passed *en route* for home.

As it happened the stuff proved more of a hindrance than a help for I was not quite sure, strange though it may sound, how to turn my windfall into cash. Passing gold dust was not an act that had previously entered readily into my orbit and was hardly one upon which I could seek advice. I had walked boldly up to the counter of a city branch of one of the leading 'big five' banks on a quiet Saturday morning, when no other customers were around, *en route* for my beloved Potter's, and asked an astonished clerk if he could 'weigh this up and kindly give me the cash equivalent'. Yes, there remained I supposed a delightful naïvety on the part of most merchant seamen, notwithstanding whether they are officers or ratings. Blanching slightly under the open-eyed glances of nearby bank workers, my musings as to whether or not this was quite the correct form was interrupted by overhearing quiet mutterings between the clerk and a manager in a nearby office, and then the sound of a telephone dial stuttering its fragmented course. Without waiting further developments, I grabbed my little plastic bag off the highly varnished counter and ran out of the building, soon to lose myself conveniently in the back streets behind Fenchurch Street railway station. Sweating slightly, it was with considerable relief that I found myself facing Ibex House in the Minories from whence, equally as slickly, I sidled into the refuge of my bookshop for the next couple of hours.

Two weeks into my leave I received an unexpected summons to the Kremlin. Upon my arrival and, as I thought, safely ensconced with Captain Ford, he shook me enthusiastically by the hand and, with beaming smile, told me he and I were about to part company. Whilst wondering which of us was about to be sacked, I realised he was directing our passage towards the office of the senior marine superintendent, where he introduced us and then promptly left. Captain Marshall looked up at me and smilingly invited me towards a chair on the other side of his desk. The by now traditional coffee and biscuits were already temptingly waiting, I was pleased to note, so did as required. Passing across the latter, he gave me that very penetrating look with which he was always associated in my mind from the few occasions we had met. He paused again and, following a few pleasantries concerning family matters and how my present leave was going, made the following pronouncement (to say I was all agog put my feelings very mildly, I really had little idea what was to come, but guessed it could not be bad news): 'It has been my pleasure to follow your progress with the Ellerton Group since the days when my selection panel interviewed you whilst you were at Keddleston Navigation School. You may remember that occasion?'

I confirmed that the memory indeed was, if not daisy fresh, at least still rambling somewhere around the parameters of my mind. He continued: 'It was good to see that we were then proved correct in our judgement. As you may have heard, I am due to retire soon and, with good wife, intend to move to the cottage in Cornwall we have been fortunate in enjoying so far as a holiday home. Nevertheless, I tell you this only to reinforce the pleasure it gives me, as almost a final task, to offer you promotion to senior second officer once you have enjoyed a few more weeks of leave. I know you have not yet obtained Masters', but we feel that you are ready for this next move, the experience of which will stand you in extremely good stead for that examination when you finally feel ready to attempt this.'

In the silence that followed I could hear the clock on the bulkhead passing away the seconds. To my astounded ears it sounded like the chimes of Big Ben as my mind tried to cope with such unexpected news. I mean, Ellertons simply did not promote until the candidate held his next higher qualification, so I felt slightly bemused. I expressed these passing thoughts directly to him, and received reassurance that the Group had not taken leave of its collective maritime senses but was merely following a recently introduced boardroom policy intended to retain promising officers and groom them for ultimate command. Of course, I was flattered, but was not at all certain if I was ready for this promotion. Anyway, the 'optimistic mode' with which Sue reckoned I was blessed soon switched into gear, and I found myself accepting my next step up. Captain Ford afterwards wheeled me along to the office of a Captain Henshaw, the super responsible for senior second and chief officers, to discuss, as he put it, 'the finer points involved'.

The promotion meant also a visit to my naval outfitters to have another thinner half-bar fitted between my existing two thick stripes and also, far more welcome, a substantial increase in salary.